S0-AIB-519

The Salisbury Plain Poems

WITHDRAWN

The Cornell Wordsworth

General Editor: Stephen Parrish
Associate Editor: Mark L. Reed

Advisory Editors: M. H. Abrams, Geoffrey Hartman, Jonathan Wordsworth

---

THE SALISBURY PLAIN POEMS, edited by Stephen Gill

The Salisbury Plain Poems of William Wordsworth

Salisbury Plain, or *A Night on Salisbury Plain*
Adventures on Salisbury Plain (including *The Female Vagrant*)
Guilt and Sorrow; or, *Incidents upon Salisbury Plain*

Edited by STEPHEN GILL

CORNELL UNIVERSITY PRESS
ITHACA, NEW YORK

PR
5869
G9
1975

THIS BOOK HAS BEEN PUBLISHED WITH THE AID OF A GRANT FROM THE
HULL MEMORIAL PUBLICATION FUND OF CORNELL UNIVERSITY.

Copyright © 1975 by Cornell University

All rights reserved. Except for brief quotations in a review, this book, or parts thereof, must not
be reproduced in any form without permission in writing from the publisher. For information
address Cornell University Press, 124 Roberts Place, Ithaca, New York 14850.

First published 1975 by Cornell University Press.

International Standard Book Number 0-8014-0892-X
Library of Congress Catalog Card Number 74-4865

Printed in the United States of America by Vail-Ballou Press, Inc.

To the memory of
John Finch and George Healey
this series is dedicated

Contents

Foreword

Our aim in the series which this volume inaugurates is to present—for the first time—full and accurate texts of Wordsworth's long poems, together with all variant readings from first drafts down to the final lifetime (or first posthumous) printings.

When Ernest de Selincourt set down comparable aims in 1940 as editor of *The Poetical Works of William Wordsworth*, he remarked: "It is probable that no poet ever paid more meticulous or prolonged attention to his text than Wordsworth." Evidence of that attention, as de Selincourt went on to say, can be found not only in the multitude of revisions Wordsworth introduced into editions of his poems from 1800 onward, but in the thousands of variant draft readings that swarm through his manuscripts. These manuscripts, most of them in the Wordsworth Library at Grasmere, form a singularly rich archive: the material they provide for the study of a great poet's art is unmatched in its abundance and its detail. The readings stretch across some sixty years of the poet's career, from juvenilia written at Cambridge or earlier to his last unflagging efforts to perfect the great poem on his own life and the smaller poems he wrote in his old age.

The poet's persistent habit of revision—de Selincourt called it "an obsession"—makes an editor's choice of basic text difficult: Shall he print the earliest complete versions of Wordsworth's poems or the final revised versions? The editor is faced, moreover, with another complicating fact: from his first collected edition onward, Wordsworth arranged his poems in classes defined, variously, by the poems' subjects, or by the powers of mind thought to be predominant in their composition, or by their occasion, or simply by their form. Although these classes altered somewhat, and certain poems drifted from one class to another, Wordsworth never lost his conviction that they afforded an important insight into his poetic intentions. The editor is thus obliged to make a second hard choice at the outset of his undertaking: Shall he preserve the classes into which the poet arranged his works, or shall he break up the classes and arrange the poems chronologically in order to reveal Wordsworth's artistic growth?

These choices were summed up cogently by de Selincourt, who elected to print the final revised text and to preserve Wordsworth's classes in the five-volume edition which he began to issue in 1940 and Helen Darbishire completed in 1949. To make possible study of the poet's artistic growth from apprenticeship into maturity, de Selincourt accompanied Wordsworth's final text with "an *apparatus criticus* which will record its development from the earliest existing copy, through its successive stages in manuscript and print, till it received its final revision." While he had, he said, omitted "some trivial variants," he went on to declare: "I have included everything which seemed to me of the least significance, and I have erred on the side of fullness."

This declaration, together with the massive bulk and fine detail of the *apparatus* provided by de Selincourt, has misled readers into supposing that they can in de Selincourt's volumes trace accurately and fully the stages of a poem's growth. It is not easy to find fault with de Selincourt's management of literary problems: his sure taste and formidable learning make his accounts of a poem's history, for example, acute and informative. But one must find other terms to describe his presentation of texts. One scarcely wants to say of him what his partner, Helen Darbishire, harshly said of their predecessor, the unfortunate Professor Knight: "He probably jotted down the readings hurriedly and afterwards misread his own handwriting, if he had not first misread Wordsworth's." Yet to examine a case can be somberly instructive. A pertinent case is the way in which de Selincourt presented MS. 2 of the Salisbury Plain poems, *Adventures on Salisbury Plain*, looked upon as complete by Wordsworth in 1799 and set down in a fair copy by Dorothy. This manuscript represents an important state of an interesting poem, as de Selincourt recognized in his comments on it.

But to reconstruct this state of the poem from the readings and the *apparatus* which de Selincourt provides would be impossible. MS. 2, *Adventures on Salisbury Plain*, consists of 62 stanzas, though 30 more are implied, consisting of the Female Vagrant's tale to be inserted in two segments, making up a poem of 92 stanzas. Stanzas 1–5 and half of Stanza 6 de Selincourt prints in his Notes at the back of *Poetical Works*, Volume I (pp. 335–336). For the second half of Stanza 6 and for Stanzas 7–11 he offers MS. 2 readings in his *apparatus criticus* (pp. 96–98). Stanzas 12 and 13 he makes no attempt to reproduce, explaining that Stanza 12 is "a revised version" of MS. 1 (which he does print) and that Stanza 13 is "a version of [MS. 1] intermediary between MS. 1 and text." For Stanzas 14–24 and the first half of Stanza 25 he again provides readings in the *apparatus* (pp. 99–103). The remainder of Stanza 25 and the whole of Stanzas 26 and 27 are passed over, though the version of MS. 1—MS. 2 having only what de Selincourt calls "unimportant variants"—can be read in the *apparatus* (pp. 104–105). Stanza 28 is printed in full in the *apparatus* (p. 105), and Stanza 29 may be reconstructed from quotations in the *apparatus* (pp. 105–106).

At this point, MS. 2 allows for the insertion of the first half of the Female

Vagrant's tale, and the text resumes with Stanza 45 to close this half; seven leaves farther on in the notebook Stanzas 46 and 47 introduce the second half of the tale. De Selincourt prints these three stanzas (45–47) in his Notes (pp. 337–338) without reporting the distance which separates them, then asserts: "Here follow asterisks, denoting the rest of the woman's story [334–450],[1] and then MS. 2 goes on:

> The woman from the ruined tenement
> Did with a light and chearful step depart . . .''

(The quotation runs on through Stanzas 66–68 of MS. 2.) The asterisks are there in MS. 2, but the stanzas that follow them are not the ones de Selincourt prints but three preceding stanzas in that manuscript (63–65). The three stanzas thus lost, which were intended to follow the second half of the Female Vagrant's tale in MS. 2, actually have their equivalents in *Guilt and Sorrow*— Stanzas 35–37, which there *precede* the second half of the Female Vagrant's tale. Inexplicably, though he ignores the first two "lost" stanzas, de Selincourt does provide some MS. 2 readings from the third, in the *apparatus* to Stanza 37 of *Guilt and Sorrow* (p. 112). For Stanzas 69 to 92 (the end of MS. 2) readings are routinely given in the *apparatus* (pp. 119–127).

This complicated account may be briefly summarized: of the 62 stanzas in MS. 2, de Selincourt reproduces 11 in his Notes, provides an *apparatus* for reconstructing 44 others (though he neglects to place one of these), and passes over the remaining seven. Five of these seven can be read in the version of MS. 1; the other two might be read in the version of *Guilt and Sorrow*, if they could be located.

But the difficulties of finding the stanzas and putting them in order are only the beginning. In transcribing texts, de Selincourt misreads an occasional word, reading "home" for "house" (MS. 2, l. 22), "blowing" for "blinding" (165), "glow" for "gloom" (192), "wickedness" for "wretchedness" (767), "thoughts" for "things" (783), and a few others. More numerous are instances in which he reports not the original reading of MS. 2 but a revised reading, so that the original reading is lost: he gives us "open" for "wilder" (l. 29), "wan" for "pale" (665), "hut" for "house" (744), "sheltering" for "lonesome" (745), "within his bosom strive" for "in his heart revive" (771), "parting soul has" for "dying thoughts have" (782), and several more.

Yet even these losses may seem inconsequential in comparison to the losses that result from de Selincourt's omissions. Dozens of readings of MS. 2, some deleted, some added in revision, are unaccountably left out, as though the editor had wearied of his labor, and have therefore remained unpublished. Some of these we may accept as "trivial variants," like "for" for "now," "by"

---

[1] De Selincourt gives line numbers from *Guilt and Sorrow*.

for "in," "as" for "while," and others of the same order. But many omitted readings stretch that elastic category. Consider "He mark'd" for "And see" (l. 59), "ragged" for "spreading" or "lowly" (68), "the huge plain" for "a huge waste" (71), "view" for "sight" (96), "foregoes" for "forbears" (100), "heath" for "waste" (179), "forth sent" for "to come" (199), "on the pediment" for "in the naked room" (201), "from uneasy" for "on a restless" (202), "his horse's" for "incessant" (210), "Quickly she" for "And much they" (223), "the breaking day" for "this happy change" (569), "the boy" for "his son" (655), "And soon" for "A dire" (754), "kind" for "mild" (761), "milder" for "gentler" (762), "nerveless" for "burning" (789), "hands" for "doom" (814). There are others of equal importance. One can even instance whole lines like

> To bid his weary limbs new force assume [MS. 2, l. 173]

for de Selincourt's

> To stay his steps with faintness overcome

or

> Him further to allure to purpose kind [MS. 2, l. 222]

for

> Addressed. With joy she heard such greetings kind

or

> She said as through a bottom bare & deep
> That day she journey'd on the houseless moor [MS. 2, ll. 226–227]

for

> The woman told that through a hollow deep
> As on she journeyed far from spring or bower.

Finally, in addition to these scattered omissions are a few longer passages of MS. 2 nowhere shown in de Selincourt, such as this one from a "lost" stanza:

> His wither'd cheek was ting'd with ashy hue
> He stood, & trembled both with grief and fear
> But she felt new delight and solace new
> And from the opening east a pensive chear
> Came to her [weary thoughts] while the lark warbled near [MS. 2, ll. 572–576]

for

> Upon her cheek, to which its youthful hue
> Seemed to return, dried the last lingering tear,
> And from her grateful heart a fresh one drew:
> The whilst her comrade to her pensive cheer
> Tempered fit words of hope; and the lark warbled near.

The point of this melancholy catalogue is not to expose the lapses of a great scholar who struggled with notable success to bring order into an overwhelming mass of materials, but to show the need for a fresh presentation of those materials. We are at the outset concerned to rescue the long poems that Wordsworth wrote during his most interesting and brilliant years, then left unpublished—poems like *Salisbury Plain*, *The Ruined Cottage*, *Home at Grasmere*, *Peter Bell*, *The Borderers*, and *The Prelude*. Quite apart from its lapses, de

Selincourt's edition, based on Wordsworth's final text, has the grave disadvantage of relegating the early Wordsworth to footnote collations, where his work can be read only imperfectly, and then only by an intricate process of reconstruction.

Thus our first purpose is to bring the early Wordsworth into view. To that end, we provide continuous "reading texts" of the important long poems as they stood at their completion; an *apparatus criticus* is used to show later readings. Our second purpose is to be inclusive: to present all the manuscript readings that can be deciphered and all the changes in authorized editions of Wordsworth's printed texts up to the time of his death in 1850. Our third purpose is to make possible the study of Wordsworth's revisions—which is the study of the development of his poetic art. Since transcription can fail to reveal all the complexities of Wordsworth's manuscripts, we supply facing photographs of the most important and difficult texts. Besides the photographs, on which draft revisions can be looked at, and besides the *apparatus criticus*, in which later (or earlier) variants can be followed, we adopt a third device for the study of revisions: where two versions of a poem match sufficiently, we arrange them on facing pages so that the steps by which one was converted into the other become visible. All these devices are employed in our presentations of the Salisbury Plain poems. MSS. 1 and 2 are shown in photographs; printed readings of *The Female Vagrant* (through fourteen editions) are shown in an *apparatus*, as are variant readings of *Guilt and Sorrow* found in one of the later manuscripts (MS. 3), in proof sheets, and in the later editions; the text of the other late manuscript (MS. 4) and the text of the first edition of *Guilt and Sorrow* are printed on facing pages.

It may be observed that accomplishment of our three purposes will require some elaborate presentations. One needs to remember that Wordsworth's own attention to his long poems was elaborate—"meticulous" and "prolonged." We believe it proper now to give those poems equivalent attention.

This series had its origins in the agreement generously made by the Dove Cottage Trustees with George Healey, curator of the Cornell Wordsworth Collection, which brought to Cornell microfilms of the Wordsworth manuscripts. Until his death in 1971, Professor Healey served as one of the advisory editors, and this first volume benefited from his expertise and kindly wisdom. Through early stages of its planning, the series was shaped and sustained by the vision and the energy of John Finch, whose death in 1967 made all Wordsworth studies poorer. Mark Reed, who took Finch's place in the editorial group, deserves particular credit for bringing our designs to their final shape.

S. M. PARRISH

Ithaca, New York

Preface

This volume presents for the first time complete texts of the three poems that troubled Wordsworth in his youth and recaptured his imagination in old age. In 1793 and 1794, partly as a result of experiences while wandering over Salisbury Plain, Wordsworth composed the poem he called *Salisbury Plain*. Between 1795 and 1799 this work was transformed into the much more ambitious *Adventures on Salisbury Plain*. The poet's struggle with his intractable material, however, was left unresolved as Wordsworth entered the period of his greatest achievement. In 1841 he returned to this early work and revised it for publication in 1842 as *Guilt and Sorrow*.

For nearly a century this poem, the outcome of the poet's struggle, was all that was known to the general reader. In 1940, however, Ernest de Selincourt published many of the manuscript readings in the first volume of his great edition, *The Poetical Works of William Wordsworth*. Now all three poems are here presented in full. For the first time in any edition of Wordsworth all available evidence from the manuscripts and from the collation of all the authorized lifetime editions is drawn together. The edition aims to give the factual evidence of Wordsworth's efforts to be true to his developing vision; therefore in the Introduction and notes I have avoided critical pronouncements, confident that the evidence presented here will speak plainly enough to the reader of Wordsworth's artistic integrity, energy, and power.

It is a pleasure to express my gratitude to the many scholars who have helped me construct this edition. I wish to acknowledge especially the help of Jonathan Wordsworth of Exeter College, Oxford, who first steered me toward Salisbury Plain and has helped me more than he knows ever since. Mark Reed of the University of North Carolina has never stinted in sharing his time and knowledge, and his own meticulous scholarship has been a constant inspiration. Stephen Parrish spent many hours poring over my typescript at crucial stages when he could have been walking on the fells about Grasmere.

I owe much gratitude to a number of people who have supplied information and helped in various ways: Paul Betz, Geoffrey Carnall, P. G. M. Dickinson, the Reverend Harry Eastwood, the late John Finch, Norman Higham, N. Higson, Cecil Lang, Michael Lewis, and Robert Osborn.

Grateful thanks are due Professor Basil Willey and the Trustees of Dove Cottage for permission to publish manuscripts in their charge and for many other favors; the Library of the University of Bristol for permission to quote from the Pinney family papers; and the University of Virginia, Charlottesville, Virginia, for permission to examine and collate a proof copy of *Guilt and Sorrow* now in the Tracy W. McGregor Library.

I reserve my last and especial thanks for my wife for many patient hours of typing and checking. She has read these poems more often, I think, than any other person since they were composed.

STEPHEN GILL

Lincoln College, Oxford

Abbreviations

ASP	*Adventures on Salisbury Plain.*
BNYPL	*Bulletin of the New York Public Library.*
Chronology: EY	Mark L. Reed, *Wordsworth: The Chronology of the Early Years, 1770–1799* (Cambridge, Mass., 1967).
DC MS.	Dove Cottage manuscript (1785–1814, revised numbering).
DCP	Dove Cottage miscellaneous manuscript (later than 1814, original numbering).
DC Verse	Dove Cottage Verse manuscript (later than 1814, original numbering).
DW	Dorothy Wordsworth.
ELN	*English Language Notes.*
EY	*Letters of William and Dorothy Wordsworth: The Early Years, 1787–1805*, ed. Ernest de Selincourt (2d ed.; rev. Chester L. Shaver; Oxford, 1967).
FQ	Edmund Spenser, *The Faerie Queen.*
FV	*The Female Vagrant.*
G&S	*Guilt and Sorrow.*
Grosart	*The Prose Works of William Wordsworth*, ed. Alexander Grosart (3 vols.; London, 1876).
LY	*Letters of William and Dorothy Wordsworth: The Later Years, 1821–1850*, ed. Ernest de Selincourt (3 vols.; Oxford, 1939).
MLR	*Modern Language Review.*
Moorman	Mary Moorman, *William Wordsworth: A Biography* (2 vols.; Oxford, 1957, 1965).
MS. 1	*Salisbury Plain* and additions in DC MS. 10.
MS. 2	*Adventures on Salisbury Plain* and additions in DC MS. 16.
MS. 3	Stanzas from *Incidents upon Salisbury Plain* in DC Verse 92.
MS. 4	*Incidents upon Salisbury Plain* in DC Verse 102.
MW	Mary Wordsworth.
MWL	*The Letters of Mary Wordsworth*, ed. Mary E. Burton (Oxford, 1958).
Prelude (followed by book number)	*The Prelude*, 1805 text.
Prelude (followed by page number)	*The Prelude*, ed. Ernest de Selincourt; rev. Helen Darbishire (Oxford, 1959).
PW	*The Poetical Works of William Wordsworth*, ed. Ernest de Selincourt and Helen Darbishire (5 vols.; Oxford, 1940–1958).
RC	*The Ruined Cottage.*

RES	*Review of English Studies.*
SP	*Salisbury Plain.*
STC	Samuel Taylor Coleridge.
STCL	*Collected Letters of Samuel Taylor Coleridge*, ed. Earl Leslie Griggs (6 vols.; Oxford, 1956–1971).
STCP	*The Complete Poetical Works of Samuel Taylor Coleridge*, ed. Ernest Hartley Coleridge (2 vols.; Oxford, 1912).
UTQ	*University of Toronto Quarterly.*
WW	William Wordsworth.

The Salisbury Plain Poems

Introduction

I was in my twenty-fourth year, when I had the happiness of knowing Mr. Wordsworth personally, and while memory lasts, I shall hardly forget the sudden effect produced on my mind, by his recitation of a manuscript poem, which still remains unpublished, but of which the stanza, and tone of style, were the same as those of the "Female Vagrant." . . . It was not however the freedom from false taste, whether as to common defects, or to those more properly his own, which made so unusual an impression on my feelings immediately, and subsequently on my judgement. It was the union of deep feeling with profound thought; the fine balance of truth in observing with the imaginative faculty in modifying the objects observed; and above all the original gift of spreading the tone, the *atmosphere*, and with it the depth and height of the ideal world around forms, incidents, and situations, of which, for the common view, custom had bedimmed all the lustre, had dried up the sparkle and the dew drops.[1]

The poem praised so generously by Coleridge, and the poems which developed from it, are published in full in this volume.[2] That their individual identity and their quality have been long obscured is due largely to the swift development of Wordsworth's interests and skill during his formative years, which led him to discard achievements which we can value as coherent poems. In 1795, when Coleridge first encountered the poem, *Salisbury Plain* stood as a record of Wordsworth's earlier turbulent feelings, later recalled so vividly in *The Prelude*, about the war with France and the condition of England. In the story of the Female Vagrant, who loses her home through local tyranny, and her husband and children through war, Wordsworth created a powerful illustration for the homily he addresses to the statesmen of England on the corruption and oppression that are ravaging the nation.

The poem satisfied Wordsworth, however, for a very short time only, and in the autumn of 1795 he revised it extensively. The new poem was described to a friend who already knew *Salisbury Plain* as now "almost . . . another work,"[3] and so it is. In the second poem the poet as homilist has almost disappeared, and the Female Vagrant's story is subordinated to a more elaborately developed narrative that displays the torments of a good man driven by injustice to murder. Attempts were made to publish this poem in 1796 and

---

[1] S. T. Coleridge, *Biographia Literaria* (2 vols., 1817), I, 82–85.

[2] I have published a "reading text" of *Salisbury Plain* with manuscript collation in *Bicentenary Wordsworth Studies*, ed. Jonathan Wordsworth (Ithaca, 1970), 142–179.

[3] WW to Francis Wrangham, 20 November 1795, *EY*, 159.

1798, but when copied in 1799 or 1800 into the only manuscript that remains, DC MS. 16, it was still unpublished. In the manuscript the poem is entitled *Adventures on Salisbury Plain*.

The story of the woman was extracted and published as *The Female Vagrant* in *Lyrical Ballads*, 1798. Nothing more was published, however, until over forty years later. Two late manuscripts, DC Verse 92 and 102, show Wordsworth converting *Adventures on Salisbury Plain* into the poem published in 1842 as *Guilt and Sorrow; or Incidents upon Salisbury Plain*. His poetic treatment of experiences on Salisbury Plain thus occupied Wordsworth at widely differing periods of his career. Of the three poems presented in this volume, the two early ones are of most interest. They span some of the most exciting and creative years of Wordsworth's life and can tell us much about his development toward the great achievements of his maturity.

Salisbury Plain was the result of a happy accident. Throughout the early part of 1793, Wordsworth had been suffering the agony of a man who is opposed to the national mood yet is powerless to change it. In February war had been officially declared between France and England. For Wordsworth this was proof that his country had become the enemy of liberty, in contempt of all her proudest traditions. The war was "unnatural strife," and the thought of it ravaged his heart: "there lay it like a weight / At enmity with all the tenderest springs / Of my enjoyments."[4] By June or shortly after, his feelings had erupted in *A Letter to the Bishop of Llandaff*, but the very feebleness of any protest he could make was immediately brought home to Wordsworth as he watched the fleet preparing for war off the Isle of Wight, during his stay there in July. Unemployed, uncertain of the future, hostile to the great national crusade, the war, Wordsworth was, as he later imaged it, like a man who could feel lonely in a crowded church, "like an uninvited guest / Whom no one own'd," one who sat silent and "Fed on the day of vengeance yet to come."[5]

What released these feelings and made their energy available to the poet's creating imagination was, literally, an accident. A recalcitrant horse and a shattered carriage brought to an early end on Salisbury Plain the tour of the West Country started by Wordsworth and William Calvert in late July or early August 1793. Calvert rode away, and Wordsworth prepared to make his way over the immense waste by the help only of his "firm Friends, a pair of stout legs."[6] The account of this journey Wordsworth wrote in a letter later in life was studiously unsensational,[7] but *The Prelude*, XII, 312–353, gives a

---

[4] *Prelude*, X, 251–254.
[5] *Prelude*, X, 273–275.
[6] See DW's account of the accident to Jane Pollard, 30 August 1793, *EY*, 109.
[7] WW to John Kenyon, 1838, in Russell Noyes, "Wordsworth: An Unpublished Letter to John Kenyon," *MLR*, LIII (1958), 546–547.

more highly wrought account, in which the lonely traveler encounters the long-dead inhabitants of the Plain, sees the ancient Britons stride across the wold, and hears the shrieks of victims sacrificed by the Druids. What actually happened, of course, remains uncertain. What is sure is that the encounter with the Plain provided Wordsworth's imagination with a focusing image through which he could express much of what he had been feeling so impotently about the nature of man in society, and that the intensity of the encounter summoned up and fused dormant knowledge of many kinds to elaborate and sharpen this image. It seems likely that the poem in some form was composed at once, for in a letter of 23 May 1794, Wordsworth referred to it as "written last summer."[8] The work was called *Salisbury Plain*, though, as Wordsworth told his friend Mathews, "A night on Salisbury plain, were it not so insufferably awkward would better suit the thing itself."[9]

Salisbury Plain is rooted in its time. Along with the *Letter to the Bishop of Llandaff* it deserves a place with more famous works, both of a similar and a very different character, which reflected the radical and humanitarian opposition of the 1790s. In many respects Wordsworth was very different from the authors of *Political Justice* and *The Rights of Man*, but for a brief period he was united with them and with many others in a crusade against the follies and corruption hidden within the apparently ordered and just structure of English society. The revolutionary spirit brought old conditions into new perspectives, and the oppression of one female vagrant was suddenly seen to have intimate links with the reasons why, for instance, the country was plunging into an unjust war. The poem makes these links, emphasizing the disaster that threatens a country that has divided into two nations.

This attack on the oppression of the poor is the center from which all of the poem's questioning radiates. The woman's story of how she and her father were pauperized indignantly refutes the complacent assertions of the Bishop of Llandaff in the Appendix to his sermon "On the Wisdom and Goodness of God in having made both Rich and Poor."[10] The old father's impotence under the oppression of the wealthy, the destruction of the woman's family in the war, the inadequacy of provisions for the sick and needy—all of these *facts* are the basis for the poet's declamations which open and close the poem.[11]

---

[8] WW to William Mathews, *EY*, 120.

[9] WW to Mathews, 7 November 1794, *EY*, 136.

[10] The Appendix is in Grosart, I, 24–30. See especially "The provision which is made for the poor in this kingdom is so liberal, as, in the opinion of some, to discourage industry" (p. 27).

[11] See Grosart, I, 26, for Bishop Watson's assertion that property, acquired by "industry and probity," is secured by the constitution against the "oppression of the noble, the rapacity of the powerful, and the avarice of the rich. The courts of British justice are impartial and incorrupt . . .; with inflexible integrity they adjudge to every man his own." See also page 27 for an extraordinary discussion of the "immense sums annually subscribed by the rich for the support of hospitals, infirmaries, dispensaries."

But *Salisbury Plain* is more than a realistic account of distress.[12] A moving account of individual suffering is the focus of the poem, but around it plays a prophetic voice, which speaks of another world to which man could aspire and to which the artist as prophet must point, and which eventually includes the whole world in its apocalyptic vision:[13]

> Heroes of Truth pursue your march, uptear
> Th'Oppressor's dungeon from its deepest base;
> High o'er the towers of Pride undaunted rear
> Resistless in your might the herculean mace
> Of Reason; let foul Error's monster race
> Dragged from their dens start at the light with pain
> And die; pursue your toils, till not a trace
> Be left on earth of Superstition's reign,
> Save that eternal pile which frowns on Sarum's plain. [ll. 541–549]

The manuscript into which Wordsworth and Dorothy copied the poem is DC MS. 10. The homemade notebook has 37 leaves intact: 1–32, 35 and 37–39. Only stubs are left at 33–34, 36 and 40.[14] The notebook is made from white laid paper, with chain lines at intervals of 2.5 centimeters. It is watermarked with an image of Britannia in a circle surmounted with a crown, and countermarked with the monogram JA within a double circle containing the inscription COWEN HEAD. The poem, which was the first entry in the manuscript, runs from 1^r through 37^r. Lines 1–73, 78–108, and 226–324 are in the hand of Dorothy Wordsworth; the rest are in Wordsworth's hand. Drafts for a projected enlarged version of the poem begin on 20^v and run continuously 23^v–32^v, 37^v–38^v, 39^r–39^v. The inside front cover also contains a few draft lines. The rest of the notebook comprises other early work.[15] Dorothy Wordsworth most probably made the fair copy of *Salisbury Plain* while she and

---

[12] It should be stressed that it is a realistic account. WW claimed, "All that relates to her [the Female Vagrant's] sufferings . . . were faithfully taken from the report made to me of her own case by a friend" (*PW*, I, 330), and he felt confident enough to quote some lines from it when arguing against the real effects of the Poor Law Amendment Act in 1835 (*PW*, II, 448).

[13] The poet's double vision is presented so successfully largely because WW draws on Spenser. Eighteenth-century apologists and imitators praised Spenser's "sweetness" and pictorial charm, but neglected the visionary and prophetic aspects of *The Faerie Queene*. See WW's praise of Spenser in his 1815 Preface, which illuminates his own intentions in his Spenserian poem: Spenser "maintained his freedom by aid of his allegorical spirit, at one time inciting him to create persons out of abstractions; and, at another, by a superior effort of genius, to give the universality and permanence of abstractions to his human beings, by means of attributes and emblems that belong to the highest moral truths and the purest sensations" (*PW*, II, 440).

[14] In describing the manuscripts I have included stubs in the numbering of leaves and, where they exist, free end papers. I do not include pasted-down end papers, although any relevant writing on them is, of course, reproduced.

[15] The major items are (1) "Corrections and Additions" to *An Evening Walk*, (2) *Septimi Gades*, (3) *From the French*, (4) *From the Greek*, and (5) *Inscription for a Seat by the Pathway side ascending to Windy Brow*. One page of *Prelude* drafting remains, which suggests that the missing leaves may have been removed during work on that poem rather than on *Salisbury Plain*.

William were together at Windy Brow between early April and mid-May
1794.

The composition of the poem presents few problems of dating. Examination
of Wordsworth's various statements in the Advertisement to *Guilt and Sorrow*,
and in the Fenwick notes to that poem, *The Female Vagrant*, and *The Excursion*,[16]
shows that late in life Wordsworth was confused about the dating of the poem.
But although exact dates were hazy, it is likely that the poet would have
remembered a sequence of composition correctly. In the Fenwick note to
Guilt and Sorrow he dates the Female Vagrant's story "at least two years before"
the rest of the poem, and although the evidence is doubtful, it is possible to
find support for this statement. Around 1788, Wordsworth worked on a blank-
verse description of a vagrant family, in DC MS. 7.[17] It seems possible that in
1843, Wordsworth was remembering this work and confusing it with "The
Female Vagrant" stanzas in *Salisbury Plain*. On the other hand, it is equally
likely that these descriptive passages were worked into something like *The
Female Vagrant* before 1793 in a lost manuscript and that this was incorporated
into the larger poem.

In September 1795, Wordsworth and Dorothy began life together at
Racedown, and within two months what had seemed a poem ready for the
press was dismissed as a mere "first draught," and revision was begun.[18] The
reshaping of the poem began tentatively enough. Drafts on 29ᵛ–30ᵛ of MS. 1
show that Wordsworth considered for a time altering the shape but not the
substance of the poem. The next step, however, was more radical. A prose
outline of new incidents for the poem was entered in the Racedown Notebook,
DC MS. 11.[19] Here the meeting of the traveler and the woman is elaborated.
Attempts were then made to shape the details of the new story in the blank
spaces in MS. 1 itself. Quickly the whole poem was revised to incorporate the
new center of interest, so that by 20 November 1795, Wordsworth could write
of his poem: "Since I came to Racedown I have made alterations and addi-
tions so material as that it may be looked on almost as another work. Its object
is partly to expose the vices of the penal law and the calamities of war as they
affect individuals."[20] In MS. 2 the poem is called *Adventures on Salisbury Plain*,
and this title is used hereafter to refer to the new and revised poem.

It is strange that *Adventures on Salisbury Plain* was not published very soon
after completion, for Wordsworth and his friends were actively working to
this end. On 20 November, in the letter just cited, Wordsworth solicited

[16] See pp. 214–215 and 131, below, and *PW*, V, 376.
[17] See *Chronology: EY*, 21, 307–312.
[18] WW to Francis Wrangham, 20 November [1795], *EY*, 159.
[19] See Appendix II, below.
[20] WW to Francis Wrangham, *EY*, 159.

Wrangham's help and told him that he hoped to make money with the poem. Early in 1796 it seemed possible that it would soon go to press. In January a courteous letter from Wordsworth opened a correspondence with Coleridge's publisher, Joseph Cottle, and promised the revised poem. On 6 March, Azariah Pinney carried the manuscript to Bristol. On the seventh Wordsworth explained to Wrangham his hopes for subscription publication, and on the twenty-fifth Pinney reported that Coleridge "feels so lively an interest to bring forward so valuable a poem (as he terms it) that he assures me that his Bookseller will assist him in such a manner in the publication that he can secure you from every Expence." On 12 April, Pinney promised James Tobin that he would see the poem in print "within the duration of a few Weeks." But the haste for publication slowed. After keeping the manuscript for two weeks, Coleridge sent it to Charles Lamb. Replying at once that he had hurried through it "not without delight," Lamb promised to return it when Wordsworth should come to London. With the failure of *The Watchman*, hopes for Coleridge's help in the distribution of the poem died, and by October, Pinney had to write that the "Poem, written by a Mr. Wordsworth, that I promised to send to Ireland, has not yet appeared."[21]

One more opportunity for publication occurred, but unfortunately only after the poet's genius had already developed beyond *Salisbury Plain*. During late 1795 and early 1796 Wordsworth had worked, among other things, on Spenserian and blank-verse pieces which seem to represent attempts at re-working parts of the "Salisbury Plain" story.[22] By autumn 1796 he was engrossed in his most ambitious project yet, *The Borderers*, and after that in one still more ambitious, *The Ruined Cottage*. But when in 1798 plans for a trip to Germany clearly meant that money had to be found, *Salisbury Plain* was brought out again for negotiation. In March 1798, Coleridge offered Wordsworth's poems *Salisbury Plain* and the "Tale of a Woman" to Cottle to make a possible volume. On 9 May, Wordsworth urged Cottle to visit him, adding, "I say nothing of the Salisbury Plain 'till I see you, I am determined to finish it, and equally so that You shall publish."[23] But Wordsworth's determination came to nothing, for the negotiations ended, not with the publication of *Salisbury Plain* but of *Lyrical Ballads*, which included an extract from the longer

[21] See WW to Joseph Cottle, [January 1796], *EY*, 163; *Chronology: EY*, 179; WW to Francis Wrangham, 7 March [1796], *EY*, 168; Bergen Evans and Hester Pinney, "Racedown and the Wordsworths," *RES*, VIII (1932), 13; Azariah Pinney to James Tobin, 12 April 1796, Pinney Papers, Bristol University Library; F. W. Bateson, *Wordsworth: A Re-Interpretation* (London, 1954), 15n; Charles Lamb to STC, 24 or 31 May [1796], *The Letters of Charles Lamb*, ed. E. V. Lucas (3 vols.; London, 1935), I, 8–9; Azariah Pinney to H. Cole, 25 October 1796, Pinney Papers.
[22] See Appendix I, below.
[23] See STC to Joseph Cottle [c. 13 March 1798], *STCL*, I, 400; WW to Joseph Cottle, 9 May 1798, *EY*, 218.

poem, called *The Female Vagrant*.[24] Although tantalizing bait was dangled before the public in the coming years, nothing more was heard of publication of *Salisbury Plain* for forty years.[25]

The only manuscript which records the poem in its second phase, MS. 2, is DC MS. 16, one of Dorothy's pocketbooks. This notebook has 59 leaves intact: 1, 4–7, 10–12, 28–34, 39–69, 74–82, and 87–90. Only stubs remain at 2–3, 8–9, 13–27, 35–38, 70–73, and 83–86. The white laid paper, with chain lines at intervals of 2.1 centimeters, is watermarked with a design which suggests, from the little that is visible, the fleur-de-lis. An extensive account of the contents of the manuscript and its relation to other manuscripts of the period is given in Appendix IX of Reed's *Chronology*, so only those parts of the notebook which have a particular bearing on *Adventures on Salisbury Plain* will be dealt with here.

The poem, now headed *Adventures on Salisbury Plain*, is copied neatly in Dorothy's hand in two parts. Part First runs from 28^r through versos and rectos to 33^r, and Part Second from 40^r to 45^v. Outside the main text, drafts occur on 11^v–12^r in William's hand, representing work on alternative openings for Stanza 3, and on 39^r, work on Stanza 64; on 39^v, in Dorothy's hand, appear fair copies of two stanzas ultimately not used, tying the Soldier and the Female Vagrant more closely into the poem; on 79^v, in the later hand of Mary Wordsworth, is a copy of *Guilt and Sorrow*, Stanza LXXII, and the opening of Stanza LXIII.

The manuscript itself raises a number of questions of interest about *Adventures on Salisbury Plain*. The first concerns the dating of the manuscript and thus of the only known copy of the poem in its second state. De Selincourt suggested[26] that MS. 2 belonged to summer 1798 or to winter 1799, but not later than Wordsworth's comments to Coleridge in February 1799 on the progress of revision of the poem:

I also took courage to devote two days (O Wonder) to the Salisbury Plain. I am resolved to discard Robert Walford and invent a new story for the woman. The poem

---

[24] For full details of various aspects of the genesis of *Lyrical Ballads* see Stephen M. Parrish, "The Wordsworth-Coleridge Controversy," *PMLA*, LXXIII (1958), 367–374, revised in *The Art of the Lyrical Ballads* (Cambridge, Mass., 1973); Mark L. Reed, "Wordsworth, Coleridge and the 'Plan' of the *Lyrical Ballads*," *UTQ*, XXXIV (1965), 238–253; *Wordsworth and Coleridge: Lyrical Ballads 1798*, ed. W. J. B. Owen (Oxford, 1967), vii–xx.

[25] In 1816, Coleridge recalled in *Biographia Literaria* the astounding quality of *Salisbury Plain*, in the passage quoted at the beginning of this Introduction. Joseph Cottle, in 1837, went further and expressed the view that *Salisbury Plain* was "with the exception of the 'Excursion,' the poem of all others, on which I thought Mr. Wordsworth might most advantageously rest his fame as a poet" (*Early Recollections*; *Chiefly Relating to the Late Samuel Taylor Coleridge* [2 vols.; London, 1837], I, 314n).

[26] *PW*, I, 331.

is finished all but her tale. Now by way of a pretty moving accident and to bind together in palpable knots the story of the piece I have resolved to make her the widow or sister or daughter of the man whom the poor Tar murdered. So much for the vulgar. Further the Poets invention goeth not. This is by way of giving a physical totality to the piece, which I regard as finish'd minus 24 stanzas the utmost tether allowed to the poor Lady.[27]

The manuscript evidence, however, suggests another line of reasoning. In de Selincourt's view the revision work in the manuscript at 39^v and 46^v must represent the two days' work to which Wordsworth refers in the letter to Coleridge just mentioned. But this supposition seems mistaken, for whatever the relation of these stanzas to Wordsworth's growing conception of the poem, they are not draft. They are entered neatly into blank spaces after the completion of some work on *The Prelude* and of the copying of Part Second of *Adventures on Salisbury Plain*. They are fair copies of the corrections Wordsworth may have been making in February 1799 and, like all fair copies, may have been entered after the original date of composition.

One may perhaps go further. The letter to Coleridge shows Wordsworth planning a story for the woman to replace the extract printed in *Lyrical Ballads*, 1798. But in the MS. 2 copy of the poem there is no space for any story. In Part Second asterisks are left to show that some necessary episode is missing; in Part First there are not even these. MS. 2 is a fair copy of the poem made after Wordsworth has decided that, for the time being at least, invention does not run to another story for the woman. Work on the second edition of *Lyrical Ballads* absorbed the Wordsworths through the summer of 1800. The copy of *Adventures on Salisbury Plain* was thus most likely made after April 1799 and before summer 1800, most probably after the beginning of May 1799, when the Wordsworths began their visit to Sockburn.

If the letter of February 1799 does not help after all, what date can be assigned? Mark Reed has demonstrated that the poems in the Alfoxden, Christabel, and DC MS. 16 notebooks are usually in their most developed form in DC MS. 16, and that most of the copies in this manuscript can be dated after the visit to Goslar.[28] There is no need to repeat his detailed arguments here, but it is worth while to touch on the nature of the evidence that helps us to date this copy of *Adventures on Salisbury Plain*. Parts First and Second are divided at 33^v and 34^r–34^v by draft work on lines appearing in *Prelude*, V, and then by four stubs of pages which contained work on *Prelude*, I. Leaf 39^r contains the end of Book I, and 39^v the abortive opening of Book II.[29] It seems unlikely that these opening lines preceded Wordsworth's meeting with

---

[27] See WW and DW to STC, 27 February [1799], *EY*, 256–257.
[28] *Chronology: EY*, 321–328.
[29] See *Prelude*, II, 1, *app. crit.*

Coleridge in Göttingen in April 1799, but likely that the copy of *Adventures on Salisbury Plain* followed their entry into the notebook.

Some comments need to be made also about the nature of the revisions in the manuscript. The first, and most important, is that there are two main levels of revision, which must be clearly differentiated. Study of the facsimiles presented below shows that early revisions are to be distinguished from the late revisions in the hand of Mary Wordsworth. The first tamper piecemeal with the poem, but the second attempt considerable reconstruction and can probably be assigned to 1841–1842, when Wordsworth was revising the poem for the 1842 volume, *Poems, Chiefly of Early and Late Years*. Some of this revision is puzzling. Lines on 39ᵛ and 46ᵛ show Wordsworth, as he says, trying to "bind together in palpable knots the story of the piece."[30] The soldier now becomes the father of the woman brought in dying, so that his earlier explanation that he was journeying to meet a daughter in distress is verified. The female vagrant is called Rachael, and it is her husband the sailor has murdered. These lines offer a coherent restatement of the relationships of the characters. Two more stanzas, however, are much less easily fitted into the framework of the poem as it stands. On 11ᵛ some lines seem to reverse all the earlier attitudes toward the old soldier. He speaks of having a pension and of living well in his own home. But he speaks in the past tense, and it may be that Wordsworth meant the old man's previous security to contrast with his present destitution. One must be as tentative about the stanza on 33ʳ, describing the "man of knotty joints." The details of the scene described do not fulfill any obvious need in the poem.

The most important question remains: what stage of the poem does this MS. 2 copy represent? Caution is needed in weighing the evidence, for some details are difficult to assess with confidence. One problem concerns the make-up of the story at a given date. In February 1799, Wordsworth had written to Coleridge that as part of the revision of *Adventures on Salisbury Plain* he was resolved to "discard Robert Walford."[31] Wordsworth had used part of this name before. Shortly after March 1797, Thomas Poole told him the story of one John Walford, and Wordsworth incorporated the pathetic story into his poem *A Somersetshire Tragedy*.[32] In 1799, in the letter quoted earlier, Wordsworth drew on the name again to distinguish for Coleridge one of the characters in *Adventures on Salisbury Plain*, the poem Coleridge already knew. He must have been referring to the old soldier, since the sailor, far from being discarded in the revisions, is tied into the story more tightly than before. It

---

[30] WW and DW to STC, 27 February [1799], *EY*, 256.
[31] *EY*, 256.
[32] See Jonathan Wordsworth, "A Wordsworth Tragedy," *Times Literary Supplement*, 21 (July 1966), 642.

is improbable that Wordsworth would have stumbled on the name Walford before hearing it from Poole, and if he did not, an approximate date can be fixed for the soldier's entry into the poem.[33] In this particular, then, MS. 2 does not represent the poem of 1795.

The second reason for caution is that some lines found in *Adventures on Salisbury Plain* are also found in the fragments edited below in Appendix I and in de Selincourt's "Fragment of a 'Gothic' Tale."[34] The fragments are the work of late 1795 to October 1796, that is, of the period after the completion of the version of *Adventures on Salisbury Plain* mentioned to Wrangham on 20 November 1795, but before the copying of MS. 2 in 1799. The lines can thus be seen in two ways: either as belonging to 1795, worked into the drafting of 1795–1796, and recorded in the manuscript of 1799; or as having been composed during the drafting of 1795–1796 and incorporated by Wordsworth into *Adventures on Salisbury Plain* sometime before the fair copy of 1799. If the latter is the case, the manuscript of 1799 again does not represent exactly the poem of 1795. Although such evidence suggests that the 1795 poem is now lost to us, there is no doubt that substantially, if not in every detail, it has survived in the poem in MS. 2, *Adventures on Salisbury Plain*.

Adventures on Salisbury Plain is both a continuation and a consummation of *Salisbury Plain*. It continues the social and political interests of the poem, and even extends them, but this continuing attack on the government of the country does not draw on any really new response to contemporary conditions. There were many good reasons why the attack should continue,[35] and it is successful because the rhetoric of *Salisbury Plain* has been replaced by a fully dramatized presentation of the human calamities consequent upon war, but Wordsworth's interest was rapidly shifting from social and political phenomena to the more complex phenomena of human motives and behavior.

The dramatic structure of *Adventures on Salisbury Plain*, in which the poet's intrusive voice has largely disappeared, enables Wordsworth to develop this interest in characters who are felt to be independent of the strictly didactic patterning which determines the shape of *Salisbury Plain*. The poem now

---

[33] It will be seen from the transcript of the additions to MS. 1, below, that the revisions touch on the sailor and the woman but do not mention a soldier. Bateson noted the letter, but, I think, misinterpreted the evidence when he wrote that in 1799 the "only name he [WW] could think of for his murderer-hero was Walford" (*Wordsworth*, 134).

[34] See (1) "'Gothic' Tale," ll. 200–202, *PW*, I, 292, and *ASP*, ll. 412–414; and (2) the fragments in Appendix I, ll. 88–90, below, and in the MS. 2 transcription, below. The same argument as to priority applies to *The Ruined Cottage*, MS. B, ll. 353–354, *PW*, V, 390, and *ASP*, ll. 743.

[35] At the end of *Salisbury Plain* WW prophesied that "Error's monster race," once dragged from its den, would "start at the light with pain / And die." Actually, the war continued; habeas corpus was not restored, and the 1794 treason trials did nothing to restore the liberties of the people, which were further eroded by the acts of 1795; social distress markedly worsened during 1794 and 1795.

proofs of Stanza 56 to the end.[46] DC Verse 92, referred to hereafter as MS. 3, is a half-leather bound notebook with 96 leaves, including free end papers, intact: 1–6, 13–18, 20–21, 23–51, 56–65, 67–72, 75–82, 89–99, 107–110, 114–125, and 129. Stubs remain at 7–12, 19, 22, 52–55, 66, 73–74, 83–88, 100–106, 111–113, and 126–128. After 129 an indeterminate number of leaves have been removed. The gathering 89–106 of blue-tinted laid paper, with chain lines at intervals of 2.5 centimeters, has been crudely sewn with green tape onto the last of the stubs 83–88. The white wove paper of leaves 1–88 and 107 to the end is watermarked RR 1803. The inserted gathering is watermarked with an image of Britannia in a circle surmounted by a crown and countermarked with the monogram EH 1838. The volume consists of fair copies, almost entirely in the handwriting of Mary Wordsworth, of mis-cellaneous late poems and the Scotch and Italian tour sequences. These poems are all in fair copies running on rectos from front to back. Part of *Guilt and Sorrow* runs, with notebook inverted, on the versos from 51^v back to 47^v, including only Stanza 61 to the end of the published version of the poem. Stanzas 71–72 were not included in the consecutive fair copying, but they were copied on 47^v after the end of the poem. It will be noted that the episode of the beaten boy is not included in the stanzas mentioned here. The episode was thought of as part of the poem at some stage, however, for Stanzas 54–57 are found on a loose sheet of the blue-tinted paper, which was at one time pinned into MS. 3. The manuscript presents a fragmentary text and seems to be a fair copy of the corrected Part Second of MS. 2. Comparative readings across the last manuscripts, however, reveal that MSS. 2 and 3 must have been in use at the same time. It is possible to see also by comparison of hand-writing in developing revisions that Mary Wordsworth was using both manu-scripts to write out the poet's corrections.

One very puzzling question is, What were these revisions? The problem can be simply put. Calculations on the end papers of MS. 3 show that Words-worth was thinking of a poem of 47 nine-line stanzas. *Guilt and Sorrow* was published with 74. In MS. 2 the stanzas of Part First are corrected and numbered to 20; in MS. 3 they are numbered 28–41. What version of the poem can this numbering represent? We can only conjecture, but the evidence does suggest that for a while Wordsworth considered very drastic revision indeed. He did not want to duplicate *The Female Vagrant*,[47] yet had not been able to make up another story for the woman. Without her narrative, however, the poem is unbalanced, so it seems that Wordsworth contemplated altering it still further. MS. 2 shows that after extensive deletion what remained was

---

[46] The first-stage proofs are now in the Tracy W. McGregor Library, University of Virginia, Charlottesville, Virginia. The second-stage proofs are at Dove Cottage.

[47] See WW to Edward Moxon, 18 January 1842 and 22 July 1843, *LY*, III, 1111–1112 and 1172, for WW's changing attitudes about the subject of reprinting *The Female Vagrant*.

a poem of 46 to 48 stanzas.[48] If we accept the idea that the late corrections in MS. 2 and the copy in MS. 3 together represent an intermediate version between *Adventures on Salisbury Plain* and *Guilt and Sorrow*, then it is possible to work out a cut-down version of the story which would make sense of the numbering of the stanzas. MS. 2 ends with Stanza 20. MS. 3 begins with 28. Seven stanzas are missing in which the sailor and the woman can cross the plain, descend to the valley, and arrive at the stream. Later, when the idea of a truncated poem was abandoned, the stanzas giving the episode of the beaten boy were copied onto a loose sheet, which was then put with MS. 3.

DC Verse 102 (referred to hereafter as MS. 4) is, by contrast, straightforward. The portion which contains *Guilt and Sorrow* is a crudely sewn collection, of different-sized leaves, of fair copies of poems for the 1842 volume. Thirty-six leaves are intact: 1–14, 16–29, and 31–36. Stubs remain at 16 and 30. One loose sheet remains also. The collection is made up of various papers. 1–2, 23–25, and 36 are of blue-tinted wove. 3–22, 26–35, and the loose sheet are of white wove, embossed "London Superfine." "Incidents upon Salisbury Plain," as the poem is now headed, runs on rectos and versos from 2^r through 20^r. The Advertisement occupies 1^r and 1^v. The poem is in the hand of Mary Wordsworth, except for the Female Vagrant's story, which has been copied in by an as yet unidentified amanuensis. Stanzas 12 and 13 are copied in an order the reverse of that in which they were published in *Guilt and Sorrow*. The original copy of the opening stanzas was so heavily corrected that it was not sewn into the final collection, and it remains loose, as mentioned above. Another legible copy was made of the opening for the final sewing-up. The manuscript presents a skillful revision of *Adventures on Salisbury Plain*. Wordsworth has composed very little afresh, and it would be idle to argue that the manuscript represents a major imaginative effort. There is evidence, however, of a major exercise of artistic self-discipline and of refined technical skill, as the redundancies of the earlier work are trimmed away.

The poems presented in this volume belong to some of the most formative and creative years of Wordsworth's life. They draw on his knowledge of past literature, refreshed by his own current experience. They reveal the progress of a great mind from indebtedness of various kinds to the more original exercise of its powers. Each new version records a triumph over artistic problems. Some stages in the development of the poems remain unclear, and we can never recapture exactly the experience of Wordsworth's earliest readers, such as Cottle, Pinney, and Coleridge, but it is now more nearly possible to see the early poems as they saw them and, like Lamb, to "hurry through" them "not without delight."

---

[48] The doubt arises because it is not certain whether some stanzas are to be considered as entirely or only partly deleted.

Editorial Procedure

This edition provides (1) underlying basic texts, or "reading texts," of *Salisbury Plain, Adventures on Salisbury Plain,* and *Guilt and Sorrow*; and (2) full transcriptions of the early manuscripts, sometimes with facing photographic reproductions, for study of the composition and development of the poems. Editorial procedures have been adapted to the different aims of the two styles of presentation.

The reading texts of *Salisbury Plain* and *Adventures on Salisbury Plain* present the text of the fair copies of the poems in their earliest complete state, save for a few silent corrections of obvious errors or false starts. The text of *Adventures on Salisbury Plain* has been supplemented by *The Female Vagrant*, which was not copied into the manuscript (see Introduction and the Prefatory Note to the reading text, below). Punctuation and stanza and line numbering are editorial, but accidentals otherwise follow the original, except that ampersands have been spelled out. Square brackets enclosing blank spaces indicate words or a line missing in the text. The text of *Guilt and Sorrow* follows the text of its first publication, in 1842, in *Poems, Chiefly of Early and Late Years*.

Presentation of the transcriptions is rather more complex. A major peculiarity of Wordsworth's manuscripts is that much of the writing is not in the poet's own hand but in that of amanuenses or copyists, generally Dorothy or Mary Wordsworth or Sara Hutchinson. The transcriptions present the passages that are in Wordsworth's hand in roman type, all others in italic (although in the case of occasional scattered words and phrases identification of the hand can only be conjectural). Where transcripts face photographs, doubled-back lines are transcribed roughly as they appear. Revisions are in smaller type, above or below the line to which they pertain, whenever that can be determined. The primary object of the transcriptions, to aid reading of the manuscripts, is of course not always served by exact duplication of the arrangement of the original writing. Spacing has occasionally, therefore, been simplified, and stanza numbers set apart. Line numbers are assigned to each complete line of the fair copy, but lines of correction are not numbered and are normally indented. In the separate transcriptions of the frequently jumbled additions to MSS. 1 and 2—written on pages where no fair copy appears—the numbers of corresponding lines in the main texts are indicated in the right-hand margin.

Deletions are indicated either by a horizontal line drawn through a word or phrase, or by vertical or diagonal lines which simulate the larger deletion marks actually in the manuscript. Deletion marks have been extended or shortened if reproducing them exactly would introduce confusion about Wordsworth's intentions. Random marks, reinforced letters, or overwritten partial letters are not normally recorded.

An *apparatus criticus* supplies a record of printed textual variants of *The Female Vagrant* and of variants in MS. 3 and the proof, as well as the printed texts, of *Guilt and Sorrow*.

Although in describing the manuscripts I have included stubs in the numbering of leaves and, where they exist, free end papers, I do not include pasted-down end papers, but any relevant writing on them is transcribed.

The following symbols are used in transcription of manuscripts:

[?patient]	Doubtful word.
[? ?]	Illegible words; each question mark represents one word.
[——?——]	Illegible word deleted.
t⎫ As⎭	An overwriting; the original letter "s" is overwritten "t" so as to convert "As" to "At".
s⎱ ⎰	A short addition, sometimes only a mark of punctuation.
He bore a scythe	Words written over an erasure; the original is now illegible.
[ ]	Used only in the transcription of MS. 4 to indicate words concealed by sealing wax.

Salisbury Plain (1793–1794)

Reading Text

Salisbury Plain

1

Hard is the life when naked and unhouzed
And wasted by the long day's fruitless pains,
The hungry savage, 'mid deep forests, rouzed
By storms, lies down at night on unknown plains
And lifts his head in fear, while famished trains   5
Of boars along the crashing forests prowl,
And heard in darkness, as the rushing rains
Put out his watch-fire, bears contending growl
And round his fenceless bed gaunt wolves in armies howl.

2

Yet is he strong to suffer, and his mind   10
Encounters all his evils unsubdued;
For happier days since at the breast he pined
He never knew, and when by foes pursued
With life he scarce has reached the fortress rude,
While with the war-song's peal the valleys shake,   15
What in those wild assemblies has he viewed
But men who all of his hard lot partake,
Repose in the same fear, to the same toil awake?

3

The thoughts which bow the kindly spirits down
And break the springs of joy, their deadly weight   20
Derive from memory of pleasures flown
Which haunts us in some sad reverse of fate,
Or from reflection on the state
Of those who on the couch of Affluence rest
By laughing Fortune's sparkling cup elate,   25
While we of comfort reft, by pain depressed,
No other pillow know than Penury's iron breast.

4

Hence where Refinement's genial influence calls
The soft affections from their wintry sleep

And the sweet tear of Love and Friendship falls   30
The willing heart in tender joy to steep,
When men in various vessels roam the deep
Of social life, and turns of chance prevail
Various and sad, how many thousands weep
Beset with foes more fierce than e'er assail   35
The savage without home in winter's keenest gale.

5

The troubled west was red with stormy fire,
O'er Sarum's plain the traveller with a sigh
Measured each painful step, the distant spire
That fixed at every turn his backward eye   40
Was lost, tho' still he turned, in the blank sky.
By thirst and hunger pressed he gazed around
And scarce could any trace of man descry,
Save wastes of corn that stretched without a bound,
But where the sower dwelt was nowhere to be found.   45

6

No shade was there, no meads of pleasant green,
No brook to wet his lips or soothe his ear,
Huge piles of corn-stack here and there were seen
But thence no smoke upwreathed his sight to cheer;
And see the homeward shepherd dim appear   50
Far off—He stops his feeble voice to strain;
No sound replies but winds that whistling near
Sweep the thin grass and passing, wildly plain;
Or desert lark that pours on high a wasted strain.

7

Long had each slope he mounted seemed to hide   55
Some cottage whither his tired feet might turn,
But now, all hope resigned, in tears he eyed
The crows in blackening eddies homeward borne,
Then sought, in vain, a shepherd's lowly thorn
Or hovel from the storm to shield his head.   60
On as he passed more wild and more forlorn
And vacant the huge plain around him spread;
Ah me! the wet cold ground must be his only bed.

38   Sarum's] Salisbury's.

8

Hurtle the rattling clouds together piled
By fiercer gales, and soon the storm must break.   65
He stood the only creature in the wild
On whom the elements their rage could wreak,
Save that the bustard of those limits bleak,
Shy tenant, seeing there a mortal wight
At that dread hour, outsent a mournful shriek   70
And half upon the ground, with strange affright,
Forced hard against the wind a thick unwieldy flight.

9

The Sun unheeded sunk, while on a mound
He stands beholding with astonished gaze,
Frequent upon the deep entrenched ground,   75
Strange marks of mighty arms of former days,
Then looking up at distance he surveys
What seems an antique castle spreading wide.
Hoary and naked are its walls and raise
Their brow sublime; while to those walls he hied   80
A voice as from a tomb in hollow accents cried:

10

"Oh from that mountain-pile avert thy face
Whate'er betide at this tremendous hour.
To hell's most cursed sprites the baleful place
Belongs, upreared by their magic power.   85
Though mixed with flame rush down the crazing shower
And o'er thy naked bed the thunder roll
Fly ere the fiends their prey unwares devour
Or grinning, on thy endless tortures scowl
Till very madness seem a mercy to thy soul.   90

---

68   bustard] The great bustard (*Otis tarda*), formerly common in England.

70   outsent] The use of such compounds as "outsent" is common in eighteenth-century Miltonic and Spenserian verse. For the fullest discussion of eighteenth-century Spenserianisms see Earl R. Wasserman, *Elizabethan Poetry in the Eighteenth Century*, Illinois Studies in Language and Literature, XXXII, Nos. 2–3 (Urbana, 1947). For WW's comments on the Spenserian stanza later in life see his considered statement to Catherine Grace Godwin in 1829 (*LY*, I, 439).

88   unwares] A Spenserian turn which appears many times in *FQ*, e.g., "The faire Enchauntresse, so unwares opprest" (II, xii, lxxxi, 8).

11

"For oft at dead of night, when dreadful fire
Reveals that powerful circle's reddening stones,
'Mid priests and spectres grim and idols dire,
Far heard the great flame utters human moans,
Then all is hushed: again the desert groans,   95
A dismal light its farthest bounds illumes,
While warrior spectres of gigantic bones,
Forth-issuing from a thousand rifted tombs,
Wheel on their fiery steeds amid the infernal glooms."

12

The voice was from beneath but face or form   100
He saw not, mocked as by a hideous dream.
Three hours he wildered through the watery storm
No moon to open the black clouds and stream
From narrow gulph profound one friendly beam;
No watch-dog howled from shepherd's homely shed.   105
Once did the lightning's pale abortive beam
Disclose a naked guide-post's double head,
Sole object where he stood had day its radiance spread.

13

'Twas dark and waste as ocean's shipless flood
Roaring with storms beneath night's starless gloom.   110
[   ]
Where the wet gypsey in her straw-built home
Warmed her wet limbs by fire of fern and broom.
No transient meteor burst upon his sight
Nor taper glimmered dim from sick man's room.   115
Along the moor no line of mournful light
From lamp of lonely toll-gate streamed athwart the night.

14

At length, deep hid in clouds, the moon arose
And spread a sickly glare. With flight unwilled,

---

92   powerful circle's] Stonehenge's.
117   One of the many instances in this poem where an exact observation is couched in consciously poetic language. Cf. *Rape of the Lock*, II, 82: ". . . stars that shoot athwart the Night." For comments on the diction of *The Female Vagrant* see Emile Legouis, "Some Remarks on the Composition of the *Lyrical Ballads* of 1798," *Wordsworth and Coleridge: Studies in Honor of George McLean Harper*, ed. Earl Leslie Griggs (Princeton, 1939), 6–7. See also note to l. 228 below.

Worn out and wasted, wishing the repose   120
Of death, he came where, antient vows fulfilled,
Kind pious hands did to the Virgin build
A lonely Spital, the belated swain
From the night-terrors of that waste to shield.
But there no human being could remain   125
And now the walls are named the dead house of the plain.

15

Till then as if his terror dogged his road
He fled, and often backward cast his face;
And when the ambiguous gloom that ruin shewed
How glad he was at length to find a place   130
That bore of human hands the chearing trace:
Here shall he rest till Morn her eye unclose.
Ah me! that last of hopes is fled apace;
For, entering in, his hair in horror rose
To hear a voice that seemed to mourn in sorrow's throes.   135

16

It was the voice of one that sleeping mourned,
A human voice! and soon his terrors fled;
At dusk a female wanderer hither turned
And found a comfortless half-sheltered bed.
The moon a wan dead light around her shed;   140
He waked her and at once her spirits fail
Thrill'd by the poignant dart of sudden dread,
For of that ruin she had heard a tale
That might with a child's fears the stoutest heart assail.

---

123   Spital] House for the indigent; here, a shelter for travelers.
127–128   Cf. *FQ*, I, ix, xxi, 5–6:
    Still as he fled, his eye was backward cast,
    As if his feare still followed him behind.
The image is fairly common in *FQ*; see III, i, xvi, 1; and V, viii, iv, 9.
   134   his hair in horror rose] Cf. the moment in *FQ*, I, ii, xxxi, 8–9, when the Redcrosse Knight
plucks at the man-tree Fradubio:
    Astound he stood, and up his hair did hove
    And with that suddein horror could no member move.
   142   WW's metaphor has an accuracy which is now unrecognized. "Thrill'd" comes from a
form of the OE word for "pierce." The meaning was quite clear to Spenser, as many examples
show: e.g., *FQ*, I, viii, xxxix, 1–2: "Which when that Champion heard, with percing point / Of
pitty deare his hart was thrilled sore," and *FQ*, II, i, xxxviii, 5: "Or thrild with point of thorough
piercing paine." *SP*, l. 186, however, fails to respect the metaphoric use.

17

Had heard of one who forced from storms to shroud   145
Felt the loose walls of this decayed retreat
Rock to his horse's neighings shrill and loud,
While the ground rang by ceaseless pawing beat,
Till on a stone that sparkled to his feet
Struck and still struck again the troubled horse.   150
The man half raised that stone by pain and sweat,
Half raised; for well his arm might lose its force
Disclosing the grim head of a new murdered corse.

18

Such tales of the lone Spital she had learned,
And when that shape with eyes in sleep half-drowned   155
By the moon's sullen lamp she scarce discerned,
Cold stony horror all her senses bound.
But he to her low words of chearing sound
Addressed. With joy she heard such greeting kind
And much they conversed of that desert ground,   160
Which seemed to those of other worlds consigned
Whose voices still they heard as paused the hollow wind.

19

The Woman told that through a hollow deep
As on she journeyed, far from spring or bower,
An old man beckoning from the naked steep   165
Came tottering sidelong down to ask the hour;
There never clock was heard from steeple tower.
From the wide corn the plundering crows to scare
He held a rusty gun. In sun and shower,
Old as he was, alone he lingered there,   170
His hungry meal too scant for dog that meal to share.

20

Much of the wonders of that boundless heath
He spoke, and of a swain who far astray
Reached unawares a height and saw beneath
Gigantic beings ranged in dread array.   175

---

157   Cf. *FQ,* I, vi, xxxvii, 2–3:
      That suddein cold did runne through every vaine,
      And stony horrour all her senses fild.
(See *PW,* I, 334.)

Such beings thwarting oft the traveller's way
With shield and stone-ax stride across the wold,
Or, throned on that dread circle's summit gray
Of mountains hung in air, their state unfold,
And like a thousand Gods mysterious council hold.   180

21

And oft a night-fire mounting to the clouds
Reveals the desert and with dismal red
Clothes the black bodies of encircling crowds.
It is the sacrificial altar fed
With living men. How deep it groans—the dead   185
Thrilled in their yawning tombs their helms uprear;
The sword that slept beneath the warrior's head
Thunders in fiery air: red arms appear
Uplifted thro' the gloom and shake the rattling spear.

22

Not thus where clear moons spread their pleasing light.   190
—Long bearded forms with wands uplifted shew
To vast assemblies, while each breath of night
Is hushed, the living fires that bright and slow
Rounding th'aetherial field in order go.
Then as they trace with awe their various files   195
All figured on the mystic plain below,
Still prelude of sweet sounds the moon beguiles
And charmed for many a league the hoary desart smiles.

23

While thus they talk the churlish storms relent;
And round those broken walls the dying wind   200
In feeble murmurs told his rage was spent.
With sober sympathy and tranquil mind
Gently the Woman gan her wounds unbind.
Might Beauty charm the canker worm of pain
The rose on her sweet cheek had ne'er declined: 205
Moved she not once the prime of Keswick's plain
While Hope and Love and Joy composed her smiling train?

24

Like swans, twin swans, that when on the sweet brink
Of Derwent's stream the south winds hardly blow,

'Mid Derwent's water-lillies swell and sink   210
In union, rose her sister breasts of snow,
(Fair emblem of two lovers' hearts that know
No separate impulse) or like infants played,
Like infants strangers yet to pain and woe.
Unwearied Hope to tend their motions made   215
Long Vigils, and Delight her cheek between them laid.

25

And are ye spread ye glittering dews of youth
For this,—that Frost may gall the tender flower
In Joy's fair breast with more untimely tooth?
Unhappy man! thy sole delightful hour   220
Flies first; it is thy miserable dower
Only to taste of joy that thou may'st pine
A loss, which rolling suns shall ne'er restore.
New suns roll on and scatter as they shine
No second spring, but pain, till death release thee, thine.   225

26

"By Derwent's side my father's cottage stood,"
The mourner thus her artless story told.
"A little flock and what the finny flood
Supplied, to him were more than mines of gold.
Light was my sleep; my days in transport rolled: 230
With thoughtless joy I stretched along the shore
My parent's nets, or watched, when from the fold
High o'er the cliffs I led his fleecy store,
A dizzy depth below! his boat and twinkling oar.

215–216   In revision these lines read:
    Their sensible warm motions transport swayed
    By day, and Peace at night her cheek between them laid.
WW also used the phrase "sensible warm motion" in the 1794 revisions of *An Evening Walk* in
the Windy Brow notebook, DC MS. 10. See *PW*, I, 7. De Selincourt notes that WW echoes
Claudio's words in *Measure for Measure*, III, i, 119–120: "This sensible warm motion to become / A
kneaded clod." See *The Early Wordsworth*, The English Association Presidential Address (n.p.,
1936), 28, n. 16.
214–223   An image of the transience of man's early life used earlier by WW in *In Part from
Moschus: Lament for Bion* (c. 1788), *PW*, I, 286:
    Man's sweet and pleasant time, his morn of life
    Flies first, and come diseases on and age.
228   finny flood] Cf. *FQ*, III, vııı, xxix, 9: "driving his finny drove." De Selincourt comments
on the poetic diction of this and other phrases, *PW*, I, 337. See also note to l. 117, above.

27

"Can I forget my seat beneath the thorn,   235
My garden stored with peas and mint and thyme,
And rose and lilly for the sabbath morn;
The church-inviting bell's delightful chime,
The merriment and song at shearing time,
My hen's rich nest with long grass overgrown,   240
The cowslip gathering at the morning prime,
The hazel copse with teeming clusters brown,
[   ]

28

"Can I forget the casement where I fed
The red-breast when the fields were whitened o'er,   245
My snowy kerchiefs on the hawthorn spread
My humming wheel and glittering table store,
The well-known knocking at the evening door,
The hunted slipper and the blinded game,
The dance that loudly beat the merry floor,   250
The ballad chaunted round the brightening flame
While down the ravaged hills the storm unheeded came?

29

"The suns of eighteen summers danced along
Joyous as in the pleasant morn of May.
At last by cruel chance and wilful wrong   255
My father's substance fell into decay.
Oppression trampled on his tresses grey:
His little range of water was denied;
Even to the bed where his old body lay
His all was seized; and weeping side by side   260
Turned out on the cold winds, alone we wandered wide.

30

"Can I forget that miserable hour
When from the last hill-top my sire surveyed,

---

258   WW's note, *Lyrical Ballads*, 1798–1800: "Several of the Lakes in the north of England
are let out to different Fishermen, in parcels marked out by imaginary lines drawn from rock
to rock."

261   See Z. S. Fink, *The Early Wordsworthian Milieu* (Oxford, 1958), 88–89 and 134–135, for
a story of local oppression, known to WW, in which an old couple are tyrannized because they
will not sell a field to a local landowner.

Peering above the trees, the steeple-tower
That on his marriage-day sweet music made?   265
There at my birth my mother's bones were laid
And there, till then, he hoped his own might rest.
Bidding me trust in God he stood and prayed:
I could not pray, by human grief oppressed,
Viewing our glimmering cot through tears that never ceased.   270

31

"There was a youth whose tender voice and eye
Might add fresh happiness to happiest days.
At uprise of the sun when he was by
The birds prolonged with joy their choicest lays,
The soft pipe warbled out a wilder maze,   275
The silent moon of evening, hung above,
Showered through the waving lime-trees mellower rays;
Warm was the breath of night: his voice of love
Charmed the rude winds to sleep by river, field, or grove.

32

"His father bid him to a distant town   280
To ply remote from groves the artist's trade.
What tears of bitter grief till then unknown,
What tender vows our last sad kiss delayed!
To him our steps we turned, by hope upstayed.
Oh with what bliss upon his neck I wept;   285
And her whom he had loved in joy, he said,
He well could love in grief: his faith he kept,
And sheltered from the winds once more my father slept.

33

"Four years each day with daily bread was blessed,
By constant toil and constant prayer supplied.   290
Three lovely infants lay within my breast
And often viewing their sweet smiles I sighed
And knew not why. My happy father died
Just as the children's meal began to fail.
For War the nations to the field defied.   295
The loom stood still; unwatched, the idle gale
Wooed in deserted shrouds the unregarding sail.

34

"How changed at once! for Labor's chearful hum
Silence and Fear, and Misery's weeping train.
But soon with proud parade the noisy drum   300
Beat round to sweep the streets of want and pain.
My husband's arms now only served to strain
Me and his children hungering in his view.
He could not beg: my prayers and tears were vain;
To join those miserable men he flew.   305
We reached the western world a poor devoted crew.

35

"Oh dreadful price of being! to resign
All that is dear in being; better far
In Want's most lonely cave till death to pine
Unseen, unheard, unwatched by any star.   310
Better before proud Fortune's sumptuous car
Obvious our dying bodies to obtrude,
Than dog-like wading at the heels of War
Protract a cursed existence with the brood
That lap, their very nourishment, their brother's blood.   315

36

"The pains and plagues that on our heads came down,
Disease and Famine, Agony and Fear,
In wood or wilderness, in camp or town,
It would thy brain unsettle even to hear.
All perished, all in one remorseless year,   320
Husband and children one by one, by sword
And scourge of fiery fever: every tear
Dried up, despairing, desolate, on board
A British ship I waked as from a trance restored."

37

Here paused she of all present thought forlorn,   325
Living once more those hours that sealed her doom.
Meanwhile he looked and saw the smiling morn

---

306   poor devoted crew] *OED* gives, as a third meaning for "devoted," "formally or surely
consigned to evil or destruction: doomed." Cf. *Paradise Lost*, IX, 900–901:
    How art thou lost, how on a sudden lost,
    Defac't, deflourd, and now to Death devote?
325   forlorn] past participle of the obsolete verb "forlese"; much used by Spenser.

All unconcerned with their unrest resume
Her progress through the brightening eastern gloom.
Oh when shall such fair hours their gleams bestow   330
To bid the grave its opening clouds illume?
Fled each fierce blast and hellish fiend, and lo!
Day fresh from ocean wave uprears his lovely brow.

38

"Oh come," he said, "come after weary night
So ruinous far other scene to view."   335
So forth she came and eastward look'd. The sight
O'er her moist eyes meek dawn of gladness threw
That tinged with faint red smile her faded hue.
Not lovelier did the morning star appear
Parting the lucid mist and bathed in dew,   340
The whilst her comrade to her pensive chear
Tempered sweet words of hope and the lark warbled near.

39

They looked and saw a lengthening road and wain
Descending a bare slope not far remote.
The downs all glistered dropt with freshening rain;   345
The carman whistled loud with chearful note;
The cock scarce heard at distance sounds his throat;
But town or farm or hamlet none they viewed,
Only were told there stood a lonely cot
Full two miles distant. Then, while they pursued   350
Their journey, her sad tale the mourner thus renewed.

40

"Peaceful as this immeasurable plain
By these extended beams of dawn impressed,
In the calm sunshine slept the glittering main.
The very ocean has its hour of rest   355
Ungranted to the human mourner's breast.
Remote from man and storms of mortal care,

332–333 As the culmination of revisionary drafts for this stanza WW wrote between these
lines:
      The sun in view uplifts his orient head
      He feels his friendly beam a vital influence shed.
See *SP* transcriptions, 24ʳ, and 32ᵛ, below. The revision lines echo James Beattie's *The Minstrel*,
I, xxvi, 7–8, and II, xliv, 9.

With wings which did the world of waves invest,
The Spirit of God diffused through balmy air
Quiet that might have healed, if aught could heal, Despair.   360

41

"Ah! how unlike each smell, each sight and sound
That late the stupor of my spirit broke.
Of noysome hospitals the groan profound,
The mine's dire earthquake, the bomb's thunder stroke;
Heart sickening Famine's grim despairing look;   365
The midnight flames in thundering deluge spread;
The stormed town's expiring shriek that woke
Far round the griesly phantoms of the dead,
And pale with ghastly light the victor's human head.

42

"Some mighty gulf of separation passed   370
I seemed transported to another world:
A dream resigned with pain when from the mast
The impatient mariner the sail unfurled,
And whistling called the wind that hardly curled
The silent seas. The pleasant thoughts of home   375
With tears his weather-beaten cheek impearled:
For me, farthest from earthly port to roam
Was best; my only wish to shun where man might come.

43

"And oft, robbed of my perfect mind, I thought
At last my feet a resting-place had found.   380
'Here will I weep in peace,' so Fancy wrought,
'Roaming the illimitable waters round,
Here gaze, of every friend but Death disowned,
All day, my ready tomb the ocean flood.'
To break my dream the vessel reached its bound   385
And homeless near a thousand homes I stood,
And near a thousand tables pined and wanted food.

---

379   Owen notes the echo of *King Lear*, IV, vii, 63: "I fear I am not in my perfect mind"
(W. J. B. Owen, ed., *Wordsworth and Coleridge: Lyrical Ballads 1798* [Oxford, 1967], 131). In a prose
fragment in DC MS. 2, WW describes a meeting with a crazed pauper and concludes that the
wildness of her eyes "too plainly indicated that she was not in her true and perfect mind" (*The
Prose Works of William Wordsworth*, ed. W. J. B. Owen and Jane Worthington Smyser [3 vols.;
Oxford, 1974], I, 7–8). See Moorman, I, 17n; and *Chronology: EY*, 313–314.

44

"Three years a wanderer round my native coast
My eyes have watched yon sun declining tend
Down to the land where hope to me was lost;   390
And now across this waste my steps I bend:
Oh! tell me whither, for no earthly friend
Have I, no house in prospect but the tomb."
She ceased. The city's distant spires ascend
Like flames which far and wide the west illume,   395
Scattering from out the sky the rear of night's thin gloom.

45

Along the fiery east the Sun, a show
More gorgeous still! pursued his proud career.
But human sufferings and that tale of woe
Had dimmed the traveller's eye with Pity's tear,   400
And in the youthful mourner's doom severe
He half forgot the terrors of the night,
Striving with counsel sweet her soul to chear,
Her soul for ever widowed of delight.
He too had withered young in sorrow's deadly blight.   405

46

But now from a hill summit down they look
Where through a narrow valley's pleasant scene
A wreath of vapour tracked a winding brook
Babbling through groves and lawns and meads of green.
A smoking cottage peeped the trees between,   410
The woods resound the linnet's amorous lays,
And melancholy lowings intervene
Of scattered herds that in the meadows graze,
While through the furrowed grass the merry milkmaid strays.

47

Adieu ye friendless hope-forsaken pair!   415
Yet friendless ere ye take your several road,
Enter that lowly cot and ye shall share
Comforts by prouder mansions unbestowed.

---

396   De Selincourt notes the echo of *L'Allegro*, ll. 49–50 (*PW*, I, 338):
      While the Cock with lively din,
      Scatters the rear of darkness thin.

For you yon milkmaid bears her brimming load,
For you the board is piled with homely bread,   420
And think that life is like this desart broad,
Where all the happiest find is but a shed
And a green spot 'mid wastes interminably spread.

48

Though from huge wickers paled with circling fire
No longer horrid shrieks and dying cries   425
To ears of Dæmon-Gods in peals aspire,
To Dæmon-Gods a human sacrifice;
Though Treachery her sword no longer dyes
In the cold blood of Truce, still, reason's ray,
What does it more than while the tempests rise,   430
With starless glooms and sounds of loud dismay,
Reveal with still-born glimpse the terrors of our way?

49

For proof, if man thou lovest, turn thy eye
On realms which least the cup of Misery taste.
For want how many men and children die?   435
How many at Oppression's portal placed
Receive the scanty dole she cannot waste,
And bless, as she has taught, her hand benign?
How many by inhuman toil debased,

421–423   These lines show WW once again using old material. This image of life had already
appeared in *Descriptive Sketches*, ll. 590–593 (*PW*, I, 76):

    —Alas! in every clime a flying ray
    Is all we have to chear our wintry way,
    Condemn'd, in mists and tempests ever rife,
    To pant slow up the endless Alp of life.

424–427   WW is calling on the widespread belief that the Druids made human sacrifices.
In Aylett Sammes, *Britannia Antiqua Illustrata: or, the Antiquities of Ancient Britain, Derived from the
Phoenicians* (London, 1676), 103–105, WW could have found an illustration of the sacrificial
wicker and a description of the Druids in which he might have seen striking parallels with the
governing class of his day. In DC MS. 12, under the heading *Druids*, he has made the following
list:

C. Comment. Lib. 6
Plin. Nat. Hist: Lib. 16. c. 44.—Lib. 29. c. 3
Dray. PolyOlbion. Ninth Song—
Mona. Antiqua 338
Dion Chrysostom.—
Tac. annals. L. 14th. c. 29.—
Luc. Phar. L. 3.—
Ammianus Marcellinus Lib. 15th
Procopius. Goth. Lib. 4.—

Abject, obscure, and brute to earth incline   440
Unrespited, forlorn of every spark divine?

50

Nor only is the walk of private life
Unblessed by Justice and the kindly train
Of Peace and Truth, while Injury and Strife,
Outrage and deadly Hate usurp their reign;   445
From the pale line to either frozen main
The nations, though at home in bonds they drink
The dregs of wretchedness, for empire strain,
And crushed by their own fetters helpless sink,
Move their galled limbs in fear and eye each silent link.   450

51

Lo! where the Sun exulting in his might
In haste the fiery top of Andes scales
And flings deep silent floods of purple light
Down to the sea through long Peruvian vales,
At once a thousand streams and gentle gales   455
Start from their slumber breathing scent and song.
But now no joy of man or woman hails
That star as once, ere with him came the throng
Of Furies and grim Death by Avarice lashed along.

52

Oh that a slave who on his naked knees   460
Weeps tears of fear at Superstition's nod,
Should rise a monster Tyrant and o'er seas
And mountains stretch so far his cruel rod
To bruise meek nature in her lone abode.
Is it for this the planet of the pole   465
Sends through the storms its stedfast light abroad?
Through storms we ride with Misery to her goal:
Nor star nor needle know the tempests of the soul.

451–456 In the early DC MS. 2, WW has entered the following observation, which is the genesis of the imagery of this stanza: "The rivers in Peru are observed to quicken their currents with the first approach of morning; an effect produced by the rays of the sun melting the snow upon the Andes. Similar appearances are striking among the Alps." The passage continues to tell at some length of WW's own experience in the Alps when he was nearly caught by such a quickening stream. WW also recalled this phenomenon in his revisions to *An Evening Walk* (*PW*, I, 20, *app. crit.*): "Spirit who guid'st that orb / . . . Roll to Peruvian Vales."

53

How changed that paradise, those happy bounds
Where once through his own groves the Hindoo strayed;   470
No more the voice of jocund toil resounds
Along the crowded banyan's high arcade.

Lines 473–504 are missing.

57

How weak the solace such fond thoughts afford,   505
When with untimely stroke the virtuous bleed.
Say, rulers of the nations, from the sword
Can ought but murder, pain, and tears proceed?
Oh! what can war but endless war still breed?
Or whence but from the labours of the sage   510
Can poor benighted mortals gain the meed
Of happiness and virtue, how assuage
But by his gentle words their self-consuming rage?

58

Insensate they who think, at Wisdom's porch
That Exile, Terror, Bonds, and Force may stand: 515
That Truth with human blood can feed her torch,
And Justice balance with her gory hand
Scales whose dire weights of human heads demand
A Nero's arm. Must Law with iron scourge
Still torture crimes that grew a monstrous band   520
Formed by his care, and still his victim urge,
With voice that breathes despair, to death's tremendous verge?

Lines 523–539 are missing.

Who fierce on kingly crowns hurled his own lightning blaze.   540

---

509   De Selincourt (*PW*, I, 341) notes the debt to Milton's sonnet *On the Lord Gen. Fairfax at the Siege of Colchester*, l. 10. The concluding lines of the sonnet anticipate WW's indictment of English society: "In vain doth Valour bleed / While Avarice, and Rapine share the land."

510–513   Cf. WW's contemporary assertion to William Mathews that the "enlightened friend of mankind" should let slip no opportunity of "explaining and enforcing those general principles of the social order which are applicable to all times and to all places" (*EY*, 124). See the phrase "social order" used in an ironic context in the revision of MS. 1, below, p. 111.

511   Cf. *FQ*, III, xi, i, 8: "self-consuming smart."

61

Heroes of Truth pursue your march, uptear
Th'Oppressor's dungeon from its deepest base;
High o'er the towers of Pride undaunted rear
Resistless in your might the herculean mace
Of Reason; let foul Error's monster race   545
Dragged from their dens start at the light with pain
And die; pursue your toils, till not a trace
Be left on earth of Superstition's reign,
Save that eternal pile which frowns on Sarum's plain.

541–549   See T. J. Gillcrist, "Spenser and Reason in the Conclusion of *Salisbury Plain*," *ELN*, VII (1969), 11–18.

Salisbury Plain (1793–1794)

Photographic Reproductions and Transcriptions

A night
Salisbury Plain on Salisbury plain
                                    Salisbury ple.
If Hard is the Life when naked

Hard is the life when naked and unhouzed
And wasted by the long day's fruitless pains
The hungry savage 'mid deep forests, rouzed
By storms, lies down at night on unknown
                                              plains
And lifts his head in fear while famished trains
Of boars along the crashing forests prowl
                          thickets
And heard in darkness as the rushing rains
Put out his watch-fire bears contending growl
And round his fenceless bed gaunt wolves
        in as miles howl

            2
            was that repose proson
        is he strong to suffer & his mind
        masters all his evils unsubdued
        happier days, since at the breast he
        knew, an then by pursued

A night
    on   Salisbury plain
Salisbury Plain

        Salisbury plain

I

   Hard is the life when naked

1   *Hard is the life when naked and unhouzed*
2   *And wasted by the long day's fruitless pains*
3   *The hungry savage 'mid deep forests, rouzed*
4   *By storms, lies down at night on unknown*
                            plains
5   *And lifts his head in fear while famished trains*
                  thickets
6   *Of boars along the crashing forests prowl*
7   *And heard in darkness as the rushing rains*
8   *Put out his watch-fire bears contending growl*
9   *And round his fenceless bed gaunt wolves*
       in armies howl

2

   was that savage [?]   ~~yet~~
                & ⎱
10 *Yet is he strong to suffer, —⎰ his mind*
                     d ⎱
11 *Encounters all his evils unsub[?b]⎰ued*
         ~~the~~
12 *For happier days since at the breast he pine*
13 *He never knew, and when by foes pursued*

Title   There is no apparent reason for the repetition of "Salisbury plain." See a similar repetition at l. 18. The longer title, "A night on Salisbury plain," is Wordsworth's preferred second thought (see the letter to Mathews, 7 November 1794, *EY*, 136). The penciled page numbers were written later, probably by Gordon Wordsworth.

1   As observed in the Introduction, ll. 1–72, 78–108, and 226–324 of MS. 1 are in the hand of DW, the rest in the hand of WW. Throughout MS. 1, corrections not in the hand of WW himself are in the hand of DW, unless otherwise noted.

9/10   The crosshatch mark was probably made while testing a pen; similar marks appear on the facing inside cover.

12   *pine*] The final "d" has been worn away.

With life he scarce his reached the fortress side
While with the war-songs [how] the valleys shake
What in those wild assemblies has he viewed
But men who all of his hard lot partake
Repose in the same fear to the same toil

              awake
   Repose in the same fear to the same toil awake

The thoughts which bow the kindly spirits down
And break the springs of joy, their deadly
                      weight
Derive from memory of pleasures flown
Which haunts us in some sad reverse of fate
Or from reflection on the state
Of those, who on the couch of Affluence rest
With joys
By laughing Fortune's sparkling cup elate
While we of comfort reft, by pain depressed
No other pillow know than Penury's iron
   breast

14   *With life he scarce has reached the fortress rude*

                    howl

                       a}   s}

15   *While with the war-song's pee∫l the valleys [?h]} hake*

16   *What in those wild assemblies has he viewed*

17   *But men who all of his hard lot partake*

18   *Repose in the same fear, to the same toil*

                    awake

          Repose in the same fear to the same toil awake

                      3

19   *The thoughts which bow the kindly spirits down*

                    [?rest]

20   *And break the springs of joy, their deadly*

                    weight

21   *Derive from memory of pleasures flown*

22   *Which haunts us in some sad reverse of fate*

23   *Or from reflection on the state*

24   *Of those, who on the couch of Affluence rest*

       With ~~joyous~~

           i}

25   *By laughf∫ng Fortune's sparkling cup elate*

           re}

26   *While we of comfort, be∫ft, by pain depressed*

27   *No other pillow know than Penury's iron*

                  breast

---

  20   [?rest]] This word in pencil seems unrelated to either 19 or 20 and could be the last letters
of a now partially obliterated word.

  25   joyous] First written in pencil, later reinforced in ink.

4

Hence where 'Refinements' genial influence calls
The soft affections from their wintry sleep
And the sweet tear of love and Friendship falls
The willing heart in tender joy to steep
When men in various vessels roam the deep
Of social life, and turns of chance prevail
Various and sad, how many thousands weep
Beset with foes more fierce than e'er assail
The savage without home in winter's
                                    keenest gale

Chiefly when guided by some ——
Through & ———— till ——— scattered ————

The troubled west was red with stormy fire
                              A traveller weary
Oer Sarum's plain the traveller ————
                his long some way
Measured ———————————— the distant
                                        rise

53 *Sweep the thin grass and, passing, wildly plain;*
54 *Or desert lark that pours on high a wasted*
                        strain

                        7

55 *Long had each slope he mounted seemed*
                        to hide

56 *Some cottage whither his tired feet might turn* ⎫
        such without a hope or wish
57 *But now* ~~all hope resigned in tears~~ *he eyed*
        But now perplexed disheartened, stupefied
            ~~viewed~~   [?]⎫
58 *The crows in blackening eddies homeward borne* ⎰
        watched   [?] ⎫ -cut
                        [?ragged] ⎰
59 *Then sought, in vain, a shepherds lowly thorn*
60 *Or hovel from the storm to shield his head*
        For as he onward passed more wild, forlorn
61 *On as he passed more wild and more forlorn*
62 *And vacant the huge plain around him spread*
63 *Ah me! the wet cold ground must be his*
                        only bed!

Hark! the rattling clouds together piled
By fiercer gales, and soon the storm must break
                  seems
He stood the only creature in the wild
On whom the elements their rage could wreak
Save that the bustard of those limits bleak
Shy tenant seeing there a mortal wight
At that dread hour outsent a mournful
And half upon the ground, with strange affright
                                      shriek
Forced hard against the wind a thick
                unwieldy flight

The Day unheeded sunk while on a mound
He stands beholding with astonished gaze
Frequent upon the deep entrenched ground
Strange marks of mighty arms of former
                    before him   days
Then looking up at distance he surveys

8

64 *Hurtle the rattling clouds together piled*

65 *By fiercer gales, and soon the storm must break,*
   seemed
66 *He stood the only creature in the wild*
67 *On whom the elements their rage could wreake*
68 *Save that the bustard of those limits bleak*
69 *Shy tenant seeing there a mortal wight*
    such [?late]
     late [?darkness] at such an hour
70 *At that dread hour outsent a mournful*
      shriek
71 *And half upon the ground, with strange affright,*
72 *Forced hard against the wind a thick*
     unwieldy flight

  Roofless and bare and not of earthly form
  Ill fitted did that pile for comfort
  But now when [?he] shelter [?ran]
    [? ?]

9

  Day ⎰
73 The Sun ⎱ unheeded sunk while on a mound
74 He stands beholding with astonished gaze
75 Frequent upon the deep entrenched ground
76 Strange marks of mighty arms of former
       days
    before him
77 Then looking up at distance he surveys

A brow that in the ~~setting~~ ~~gay hollow~~
~~Headless I seem~~ I can here to check the ~~gay ere it falls~~
What seems an antique castle spreading wide
Hoary and naked are its walls and raise
Their brow sublime, while to those walls he hied
A voice as from a tomb in hollow accents cried

~~Dewlowing frogs I'd uncertain leap or turn~~
" ~~That though hollow~~ ~~slow her himself fir on high~~
~~Or~~ ~~ample from piles pile by cried against they face~~
" from that mountain pile ~~avant~~ they face
~~What ere~~ ~~ancient dark~~ ~~down~~
" What e'er betide at this tremendous hour
" To hell's most cursed sprites the baleful place
" B again
" Belongs, upreared by their magic power
" Though mixed with flame rush down the ~~crazing~~
"   glower
" And o'er thy naked bed the ~~thunder~~ roll
"   at once
" Fly ere the fiends their prey ~~unawares~~ ~~at once~~ devour
" Or grinning, on thy endless tortures scowl
" Till very madness seem a mercy to thy soul

~~The boy is not sin faint now hand were~~ ~~by are~~
~~as the wild road the head that planned desire~~
~~should afried and gave her in other in burn there~~

78   *What seems an antique castle spreading wide*

79   *Hoary and naked are its walls and raise*

         ir

80   *The[?ir] } brow sublime, while to those walls he hied*

81   *A voice as from a tomb in hollow accents cried*

10

    And from that pile he cried avert thy face

82   *"Oh from that mountain-pile avert thy face*

     What er   [?avenging] at dark night [?lower]

83   *"Whate'er betide, at this tremendous hour.*

84   *" To hell's most cursed sprites the baleful place*

     Again

85   *"Belongs, upreared by their magic power.*

86   *" Though mixed with flame rush down the crazing*

                               shower

87   *"And o'er thy naked bed the thunder roll*

        at once   ~~at once~~

88   *"Fly ere*ₐ*the fiends their prey* ~~unwares~~ *devour*

89   *"Or grinning, on thy endless tortures scowl*

90   *"Till very madness seem a mercy to thy soul*

     Roofless and [?bare] & not of earthly form
     Again he wildered through the

   77/78, 81/82   The two pairs of lines of draft belong to the revisions to *An Evening Walk* on the verso opposite, as do the last three lines of the drafting at the foot of the page which are visible in the photograph.

11.   15

"For oft, at dead of night, when dreadful fire
"⟨corsairs⟩ that powerful circle's reddening stones
                                    shadows
"Amid priests and spectres grim and idols dire
"Far heard the great flame utters human moans
" ⟨Splenced⟩ ey death.
" Then all is hushed: again the desert groans
A dismal light its farthest bounds illumes,
" While warrior spectres of gigantic bones.

" Forth-issuing from a thousand lifted tombs

" Wheel on their fiery steeds amid the
                        infernal glooms
              and struggling ⟨by⟩ ⟨as⟩
     ⟨He heard no more⟩ ⟨for fear oppressd his form⟩
     ⟨Thy ⟩⟨ ⟩⟨wreath⟩⟨ ⟩⟨face⟩⟨ ⟩
     ⟨ ⟩⟨a shape more hideous than a madman's dream⟩
     ⟨Ha ⟩⟨mocked⟩⟨ as by a hideous dream⟩
     ⟨at last he fled⟩⟨ ⟩⟨through the storm⟩
     ⟨ ⟩⟨across the wilderness through the watery storm⟩

     No ⟨ ⟩ to ⟨open⟩ the black clouds and stream

     From ⟨ ⟩ gulph profound one friendly beam
     ⟨ ⟩⟨friendly⟩⟨sound⟩ his footsteps lay
     ⟨ ⟩⟨ ⟩⟨heard from shepherds⟩⟨ ⟩

11

91 "*For oft, at dead of night, when dreadful fire*
     Unfolds
     Unfolds ⎫
92 "*Reveals* ⎰ *that powerful circle's reddening stones*
          shadows
93 "*Mid priests and spectres grim and idols dire*
94 "*Far heard the great flame utters human moans*
     Silenced by death:
95 "*Then all is hushed : again the desert groans*
[96] *A dismal light its farthest bounds illumes,*
97 "*While warrior spectres of gigantic bones*
98 "*Forth-issuing from a thousand rifted tombs*
99 "*Wheel on their fiery steeds amid the*
        infernal glooms

12

     ed
  And struggling long as
           F⎱
  He ~~heard no more for f~~⎰ear ~~oppress'd his form~~
100 ~~*The voice was from beneath but face or form*~~
  In shape more hideous than a madman's dream
101 ~~*He saw not mocked as by a hideous dream*~~
  At ~~last he fled and~~ wildered ~~through the storm~~
102 ~~*Three hours he wildered through the watery storm*~~
103 *No moon to open the black clouds and stream*
104 *From narrow gulph profound one friendly beam*
  Nor any friendly sound his footsteps led
105 ~~*No watch-dog howled from shepherd's homely shed*~~

---

[96] The bracketed line number indicates a line apparently omitted by oversight from the fair copy.

17

Once did the lightning's *aery disastrous* gleam

Disclose aß naked guide-posts double head

Sole object where he stood had day its

Tußes, death, and waste as oceans shipless flood

The desert sounded to the whirlwinds sweep

Though t.....

Twas dark and void as oceans

No shuddering

No Gypsey

Nor transient meteor burst upon his sight

Nor taper glimmered dim from sick man's room,

Along the moor no line of mournful light

From lamps of lonely toll-gate streamed

athwart the night.

At length the moon arose

The down were

And spread a sickly glare.

                              faint disastrous
                                         gleam ⎫
106   *Once did the lightning's ~~pale abortive~~ beam* ⎭
107   *Disclose a naked guide-post's double head*
                              miles around
108   *Sole object where he stood had day its*

                                    a
                                    re ⎫
              radiance sp[?e]⎰d

                    in a moment lost
              ~~Though lost~~ [?as ?]   ~~the sight some comfort~~
                                                              shed
              ~~W Though~~ Sight which though lost at once
                              some gleam of comfort shed

                         13

109   Twas dark and waste as ocean's shipless flood
              Though tree
110   ~~Roaring with storms beneath nights starless gloom~~
              The desart sounded to the whirlwind's sweep
                                    labouring
              Though tree was none to top his ~~raven~~ plume
                                    barren
              Twas dark and void as ocean's ~~shipless~~ deep barren
              Roaring with storms beneath nights starless gloom
              No shivering
              ~~Where~~ ⎫
112   [?Who] ⎭ ~~the wet gypsey in her straw-built home~~
              No Gypsey cowered o er fire of fern or broom
113   ~~Might Warmed her wet limbs by fire of fern and broom~~
                              kiln ⎫
              [?farmers ?]⎭ red kiln [?glared ?upon]
              or ⎫
114   No ⎭ transient meteor burst upon his sight
                              ~~kiln~~ ⎫
              Nor [?farmers] kiln glare on [?kil ?kil]⎭ sight
115   Nor taper glimmered dim from sick man's room,
              Though nothing did to check its [?crimson][?]
116   Along the moor no line of mournful light
117   From lamp of lonely toll-gate streamed
                              athwart the night.
                    object
              Though none to thwart it

                         14

                    though   step
118   At length ~~deep~~ hid in clouds the moon arose
              The downs were [?]en   [?scarce]
119   And spread a sickly glare. With ~~flight~~
                                   scarce
                                   ~~un~~willed
                    scarce willed

---

108   miles around] First written in pencil, later reinforced in ink.
   110/112   L. 111 was not included in the fair copy. In the space left WW has written an alter-
native opening four lines, but did not complete a full revision of this stanza.
   113   Might Warmed] Probably begun as "Might warm" but altered without deletion in
original copying.
   115   sick man's] First underlined; then the underlining was deleted.
   118   step] Probably intended as an alternative to "flight," l. 119.

Worn out and weak half wishing the repose   19
Of death he came where antient vows fulfilled
And pious hands. did to the Virgin build
A lonely Spital, the belated swain
From the night-terrors of that waste to shield.
But there no human being could remain
And now the walls are named the dead house

Till then more demons dogged his road
He fled, and often backward cast his face
But when the ambiguous gloom that ruin showed
How glad he was at length to find a place
Which bore of human hands the cheering trace
Here shall he rest till Morn his eye unclose
Ah! me that last of hopes is fled apace
For, entering in his hair in horror rose
To hear a voice that seemed to mourn
                    sorrows throes.

             weak half
120 Worn out and ~~wasted~~ ‸wishing the repose
          It was a spot
121 Of death he came where antient vows fulfilled
122 Kind pious hands did to the Virgin build
123 A lonely Spital, the belated swain
      Though he had little cause to seek th'abode
      Of man or covet sight of mortal face
                   W⎫
124 From the night-terrors of that w⎰aste to shield.
125 But there no human being could remain
126 And now the walls are named the dead house
                of the plain

          cause   [?wide]
   Though he had little need on his ~~cold~~
                 wild road
   To wish for mans abode or mortal face
        he had pursued his road

        15

       ~~those demons~~
127 Till then ~~as if his terror~~ dogged ~~his road~~
     Reckless of mans abode or mortal face
128 He fled, and often backward cast his face
     But ⎫
129 And⎰ when the ambiguous gloom that ruin showed
130 How glad he was at length to find a place
     Which
131 That bore of human hands the chearing trace
132 Here shall he rest 'till Morn her eye unclose
133 Ah! me that last of hopes is fled apace
      t⎫   e⎫
    A[?s]⎰ the first st[?e]⎰p
134 For, entering in his hair in horror rose
135 To hear a voice that seemed to mourn in
            sorrows throes.

---

120   weak half] First written in pencil, later reinforced in ink.
123   The two lines below were added in pencil, probably as an alternative opening to Stanza 15.
126/127   wild] Underlined in MS.

21

16

It was the voice of one that sleeping mourned
~~nervous~~
A human voice! and soon his terrors fled
At dusk a female wanderer hither turned
And found a comfortless half sheltered bed.
The moon a wan dead light around her shed
He waked her and at once her spirits fail
Thrilled by the poignant dart of sudden dread
For of that ruin she had heard a tale
That might with a child's fears the stoutest heart
assail

17

Had heard of one who faced from storms to shroud
Felt the loose walls of this decayed retreat
Rock to his horse's neighings shrill & loud
While the loose earth in a pant ~~heavings~~ beat
~~thundering~~ ~~by scarcely~~
Till on a stone that sparkled to his feet
Struck and still struck again the troubled horse.
the
The man half raised the stone ~~with~~ pain & sweat
Half raised; for well his arm might lose its
force

16

136 It was the voice of one that sleeping mourned
　　　　[?womans]
137 A human voice! and soon his terrors fled
138 At dusk a female wanderer hither turned
139 And found a comfortless half sheltered bed
140 The moon a wan dead light around her shed
141 He waked her and at once her spirits fail
142 Thrill'd by the poignant dart of sudden dread
143 For of that ruin she had heard a tale
　　　　Which
144 That might with a child's fears the stoutest heart
　　　　　　　　　　　　　assail

17

145 Had heard of one who forced from storms to shroud
146 Felt the loose walls of this decayed retreat
147 Rock to his horse's neighings shrill & loud
　　　　loose earth incessant pawings beat
148 While the ground rang by ceaseless pawing beat
149 Till on a stone that sparkled to his feet
150 Struck and still struck again the troubled horse.
　　　　the　　　　with
151 The man half raised that stone by pain & sweat
152 Half raised; for well his arm might lose its
　　　　　　　　　　　force

137　[?womans]] Deleted in pencil.
144　Which] In pencil.　　That] Deleted in pencil.

Disclosing the grim head of a new murdered corse

23

18

Such tales of the lone Spital she had learned *hadshe*

And when that shape with eyes in sleep half drowned

By the moons sullen lamp she scarce discerned

Cold stony horror all her senses bound

~~But anon to her~~ *He by her fears* low words of chearing sound

Addressed . With joy she heard such greeting him

And much they conversed of that desert ground

Which seemed to those ~~of~~ *of* other worlds consigned

Whose voices ~~still theyheard~~ *She had* as paused the hollow

wind .

19
bottom
valley

The Woman told ~~that~~ *that* through a hollow deep

As on she journeyed far from spring or bower

An old man beckoning from the naked steep

Came tottering sidelong down, to ask the hour

153   Disclosing the grim head of a new murdered corse

18

       had she
154   Such tales of the lone Spital she had learned
155   And when that shape with eyes in sleep half-drowned
156   By the moons sullen lamp she scarce discerned
157   Cold stony horror all her senses bound
    He to her fears
158   ~~But he to her~~ low words of chearing sound
159   Addressed. With joy she heard such greeting kind
160   And much they conversed of that desert ground
161   Which seemed to those of other worlds consigned
     she had
162   Whose voices ~~still they~~ heard as paused the hollow
        wind.

19

     bottom
     valley
163   The Woman told that through a hollow deep
164   As on she journeyed far from spring or bower
165   And old man beckoning from the naked steep
166   Came tottering sidelong down to ask the hour

---

163   valley] First written in pencil, later reinforced in ink.

25

There never clock was heard from steeple tower
From the wide corn the plundering crows to scare
He held a rusty gun. In sun and shower
Old as he was alone he lingered there
His hungry meal too scant for dog that meal
                    to share.

              20
Much of the wonders of that boundless heath
He spoke, and of a swain who far astray
Reached unawares a height and saw beneath
Gigantic beings ranged in dread array
Such beings thwarting off the travellers way
With shield and stones a stride across the ground
Or throned on that dread circles summit gray
Of mountains hung in air their state unfold
And like a thousand Gods mysterious
          council hold

167   There never clock was heard from steeple tower
168   From the wide corn the plundering crows to scare
169   He held a rusty gun. In sun and shower
170   Old as he was alone he lingered there
171   His hungry meal too scant for dog that meal
                        to share.

20

172   Much of the wonders of that boundless heath
173   He spoke, and of a swain who far astray
174   Reached unawares a height and saw beneath
175   Gigantic beings ranged in dread array
176   Such beings thwarting oft the travellers way
177   With shield and stone-ax stride across the would

178   Or throned on that dread circlss$\}^{es}$ summit gra[?]$\}^{y}$
179   Of mountains hung in air their state unfold
180   And like a thousand Gods mysterious
                        council hold

27

And oft a night-fire mounting to the clouds
Reveals the desert and with dismal red
Clothes the black bodies of encircling crowds.
It is the sacrificial altar fed
With living men. How deep it groans—the
Thrilled in their yawning tombs their helms

The sword that slept beneath the warrior's head
Thunders in fiery air: red arms appear
Uplifted thro' the gloom and shake the rattling spear.

Not thus when clear moons spread their pleasing light
— Long bearded forms with wands uplifted shew
To vast assemblies; while each breath of night
Is hushed, the living fires that bright and slow
Rounding th' aetherial field in order go.
Then as they trace with awe their various file
All figured on the mystic plain below

21

at
181 And oft a night-fire mounting to the clouds
Nor less when he beheld from far
182 Reveals the desert and with dismal red
[?]
Black [?bodies] dimly with sullen red
[?tingd]
183 Clothes the black bodies of encircling crowds.
While living captive by groans [?awful]
[?heathen]   make
184 — It is the sacrificial altar fed
[?such]
That scattered [?horror] which might [?]
185 With living men. How deep it groans—the
dead
living
While the huge fire by captive fed
186 Thrilled in their yawning tombs their helms
uprear
187 The sword that slept beneath the warriours
head
188 Thunders in fiery air: red arms appear
189 Uplifted thro the gloom and shake the
rattling spear.
dire shapes of horror or

22

n⎱
190 Not thus where⎰ clear moons spread their pleas-
ing light.
with⎱
191 — Long bearded forms to⎰wands uplifted shew
eze⎱   night⎱
192 To vast assemblies; while each breath⎰ of [?morn]⎰
193 Is hushed, the living fires that bright and slow
194 Rounding th'ætherial field in order go.
y⎱
195 Then as their⎰ trace with awe their various files
196 All figured on the mystic plain below

Still prelude of sweet sounds the moon beguiles 29
And charmed for many a league the poppy desart
&c &c &c &c
friendly to all she said the traveller &c
While thus they talked the churlish storms relent
His ear &c now when round those walls the wind
And round those broken walls the dying wind
In feeble murmurs told his rage was spent.
With sober sympathy and tranquil mind
Gently the Woman gan her wounds unbind

Might Beauty charm the canker worm of pain
The rose on her sweet cheek had neer declined
Moved she not once the scene of Keswicks plain
While Hope and Love and Joy composed her
                smiling train.
          2 4   on some secret brink
Like swans twin swans that oft on the sweet
of our Derwent   where   &c &c
of Derwent stream,   the south winds hardly blow
Mid Derwents water-lillies swell I sink
In union, rose her sister breast of snow

197 Still prelude of sweet sounds the moon beguiles
198 And charmed for many a league the hoary desart
                          smiles

                          23

    So that to all she said he kindly lent
      a [?] a [?]   [?̶ ?]
    Kindly to all she said the traveller lent
              ed ⎫
199 While thus they talk[?]⎬ the churlish storms relent:
             ose ⎫
    His ear & now when round th[?]⎬ walls the wind
200 And round those broken walls the dying wind
201 In feeble murmurs told his rage was spent.
202 With sober sympathy and tranquil mind
      G ⎫
203 [?]⎬ently the Woman gan her wounds unbind
204 Might Beauty charm the canker worm of pain
205 The rose on her sweet cheek had neer declined
206 Moved she not once the prime of Keswicks plain
      en ⎫
207 While⎬ Hope and Love and Joy composed her
                          smiling train.

                          24

            on some secret brink
208 Like swans twin swans that ~~when on the sweet~~
                                        ~~brink~~
    Often oer Derwent   ,⎫ when   scarce
209 Of Derwent's stream⎬the south winds hardly blow
210 Mid Derwent's water-lillies swell & sink
211 In union, rose her sister breasts of snow

---

209   Often oer Derwent] In pencil, as are the comma and "scarce."

(Fair emblem of two Lovers hearts that know
No separate impulse, or like infants played
Like infants strangers yet to pain, and woe
Unwearied Hope to tend their motions made
Long Vigils, and Delight her cheek between
Thy day, and keep at night her cheek
them laid between them laid

And are ye spread ye glittering dews of youth
Only for this,—that Frost may gall the tender
In joys fair breast with more untimely tooth.
Unhappy Man! thy sole delightful hour
Flies first; it is thy miserable dower
Only to taste of joy that thou mayst pine
A loss, which rolling suns shall never restore
New suns roll on and scatters they shine
No second spring, but pains, till Death
New suns roll on; nor any rest is thine
Nor hope. till on the tomb thy willing limbs

Emblem to her whose breast they taught to glow

212   (Fair emblem of two lover's hearts that know

Of two hearts by no separate impulse swayed

213   No separate impulse) or like infants played

But

oh! ye were strangers then to pain & woe

214   Like infants strangers yet to pain and woe

Obedient to the breath of joy ye played &

215   Unwearied Hope to tend their motions made

Their sensible warm motions transport swayed

V }

216   Long [?]ʃigils, and Delight her cheek between

them laid.

By day, and Peace at night her cheek

you

between ~~them~~ laid

25

they   the

217   And are ~~ye~~ spread ye glittering dews of youth

218   ~~Only~~ For this,— that Frost may gall the tender

bare   flower

Springs [?]

Mornings   [?green]

219   In ~~Joys~~ fair breast with more untimely tooth.

In springs green lap

M }

220   Unhappy m ʃan! thy sole delightful hour

221   Flies first; it is thy miserable dower

222   Only to taste of joy that thou mayst pine

223   A loss, which rolling suns shall ne'er restore

224   New suns roll on and scatter as they shine

D }

225   No second spring, but pain, till dʃeath

~~release thee, thine.~~

New suns roll on; nor any rest is thine

Nor hope till on the tomb thy willing limbs

recline

---

219   In springs green lap] In pencil.

26

33

By Derwents side my father's cottage stood.
The mourner thus her artless story told
A little flock and what the finny flood
Supplied, to him were more than mines of gold
Light was my sleep, my days in transport rolled
With thoughtless joy I stretched along the shore
My parents' nets or watched when from the fold
High o'er the cliff, I led his fleecy store
A dizzy depth below! his boat and twinkling oar

27

Can I forget my seat beneath the thorn
My garden stored with peas and mint and thyme
And rose and lilly for the sabbath morn
The church-inviting bells delightful chime
The merriment and song at shearing time
My hens rich nest with long grass overgrown
The cowslip gathering at the morning prime

26

226 *By Derwent's side my father's cottage stood:*
227 *The mourner thus her artless story told*
228 *A little flock and what the finny flood*
229 *Supplied, to him were more than mines of gold*
230 *Light was my sleep; my days in transport*
                                    rolled
231 *With thoughtless joy I stretched along the shore*
232 *My parent's nets or watched when from the fold*
233 *High o'er the cliffs I led his fleecy store*
234 *A dizzy depth below! his boat and twinkling*
                            oar

27

235 *Can I forget my seat beneath the thorn*
236 *My garden stored with peas and mint and thyme*
237 *And rose and lilly for the sabbath morn*
238 *The church-inviting bells delightful chime*
239 *The merriment and song at shearing time*
     The⎫
240 *My⎬ hens rich nest with long grass overgrown*
241 *The cowslip gathering at the morning prime*

The hazel copse with teeming clusters brown   35

28

Can I forget the casement where I fed
The red-breast when the fields were whitened
My snowy kerchief on the hawthorn spread   o'er
My humming wheel and glittering table store
                                    Cloth near the stone
The well-known knocking at the evening door
The hunted slipper and the blinded game
The dance that loudly beat the merry floor
The ballad chaunted round the brightening
                                            flame
While down the ravaged hills the storm
                    unheeded came

29   twenty winters
The suns of eighteen danced along
Joyous as on the pleasant morn of may
At last by cruel chance and wilful wrong
My father's substance fell into decay
Oppression trampled on his tresses grey

242   *The hazel copse with teeming clusters brown*
[243]

28

244   *Can I forget the casement where I fed*
245   *The red-breast when the fields were whitened*
                                      o'er
246   *My snowy kerchiefs on the hawthorn spread*
         Clean hearth stone
247   *My humming wheel and glittering table store*
         My wheels loud buzz and at the
248   *The well-known knocking at the evening door*
         The low knock and the softly whispered name
249   *The hunted slipper and the blinded game*
         merry   echoing
250   *The dance that* ~~loudly~~ *beat the* ~~merry~~ *floor*
251   *The ballad chaunted round the brightening*
                                  flame
252   *While down the ravaged hills the storm*
                 unheeded came

29

         twenty winters
          ~~winters~~ ⎱
253   *The suns of* ~~eighteen summers~~ ⎰ *danced along*

         o⎱
254   *Joyous as i⎰n the pleasant morn of may*
255   *At last by cruel chance and wilful wrong*
256   *My father's substance fell into decay*
257   *Oppression trampled on his tresses grey*
258   *His little range of water was denied*

---

[243] A line is missing in the MS.

All ... the ...
Even to the bed where his old body lay   37
His All, was present, and weeping side by side
          allow
Turned out on the cold winds alone we
            wandered wide

                    30   ? x x

Can I forget that miserable hour
When from the last hill top my sire surveyed
Peering above the trees the steeple-tower
That on his marriage-day sweet music made
Till then he prest his bone weight ...
Then at my birth my mothers bones were
Gloom by sorry ...
And there, till then, he hoped his own might
                                                    wept
Bidding me trust in God he stood and prayed
I could not pray by human ... oppressed
While glistening our dear ...
Viewing our glimmering cot through tears
                    that never ceased
Glimmered our dear loved cot. our cot
There was a youth whose tender voice &
                                          eye
Might add fresh happiness to happiest days
At uprise of the sun when he was by

	All but the bed where
259	*Even to the bed where his old body lay*

<pre>
         A⎱   ,⎱ all   w
260   His a⎰ll ⎰ <del>was seized</del>; and weeping side by side
261   Turned out on the cold winds alone we
                          wandered wide
</pre>

30

262   *Can I forget that miserable hour*
263   *When from the last hill-top my sire surveyed*
264   *Peering above the trees the steeple-tower*
265   *That on his marriage-day sweet music made*

<pre>
         T⎱   there be
       [?]⎰ill then he hoped his bones might there have
                                           laid
</pre>

266   *There at my birth my mother's bones were*
                                    laid

<pre>
        Close by mother in [?their] native bowers
</pre>

267   *And there, till then, he hoped his own might*
                                      rest
268   *Bidding me trust in God he stood and prayed*

<pre>
                    through tears that fell in showers
                                       ceaseless⎱
                       [?showers]   thought ⎰
</pre>

269   *I could not pray by human <del>grief</del> oppressed*

<pre>
                       cot ⎱ home⎱
       While glimmered our dear <del>loved</del>⎰ home⎰
</pre>

270   *Viewing our glimmering cot through tears*
                    that never ceased

<pre>
                for throug grief, ceaseless alas
        Glimmered our dear [?] loved cot—our cot no
        longer ours
</pre>

31

271   *There was a youth whose tender voice &*
                              eye
272   *Might add fresh happiness to happiest days*
273   *At uprise of the sun when he was by*

259–260   All corrections are in pencil.
261/262   The r's apparently show a pen being tested.
264/265   Writing on the following page, visible in the photograph, shows through a hole in the paper.
266   there be] In pencil.
269   *grief*] Deleted in pencil, and "thought" penciled above.

The birds prolonged with joy their choicest lays
The soft pipe warbled out a wilder maze
The silent moon of evening, hung above
Showered through the waving lime-trees mellow rays
Warm was the breath of night. his voice of love
Charmed the rude winds to sleep by river field or grove

32

His father bade him to a distant town
If my sire had ~~bade him~~ slept
To ply remote from groves the artists' trade
What tears of bitter grief till then unknown
What tender vows our last sad kiss delayed
To join our steps we turned by hope upstayed
Oh with what bliss upon his neck I wept
And her whom he had loved in joy he said
He well could love in grief: his faith he kept
And sheltered from the winds once more my father slept

274 The birds p[?]ʳ}olonged with joy their choicest lays
275 The soft pipe warbled out a wilder maze
276 The silent moon of evening, hung above
277 Showered through the waving lime-trees mellower
                                    rays
278 Warm was the breath of night: his voice of ~~love~~
                                    love
279 Charmed the rude winds to sleep by river
                    field or grove

                    32
            ───────────────────
            bad   ~~seek~~
280 ~~His father bid him to~~ a distant town
                sent   i}
        His sire had [?ba] ~~ba~~}d ~~him seek~~
                sent him
281 To ply remote from groves the artist's trade
282 What tears of bitter grief till then unknown
283 What tender vows our last sad kiss delayed
284 To him our steps we turned by hope upstayed
        Like one revived
285 ~~Oh with what bliss~~ upon his neck I wept
286 And her whom he had loved in joy he said
287 He well could love in grief: his faith he kept
288 And sheltered from the winds once more
                    my father slept

──

  280 The corrected line was written out in full on the opposite verso: "His sire had sent him
to a distant town."
  285 The correction was first written in pencil, later reinforced in ink; the four words below
were canceled in pencil.

33   41

Four years each day with daily bread was ~~the~~
                                                    blessed
By constant toil and constant prayer supplied
Three lovely infants lay within my breast
And often viewing their sweet smiles I sighed
And knew not why. Thy happy father died
Just as the children's meal began to fail.
~~And round the silent loom for bye all they once~~
~~~~
~~While in the crowded port our cheerful sail~~
~~her loom stood still unwatched the idle gate~~
~~She covered the yellow mast or stayed the happy~~
~~world in deserted shrouds the uneasy wing~~

~~sail~~
34

How changed at once! for I ~~above~~ thoughtless
~~long suppliant looks and tears distracted strain~~
~~~~
But soon with proud parade the noisy drum
Beat round to sweep the streets of want & pain
Thy husband's arms now only served to strain

33

289 *Four years each day with daily bread was* ~~*bless*~~
                                              blessed
290 *By constant toil and constant prayer supplied*
291 *Three lovely infants lay within my breast*
292 *And often viewing their sweet smiles I sighed*
293 *And knew not why. My happy father died*
          When
294 *Just as the childrens meal began to fail*
          And round the silent loom for bread the[?ir]} cried
                                              y }
                 Wᵗ}
295 ~~*For w}ar the nations to the field defied*~~
          While in the crouded port no chearful sail
                             u}
296 ~~*The loom stood still: i}nwatched the idle gale*~~
                                              [?gale]
          chequered the yellow mast or stayed the passing
297 ~~*Wooed in deserted shrouds the unregarding*~~
                 sail

34
                                   thoughtless
298 *How changed at once! for Labor's* ~~*chearful*~~
                                   hum
                                   train
          Long suppliant looks and Fear's distracted
299 ~~*Silence and Fear, and Misery's weeping train*~~
300 *But soon with proud parade the noisy drum*
301 *Beat round to sweep the streets of want & pain*
302 *My husband's arms now only served to strain*

---

294 When] In pencil.
294–297 On the opposite verso WW redrafted some of these lines in pencil, then overwrote
them in ink as follows:
                       the
          When War's first threats reduced ᴧchildrens meal
          Thrice happy that from him the grave did hide
                       cold
          The empty loom ~~chill~~ hearth, and silent wheel
                 which   that }
          And tears ~~that~~ᴧflowed for ills which } Patience could not heal.

Me and his children, hungering in his view 43
To beg he was ashamed
He could not beg: my prayers and tears were vain
To join those miserable men he flew.
We reached the western world a poor
                    devoted crew

                    35
Oh! dreadful price of being! to resign
All that is dear in being; better far
In Want's most lonely cave till death
                                    to pine
Unseen, unheard, unwatched by any star
Better before proud Fortune's sumptuous car
Obvious our dying bodies to obtrude
Than dog-like wading at the heels of War
Protract a cursed existence with the brood
That lap their very nourishment their
                    brother's blood

303   *Me and his children hungering in his view*
         To beg he was ashamd my
304   *He could not beg : ~~my prayers and~~ tears were vain*
305   *To join those miserable men he flew.*
306   *We reached the western world a poor*
           devoted crew

35

307   *Oh! dreadful price of being! to resign*
308   *All that is dear in being ; better far*
309   *In Want's most lonely cave ~~to pine~~ till death*
                   to pine
310   *Unseen, unheard, unwatched by any star*
311   *Better before proud Fortune's sumptuous car*
312   *Obvious our dying bodies to obtrude*
313   *Than dog-like wading at the heels of War*
314   *Protract a cursed existence with the brood*
315   *That lap ⎰their very nourishment ⎱their*
           brother's blood

---

315   The parentheses and exclamation point were added in pencil.

36   45

The pains and plagues that on our heads
                                    came down
Disease and Famine, Agony and Fear
In wood or wilderness, in camp or town
It would thy brain unsettle even to hear
All perished, all in one remorseless year
Husband and children one by one by sword
And scourge of fiery fever: every tear
Dried up, despairing desolate, on board
A British ship I waked as from a trance
                    restored

37

Here paused she of all present thought forlorn
            on those
Living once more those hours that sealed her
                                            doom
Meanwhile he looked and saw the smiling morn
All unconcerned with their unrest resume

Her progress through the brightening eastern gloom
                        orient lustres glow
Oh when shall such fair hours their gleams bestow
And
To bid the grave its opening clouds illume

36

316 *The pains and plagues that on our heads*
                                    came down
317 *Disease and Famine, Agony and Fear*
318 *In wood or wilderness, in camp or town*
319 *It would thy brain unsettle even to hear*
320 *All perished, all in one remorseless year*
321 *Husband and children one by one by sword*
322 *And scourge of fiery fever : every tear*
323 *Dried up, despairing desolate, on board*
       A⎱
324   *a*⎰ *British ship I waked as from a trance*
                                    restored

37

325 Here paused she of all present thought forlorn
       And lived
326 Living once more those hours that sealed her
                                    doom

       M ⎱
327 [?T]⎰ eanwhile he looked and saw the smiling morn
328 All unconcerned with their unrest resume
329 Her progress through the brightening eastern gloom
                              orient lustres glow ⎱
                              orient lustre glow ⎰
330 Oh when shall such fair hours their gleams bestow
       And
331 T̶o̶ bid the grave its opening clouds illume

---

330   The first revision is in pencil.

led each ~~fierce~~ blast and hellysh fiend and so
The ~~night in irresistable~~ ~~his sweet he~~

Day fresh from ocean wave uprears his lovely brow
He ~~kneel'd his friendly~~ ~~bent a wistful~~

                    3 ⟨?⟩
                  loved
Oh! come ~~hey~~ ~~she~~ come after weary night

So numous far other scene to view

So forth she ~~came~~ and eastward ~~looked~~. The light

                    like
Oer her moist eyes ~~with~~ dawn of gladness threw

That tingod with faint red smile her faded hue

Not lovelier did the morning-star appear

Parting the lucid mist and bathed in dew
~~While the bright~~ ~~she faded~~

She whilst her comrade to her pensive chear

Tempered sweet words of hope and the lark
                    warbled near

   4?
  a   39
 30 7
They looked and saw a leghtening road and
                                        warm
Descending a bare slope not far remote

The downs all glistered dropt with fostening
                                      rain

332 Fled each fierce blast and hellish fiend and lo!
    The sun in view uplifts his orient head
333 Day fresh from ocean wave uprears his lovely brow.
    He feels his friendly beam a vital influence
                  shed

38

              cried }
              cried }
            ~~cried~~ }
334 Oh! come he ~~s said~~ } come after weary night
335 So ruinous far other scene to view
336 So }' forth she came and eastward looked }' The sight
            like
337 Oer her moist eyes ~~meek~~ dawn of gladness threw
338 That tinged with faint red smile her faded hue
              's }   seff
339 Not lovelier did the morning } ~~star~~ appear
340 Parting the lucid mist and bathed in dew
    When the bright mist he parted bathed
341 The whilst her comrade to her pensive chear
342 Tempered sweet words of hope and the lark
               warbled near.

39

              n }
343 They looked and saw a let }gthening road and
                      wain
344 Descending a bare slope not far remote
345 The downs all glistered dropt with freshening
                 rain

332–333 The blots are from the facing page of the notebook.

334 A complicated correction. It seems likely that "said" was deleted in pencil and "cried" written above in pencil; that "said" was then overwritten "cried" in ink; but that the result led WW to write "cried" in ink above, partly overwriting the penciled "cried" already there.

339 seff] In pencil, as are the "'s" added to "morning" and the deletion of "star."

340 Revision in pencil.

342/343 The calculation of lines may be related to the misnumbering of stanzas after the forty-third.

The carman whistled loud with cheerful note   49

The cock scarce heard at distance ~~sounds~~ his throat

But town or farm or hamlet none they viewed

Only were told there stood a lonely cot
    Thence three long miles. While the ...
full two miles distant. Then, while they pursue
their way my song shall tell ...
Their journey, her sad tale the mourner thus
                                        renewed.
                    40

Peaceful as this immeasurable plain

By these extended beams of dawn impressed

In the calm sunshine ... the glittering main

The very ocean has its hour of rest

.... to the human mourner's breast

Remote from man and storms of mortal care

With wings which did the world of waves invest

The Spirit of God diffused through balmy air

Quiet that might have healed if aught could
                    heal Despair.

346   The carman whistled loud with chearful note
                               blew
347   The cock scarce heard at distance ~~sounds~~ his throat
348   But town or farm or hamlet none they viewed
349   Only were told there stood a lonely cot
         Thence three long miles. While thither ~~they~~
350   Full two miles distant. Then, while they pur
                              sued
      Their way my song shall tell how she her
                      tale renewed.
351   Their journey, her sad tale the mourner thus
                         renewed.

40

352   Peaceful as this immeasurable plain
353   By these extended beams of dawn impressed
354   In the calm sunshine slept the glittering main.
355   The very ocean has its hour of rest
        ~~only~~ ⎱
    ~~that comes~~ ⎰   that comes not
356   ~~Ungranted~~ to the human mourner's breast
357   Remote from man and storms of mortal care
358   With wings whicd did the world of waves invest
359   The Spirit of God diffused through balmy air
360   Quiet that might have healed if aught could
                    heal Despair.

---

347   blew] In pencil.
358   whicd] "which" is obviously intended.

41

5

Ah how unlike each smell each sight and sound
~~That~~ Which late the stupor of my spirit broke
Of noysome hospitals the groan profound
The mine's dread earthquake the bombs thunder
                                              stroke

~~Heart sickening Famine's again declaiming look~~
Dire faces half betrayed through clouds of smoke
The midnight flames in thundering deluge spread

The stormed town's shrieking shriek that woke
Far round the griesly phantoms of the dead,
And pale with ghastly light the victors human
                                              ear
41

Some mighty gulf of separation passed
I seemed transported to another world
A ~~heaven~~ resigned with pain   when from the
                                              mast
The impatient mariner the sail unfurled
And whistling called the wind that hardly
                                              curled
The silent seas, The pleasant thoughts of home

41

361 Ah! how unlike each smell each sight and sound
      Which
362 ~~That~~ late the stupor of my spirit broke
363 Of noysome hospitals the groan profound
      dread⎫
364 The mine's dire ⎰ earthquake the bomb's thunder
                                stroke
[—— ? —— ? —— ? —— ? ——] ~~clouds of smoke~~
           ine's⎫
365 ~~Heart sickening Fame~~ ⎰ ~~grim despairing look~~
      Dire faces half betrayed through clouds of smoke
366 The midnight flames in thundering deluge spread
367 The stormed town's expiring shriek that woke
368 Far round the griesly phantoms of the dead,
369 And pale with ghastly light the victors human
                          head

42

    S⎫
370 T⎰ome mighty gulf of separation passed
371 I seemed transported to another world
    dream   ⎫
372 A th[?ing]⎰ resigned with pain   when from the
                                mast
                 r⎫
373 The impatient marine[?]⎰ the sail unfurled
374 And whistling called the wind that hardly
                           curled
         .⎫T⎫
375 The silent seas,⎰ t⎰he pleasant thoughts of home

---

365 The upper line of revision is in pencil.

53

With tears his weather-beaten cheek impearled.

For me, farthest from earthly port to roam

Was best; my only wish to shun where man might come

And oft robbed of my perfect mind I thought

At last my fate a resting-place had found

Here will I weep in peace "so Fancy wrought"

Roaming the illimitable waters round

Here gaze of every friend but Death disowned

All day my ready tomb the ocean flood.

To break my dream the vessel reached its bound

And homeless near a thousand homes I stood

And near a thousand tables pined and wanted food

Three years a wanderer round my native coast

My eyes have watched yon sun declining

Down to the land where hope to me was lost

376 With tears his weather-beaten cheek impearled.
377 For me, farthest from earthly port to roam
            could I shun the spot
              I but shun the place
378 Was best; my only wish to shun where man might
                                         fly
                              come

                      43

379 And oft robbed of my perfect mind I thought
380 At last my feet a resting-place had found
381 Here will I weep in peace "so Fancy wrought"
382 Roaming the illimitable waters round
              watch
383 Here gaze of every friend but Death disowned
384 All day my ready tomb the ocean flood.
385 To break my dream the vessel reached its bound
386 And homeless near a thousand homes I stood
387 And near a thousand tables pined and wanted
                                         food

                     4⎫
                    42⎭

388 Three years a wanderer round my native coast
         ine   orb
389 My eyes have watched yon sun declining
                                    tend
390 Down to the land where I hope to me was lost

387/388 The numbering of stanzas 44 through 47 fell behind by two in the original copy and was corrected by overwriting.
  390 WW started to capitalize the "h" in "hope" by adding a single downstroke, but did not make the connecting horizontal stroke.

And now across this waste my steps I bend   55

Oh! tell me whither for no earthly friend

Have I   no house in prospect but the tomb

She ceased. The city's distant spires ascend

Like flames which far and wide the west illume

Scattering from out the sky the rear of night.
                    ·45   then gloom

Along the fiery east the sun, a show

More gorgeous still! pursued his proud career.

But human sufferings and that tale of woe

Had dimmed the traveller's eye with pity's tear.

And in the youthful mourner's doom severe
        His lonely sufferings Present

She half forgot the terrors of the night

Striving with counsel sweet her soul to chear

Her soul for ever widowed of delight.

He too had withered young in sorrow's

That she alas for the deadly blight.
                    44

391 And now across this waste my steps I bend
392 Oh! tell me whither for no earthly friend
393 Have I   no house in prospect but the tomb
                    . ⎱ T ⎱
394 She ceased ⎰ t ⎰he citys distant Spires ascend
395 Like flames which far and wide the west illume
396 Scattering from out the sky the rear of nights
                                            thin gloom.

5 ⎱
43 ⎰

397 Along the fiery east the Sun, a show
398 More gorgeous still! pursued his proud career.
399 But human sufferings and that tale of woe

                                          s ⎱
400 Had dimmed the traveller's eye with Pity'[?]⎰ tear
        He
401 And in the youthful mourner's doom severe
        His heart forgot   [?the ?worst]
402 He half forgot the terrors of the night
                                i⎱
403 Striving with counce⎰l sweet her soul to chear
        And⎱   her ⎱ long⎱   exile⎱ invite
        [?Th]⎰ fancy from long⎰ exile⎰ to invite⎰
404 Her soul for ever widowed of Đ delight.
        But that sad soul for aye [?seem'd]
405 He too had withered young in sorrow's
        But She alas for aye was widowed
                                deadly blight.
                                    of del

44

405/406 The figure "44" belongs to the original misnumbering.

4 8

But now from a hill summit down they look 57

Where through a narrow valley's pleasant scene

A wreath of vapour tracked a winding brook
That babbled on
bebbling through groves and bows and meads of
green?

A smoking cottage peeped the trees between

The groves resound the linnets amorous lays

And melancholy lowings intervene

Of scattered herds that in the meadows graze

While through the furrowed grass the merry
milk maid strays

Adieu ye friendless hope-forsaken pair

Yet friendless ere ye take your several road

Enter that lowly cot and ye shall share

comforts by prouder mansions unbestowed

For you yon milkmaid bears her brimming
load &

For you the board is piled with homely bread

And think that life is like this desert broad

$$\left.\begin{array}{c}6\\44\end{array}\right\}$$

406 But now from a hill summit down they look

407 Where through a narrow valley's pleasant scene

408 A wreath of vapour tracked a winding brook
   That babbled on

409 Babbling through groves ~~and lawns~~ and meads of
                                                green.
   ~~One~~ A single cottage smoked

410 ~~A~~ smoking cottage peeped the trees between
            [?ring]
       fresh groves with [?ring ?at ?strife]
       groves

411 The ~~woods~~ resound the linnets amorous lays
            [?fresh]
    [?Careless ?strain] ring with
    The fresh groves ring with strife of chearful
                                          lays

412 And melancholy lowings intervene
    at [?strife] ~~the fresh groves with~~ amorous

413 Of scattered herds that in the meadows graze

414 While through the furrowed grass the merry
                           milkmaid strays

$$\left.\begin{array}{c}7\\45\end{array}\right\}$$

   How [?sweetly!] breathes the morning air

415 Adieu ye friendless hope-forsaken pair

416 Yet friendless ere ye take your several road
                   roofed   of   thatch

417 Enter that lowl~~y~~ cot and ye shall share

418 Comforts by prouder mansions unbestowed
    There not in vain has Natures bounty flowed

419 For you yon milkmaid bears her brimming
                                       load

420 For you the board is piled with homely bread

421 And think that life is like this desart broad

59

Where all the happiest find is but a shed

And a green spot mid wastes interminably

~~For here though ——~~

~~If For. Though from ——~~ wickers naked ~~——~~

~~Thought from large wickers~~ paled with circling fire

No longer horrid shrieks and dying cries

~~To ear, No more for ears, of Deamon Gods~~

~~To ear, of Deamon-Gods in peals aspire~~

~~In peals the groans of a human sacrifice~~

To Damon-Gods   a human sacrifice

Though Treachery her sword no longer dyes

~~If men or ——~~

In the cold blood of Truce, still, reason's ray

What does it more than while the tempests rise

With starless glooms, and sounds of loud ~~dismay~~

~~thread~~ with still-born ~~scant~~ glimpse the terrors of our way

For proof, if man thou lovest turn thine eye

On realms which least the cup of Misery taste

~~For proof the living ——~~

~~For want how many,~~ ~~——~~ men and children die

How many at Oppression's portal placed

Receive the scanty dole she cannot waste

422 Where all the happiest find is but a shed
423 And a green spot mid wastes interminably
                                        spread

48

    For here though naked without hope
        no more in winters keenest gale
        cold
    For, though from wickers naked without [?fire]
              or [?smoking] or [?fr]
424 — Though from huge wickers paled with circling
                                                fire
    Man in his [?breaking ?heart] no longer
      on his [?]
425 No longer horrid skrieks and dying cries
    No more to ears [?of] Deamon Gods
426 To ears of Dæmon-Gods in peals aspire
    In peals the groans of human sacrifi[?ce]
427 To Dæmon-Gods a human sacrifice

---

428 Though Treachery her sword no longer dyes
    For thoug   without home or friend
      on⎫   [?rock]
    Man [?]⎰ [?this ?vacant ?Plain] no longer [?lies]
429 In the cold blood of Truce, still, reason's ray
430 What does it more than while the tempest's rise
431 With starless glooms and sounds of loud
                                        dismay
             short
      [?scant] glimpse
432 Reveal with still-born glimpse the terrors of our
                                        way.

49

    For proof [?from] either pole to pole [?the ?living]
                [?world ?survey]
433 For proof, if man thou lovest turn thine eye
434 On realms which least the cup of Misery taste
        r⎫
    For p[?]⎰oof the living word till [?moaning] ends
             till [?moaning] ends   survey
    How many
435 For want how many, many men and children, die
436 How many at Oppression's portal placed
437 Receive the scanty dole she cannot waste

---

430 tempest's] The mistaken "'s" is presumably based on "reason's" in the previous line.
433 Revision in pencil.

And bless, as she has taught, her hand benign   61
How many by inhuman toil debased
Abject obscure and brute to earth incline
Unrespited, forlorn of every spark divine
                58

Nor only in the walk of private life
Unblessed by Justice and the kindly train
Of Peace and Truth while Injury and Strife
Outrage and deadly Hate usurp their reign

                                        forced   to
The Nations though at home in bonds they drink
The dregs of wretchedness for empire strain
      when by their own fetters crushed they sink
And crushed by their own fetters help to sink
Move their galled limbs in fear and eye each
                        silent link
                51

Lo! where the Sun exulting in his might
In haste the fiery top of Andes scales
                    pours
And flings deep silent floods of purple light
Down to the sea through long Peruvian
                                    vales
At once a thousand streams and gentle gales
Start from their slumber breathing scent and song

438   And bless, as she has taught, her hand benign
439   How many by inhuman toil debased
440   Abject obscure and brute to earth incline
441   Unrespitied, forlorn of every spark divine

50

442   Nor only is the walk of private life
443   Unblessed by Justice and the kindly train
444   Of Peace and Truth while Injury and Strife
445   Outrage and deadly Hate usurp their reign
[446]   From the pale line to either frozen [?Main]

         N⎰   forced   to
447   The n⎰ations ~~though~~ at home in bonds ~~they~~ drink
448   The dregs of wretchedness for empire strain

            when by their own fetters crushed they sink
449   And crushed by their own fetters helpless sink
450   Move their galled limbs in fear and eye each
                               silent link.

51

451   Lo! where the Sun exulting in his might
452   In haste the fiery top of Andes scales

         pours
453   And flings deep silent floods of purple light
454   Down to the sea through long Peruvian
                          vales
455   At once a thousand streams and gentle gales
456   Start from their slumber breathing scent and song.

---

[446]   A line omitted in the original fair copy was added in pencil.

But now no joy of man or Woman hails 63
That star as once, ere with him came the throng
Of Furies and grim Death by Rancie lashed
      along.
   52

Oh that a slave who on his naked knees
Weeps tears of fear at Superstition's nod
Should rise a monster Tyrant and o'ersea
And mountains stretch so far his cruel rod
To bruise meek Nature in her lone abode
Is it for this the planet of the [?]
Scatters through [?] storms   his guiding
[?] through the stars   light around
Through storms we ride with Misery to our goal
No star nor needle know the tempests of the soul
      53

How changed that paradise those happy bour[?]
Where once through his own groves the Hindoo
                                    strayed
No more the voice of jocund toil resound[?]
Along. the crouded banyans high arcade

              M⎱   W⎱

457   But now no joy of m⎰an or w⎰oman hails

458   That star as once ere with him came the throng

               led by

459   Of Furies ~~and grim~~ Death by Avarice lashed

                                 along.

                52

460   Oh that a slave who on his naked knees

461   Weeps tears of fear at Superstition's nod

462   Should rise a monster Tyrant and oer seas

463   And mountains stretch so far his cruel rod

464   To bruise meek Nature in her lone abode

465   Is it for this the planet of the pole

        Scatters through storms   his guiding

                  or⎱   [?his]⎱

466   ~~Sends through the sto⎰ms~~ ~~its~~⎰ stedfast light abroad.

467   Through storms we ride with Misery to her goal

                           T⎱

468   Nor star nor needle know the t⎰empests of the soul.

                53

469   How changed that paradise those happy bounds

470   Where once through his own groves the Hindoo

                          strayed

471   No more the voice of jocund toil resounds

472   Along the crouded banyans high arcade

---

457 "Man" appears to have been capitalized with a single stroke.

459 Deletion and addition in pencil.

465–468 On the opposite verso WW has written (the first line in pencil):

                night and storm [?s]

    Is it for this the planet of the pole

    Hangs out his stedfast lamp: Merciful God

    Who viewest us ride with Misery to her goal

               the star

    Disclose thy light of truth to guide man's erring soul

        T⎱

468   t⎰ WW capitalized the "t" simply by adding a top stroke to the existing letter.

472/505 The first of the two stubs remaining, 33ʳ, reads: "W/—/—/[?N]"; and the second, 34ʳ; "Pe/Ho/A"

How weak the solace such fond thoughts afford
When with untimely stroke the virtuous bleed
Say rulers of the nations from the sword
Can ought but murder pain and tears proceed
Oh what can war but endless war still breed
Or whence but from the labours of the sage
Can poor benighted mortals gain the meed
Of happiness and virtue how assuage
But by his gentle words their self consuming rage

Insensate they who think, at Wisdom's porch
That Exile, Terror, Bonds & Force may stand:
That Truth with human blood can feed her torch
And Justice balance with her gory hand
Scales whose dire weights of human heads demand
A Nero's arm. Must Law with iron scourge
Still torture crimes that grew a monstrous band
Formed by his care and still his victims urge
With voice that breathes despair to deaths tremendous verge

57

505 How weak the solace such fond thoughts afford
506 When with untimely stroke the virtuous bleed
507 Say rulers of the nations from the sword
508 Can ought but ~~Mur~~ murder pain and tears
                                        proceed
                  w⟩
509 Oh! what can w⟨ar but endless war still breed
510 Or whence but from the labours of the sage
511 Can poor benighted mortals gain the meed
512 Of happiness and virtue how assuage
513 But by his gentle words their self consuming
                                        rage

58

514 Insensate they who think, at Wisdom's porch
515 That Exile, Terror, Bonds & Force may stand:
516 That Truth with human blood can feed her
                                        torch
517 And Justice balance with her gory hand
518 Scales whose dire weights of human heads de:
                                        mand
519 A Nero's arm. Must Law with iron scourge
520 Still torture crimes that grew a monstrous band
521 Formed by his care and still his victims
                                        urge
522 With voice that breathes despair to deaths
                                        tremendous verge

522/540   The one stub remaining, 36ʳ, has no certainly identifiable letters on it, save possibly
"T" beginning the last line.

Who fierce on kingly crowns hurled his
                    own lightning blaze

proud 61

Heroes of Truth pursue your march uptear

Th' Oppressors dungeon from its deeper base

High oer the towers of Pride undaunted
                                    rear

Resistless in your might the herculean mace

Of Reason; let foul Error's monster race

Dragged from their dens start at the light
                                    with pain

And die; pursue your toils till not a truce

Be left on earth of Superstitions reign

Save that eternal pile which frowns
                    on Sarums plain

Which darkness . . . .

. . . .

. . . .

540   Who fierce on kingly crowns hurled his
                          own lightning blaze.

                    61

              proceed
541   Heroes ~~of Truth~~ pursue your march uptear
542   Th' Oppressors dungeon from its deepest base
543   High o'er the towers of Pride undaunted
                                   rear
544   Resistless in your might the herculean mace
545   Of Reason; let foul Error's monster race
546   Dragged from their dens start at the light
                                with pain
547   And die; pursue your toils till not a trace
548   Be left on earth of Superstitions reign
549   Save that eternal pile which frowns
                         a⎰
              on Sa⎱rums plain.

_____

541   proceed] In pencil, as is the deletion mark.
549   The three lines visible at the page foot belong to the drafting for *Prelude*, XI, 164–175,
on the opposite verso.

Additions to MS. 1

Transcriptions of the additions to MS. 1 follow. These can be dated between April–May 1794, immediately after the copying of the manuscript, and November 1795. The additions show the development of *Salisbury Plain* into the larger poem *Adventures on Salisbury Plain*. All these revisions are transcribed, in two sections. Section A shows work which, while developing the poem as it stands in MS. 1, does not reveal any great change in the poet's conception of it. Section B consists of Wordsworth's work on the more extensively developed plot, which was to include the Sailor, with the story of his crime and subsequent life. Within each section the additions are presented in the order of the manuscript leaves on which they appear. Although Wordsworth commonly used blank spaces for his revisions unsystematically, this order has the general effect here of grouping together passages which relate to the same idea or part of the poem. As indicated in Editorial Procedure, above, in the right-hand margin are given the numbers of corresponding lines in the appropriate main text—for Section A, *Salisbury Plain*; for Section B, *Adventures on Salisbury Plain*.

SECTION A

[Inside front cover]

Huge [?blea] bare & wild
Roofless & bare & not of human form
Ill fitted did that pile for [?] shelter seem

[23ᵛ]

    fitted
Ill did that naked circles form
For

                    thither forced
                    by storms to fly
And I̶ ̶h̶a̶v̶e̶ ̶h̶e̶a̶r̶d̶ ̶f̶r̶o̶m̶ travellers p̶a̶l̶e̶   c. 82–99

Inside front cover   For parallels, see 23ᵛ, below, first line and two lines preceding the last; also revisions of MS. A, lines 72/73 and 90/91.

Have said that [?what] soon as that [?hour]
Storm driven when ~~that~~ stupendous monum
                                    [?turn]
Enclosed them in its blank immensity
~~At once~~ the local genius forth has sent
Strong horrors in that [?rustic]

And travellers thither forced by storms to fly

                          orient head
He sees the sun uplift his [?lambent]   327–333
            head   comfort ⟩
And from his beams feals [?   ] ∫
           [?heads ?beams] feel
        on
And ever [?to ?him] his beam a vital
And feels his friendly beams a vital influence shed

                        earthly ⟩
Roofless and bare & not of human ∫ form
Ill fitted did such spot for shelter seem
again he wildered through the watry storm   102

[24ᵛ]

And tales are told of [?thouse ?who] forced   c. 82–99
                when that stupendous
Enclosed   stupendous ⟩
            till that [?   ]∫ monument

Enclosed him in its blank immensity
                as if
~~At once as if~~ the Genius forth had sent
            shape
Each ~~form of horror~~ in that [?wicker ?part]
      Horror seized   [?]
Strange ~~horror fear fell on him~~ [?then] round the walls
~~The thunder burst~~ earth groaned the [?thund]
Earth groaned the thunder burst

      [?]
                    when
            ~~soon as that~~ stupendous monument
Has [?close] them in its blank immensity
At once the local Genius forth hath sent
All form of horror in that [?   ]
  T ⟩
[S]∫ he earth has groaned
  T⟩
  t ∫ravellers humble when forced by storms to fly
Its shelter that stupendous monu

23ᵛ   The two lines beginning "And ever" and "And feels" are in pencil.

[25ᵛ]

He paused she of all present thought forlorn   325–333
While he in   was mute
Till Nature by excess of oerbourn
   Pour tears in floods   anguish
Did with discharge of tears hersel recruit
No other solace could such anguish suit
                      Salute
And saw the beams of breaking day upshoot
  She [?]
The yet [?]   his orient head
He feels his friendly beam a vital influence shed
       the dawn
And saw the [?   ?   ?   ]

[27ᵛ]

  Beguiled of self
Of social orders all-protecting plan   c. 400–405
  Himself forgot   [?stile]⎫
Delusion fond he spoke in tender [?]⎬
  Forgetting self
And of the general care man pays to man
~~Hope~~ Joys second spring and hopes long treasured smile
             [?sorrows]
Sounds that but served her deep breast to beguile
         [——?——?——]
And [?oft] the long sigh and oft repeated no
      along   forsaken
As wind that moan [?~~thro~~ ?a] ruined pile
Tell that the ruin is more perfect so
       brea ⎫
Did those deep [?]⎬thed sighs her desolation show

Of general care by social orders plans
[?]
of blessings unforeseen times lenient
        ever   [?lessening]
Of tears and sorrow still [?contracting] shew

Nor less when he beheld at night [?from ?far]   181–182
Black bodies dimly tinged with sullen red
  [?Exc]   [?marked]
What ~~viewed~~ he in those wild assemblies rude
The thoughts that bow the common spirit[?s] down

25ᵛ   The revisions of the fourth line and all of the last line are in pencil.
27ᵛ   The last four lines are in pencil.

[29ᵛ]

interminably spread   423

lot
Hard is the ~~life~~ when mid deep forests rouzed   1–9
By storms, the savage, weak from fruitless pains
Of the long day, alone, unclad unhoused
Lies down in the cold night on unknow plains,
And lifts his head in fear &c

time
Hard was ~~that~~ the lot when naked and unhoused
And wasted by the long days fruitless pains

                              u ⎞
The savage mid deep woods by tempests ro[?]⎰zed

        i⎞
Lay down o⎰n the cold night on these wide plains
And reared in fear, while famished trains
Of Boars along the crashing thickets prowled
And heard in darkness as the rushing rains
Put out his watchfire bears contending growled
And round his fenceless bed gaunt wolves in armies howled

Nor less when he beheld at night from far   181–189
Black bodies dimly tinged with sullen red

                        G⎞
Exulting round the idol g⎰od of war
While the great flame by living captives fed
Scattered such horror as might make the dead
Thrilled in their yawning tombs their helms uprear
The sword that slept beneath the warriors head
Thunder in fiery air red arms appear
Uplifted through the gloom & shake the rattling spear

[30ᵛ]

Yet was that savage patient and his mind   10–18
Encountered all his evils unsubdued
For happier days since at the breast he pined
He never knew and when by foes pursued
        scarce has
With life ~~has hardly reached~~ the fortress rude

          - ⎞
While with the war[?s]⎰ songs peal the vall[?ies] shook
What in those wild assemblies has he view'd
But men who all of his hard lot partook
Reposed in the same fear to the same toil awoke

The thoughts which bow the common spirit down   19–20
And break the springs of joy, their deadly weight

30ᵛ   After "their deadly weight" WW breaks off with "&c see second page/ —in winter's keenest gale," to indicate that ll. 21–36 of the original were to stand unrevised.

For here though naked, without home or friend   424–432
Man [?th] on the casual rock no longer lies
No more to ears of Demon Gods ascend
In peals the groans of human sacrifice
Though Treachery her sword no longer dies
In the cold blood of Truce still Reasons ray
What does it more than while The tempests rise
         still   horrors
Shew with ~~short~~ Glimpse the terrors of our way
For proof look round the world as far as there is day

[31ᵛ]

   On dry
~~He stretched~~ nook where fern the floor best[?rews]   c. 132
His limbs [?forth] stretch & sleep began his eyes
   [?]
His [?aching] limbs he stretchtd ~~to close~~
   began   his eyes

             [?he] shal be [?rest]
             Oh that a vain

        Night and storm[?s]

When a deep sigh he heard from [?one] that mourned   136
In sleep forth sent ~~that way he turned~~ his head
         from earth he raised his head

Till to the downs the early shepherd goes   c. 132
     sweet ⎫   ere ⎫ restless
~~Here~~ shall [?] ⎬ sleep [?his] ⎬ his frame embrace
        n⎫
In a dry d⎰ook where fern the floor bestrews
         [?frame]
He stretched ~~his~~ stiffened limbs his eyes began to close

[32ᵛ]

He paused she of all present thought forlorn   325–333
     had she
Nor had she vainly, told her wretched doom
He rose and left her silently to mourn —
One on whose [?sorrow] voice might not [?presume]

     ing ⎫
He looked ⎰ & saw the morn along the gloom
  grey or   [?]
Of the ~~dark~~ orient, opening ~~fiery~~ red
All unconcerned with their unrest resume
Her progress now the sun uplifts his [?head]
He feels his friendly beams a vital influence shed

31ᵛ   "Night and storm[?s]" is a pencil addition. It is uncertain where the words belong. See note to ll. 465–468, p. 103.

SECTION B

[26ᵛ]

c. 91–99

　Yet　　　　　　　all the power
Of ~~cold heat~~ cold and he hunger has he long [?without]
Since press'd by want in [?evile] hour
　　[?With　?　]
His hand he mingled in a [?deed] of blood
Yet [　?　?he　?murdered　?must] be mild & good
Yet to that hour he had been mild & good
　　　　　　at miserable work
And when the fatal deed of death was done
　Such　　　　him
~~Black~~ horor ~~siezed~~ Horror fell on his in [?such]
Such horror siezed him as might to [?wh]

　　　　　　　since [　?　?has　?returned]
From place to place nor known [?one] chearful sun

　　　　　as ⎱
Such pangs were his & ⎰ to relenting mood

c. 107–108

Melts the hardest since haunted has
　~~he~~ [　?　]

[28ᵛ]

　　　　　　more than before at ease
Though weak more tranquil than before he found

c. 132

　　　　　his eyes which [?where]　　it strays
　　　　　　　　[　?　?　]
His mind more calm his eye [?whereer] it strays
Marks nothing but the red suns setting [?round]
　　　　　ground　　　[　?　]
Or on the plain strange marks from former days

138–144

　[?Left]
　　　by ⎱　　　　　and
Work of ⎰ gigantic arms he ~~now~~ surveys
　　　　　　at length surveys
What seems an antique castle spreading [?wide]
Hoary and naked are its walls and raise
　　　　　　　　[?towards]
Their [?brow] sublime to those huge walls he hied
　Thinking
Hoping that sheltered there he might abide

Fled a poor vagrant since the murtherers fate to shun

99

They crossed the valley to that
　And entering
~~Entering they~~ found a good mans table spread

680–684

28ᵛ　The line beginning "Fled a poor vagrant" is in pencil.

Entering
They ~~entered~~ found a good [?] man table
Kindly the master pressed and they in comfort fed

[31ᵛ]

There not in vain has Natures bounty flowed   680–684
They entered found the good mans table spread
And in the milkmaid bore her brimming load
        housewife
The ~~daughter~~ piled with homely [?bred]
Kindly the master pressed and they in comfort

[37ᵛ]

Yet when cold fear her withering power forbears   100–106
      tend ⎫
Such comp⎰ency to pleasure known before
Does nature show that common cares
            breast ⎫
Might to his [?heart]⎰ a second spring restore
                complains of ~~misery~~
      [——?——] least complaints explore
                        wretchedness
His heartstrings trembling with responsive grief
        the best of human hearts not more

More wanted not to conjure up each shape   118–126
Of terror   substantial or vain
    To [?conjure]
All shapes of terror vain
Or solid

The stones rolled after him in train
And [?Entranced] down he fell upon the plain

[38ᵛ]

      It little grieved him
And littled ~~did~~ grieved he for the sleety shower   73–108
Cold wind and hunger he had long withstoood
Long hunted down by mans confederate power
Since phrenzy-driven he dipped his hand in blood
                        kind
Yet till that hour he had been mild and good
And when the miserable deed was done
Such pangs were his as to relenting mood
Might melt the hardest since   has he run
For years from place nor place nor known one chearful sun

Yet oft as Fear her withering grasp forbears
              [——?——]
Such tendency to pleasures loved before

Does Nature [?sho]   common cares
Might to his breast a second spring restore
The least complaints of wretchedness explore
    inmost   to   tone
His heartstrings ~~trembled with~~ responsive grief
[?T]⎱
   t ⎰rembling the best of human hearts not more
        e ⎱
~~From each ex[?f]⎰ess of pain his days have known~~
~~Well has he learned to make all others ills his~~ own
         t ⎱
He nor revenge nor ha[?v]⎰e   has ever known

[39ʳ]

        each
Yet though to ~~softest~~ sympathy inclined   109–117
Most trivial cause will rouse the keenest pang
      at [? n ?lay] ~~waste~~
Of teror and oerwhelm   his mind
   [?Sorrow]
~~For then~~ with scarce distinguishable clang
  In ⎱   rang ⎱
D[?]⎰ the cold wind a sound of irons [?]⎰
He looked and saw on a bare gibbet nigh
    clanking
In moving chains a human body hang
A hovering raven oft did round it fly
A grave the was beneath which he could not descry

[39ᵛ]

   Yet   [?shows]
~~But~~ when the [—?—?—] day break of terror   100–108

39ᵛ   On the stub of 40ʳ a number of letters or marks of composition can be made out: /[?—]
/[?—]/Cold/~~The~~/[?Sin]/Ye/And/[?See]/M/[?—]/—/—/—/Do/[?M]. On the verso the following
line endings can be recognized: s/[?—]/est/[?—]/[?—]. Marks of at least five other lines of
composition are visible, the last of which is /[?man]/. The inside back cover of the notebook has
three lines of composition and some calculations which refer to *SP*:

    A vain [?resolve] of unconfined despair
    [?Then] Now she [? ?Plain]
    For ill a covering form

    61   12 | 549   70
     9   45   9
    ---   ---   ---
    549   630

      breathe, [?on] th
To shrivel[?e] up   so fair before
      renovation buds
Such signs appear as [?the] common cares
Might to a second spring of joy restore
Such tendency appears as common cares
          n ⎱
Such tendency in m ⎰ature to restore
      that
    e⎱   [?freeze] the [?buds]
Her [?f⎰arly] spring appear [?] as common cares

And with surest touch each [?] do ex
The least complaint of sorrow doth explore
His heart trembling with [?]
And when he hears the a tale of grief
His heart strings not the best of heart not more
The best of human hearts not more
Yet there are times when fear her power forbears
  Y ⎱
[?]⎰et when bold fear his withering power forbears

Adventures on Salisbury Plain (1795–c. 1799)

Reading Text with variant readings from
The Female Vagrant (1798–1847)

The poem which follows is edited from MS. 2. Reference to the full transcription of the manuscript will show how little interference has in fact been needed to produce a reading text, although it has been necessary to renumber the stanzas. Punctuation is largely editorial. The MS. 2 poem, however, omits the story which the Female Vagrant tells to the Sailor. As indicated in the Introduction, pp. 9–10, DW did not copy the woman's story in MS. 2 because it was WW's intention to write another, once the first had been published as *The Female Vagrant* in *Lyrical Ballads*, 1798. The new story was not composed, and I have dovetailed the text of *The Female Vagrant*, 1798, at lines 262–396 and 424–558. It is presented in full, despite some repetition at lines 550–567.

An *apparatus criticus* records all variants for *The Female Vagrant* in the authorized English editions, 1798–1847; the corrections in WW's letters to Biggs and Cottle, mid-July 1800, and to Anne Taylor, 9 April 1801; and variants first appearing in the Female Vagrant's story in *Guilt and Sorrow*, 1842 and 1845, adopted in the final authorized printing of the shorter poem in 1847 (see below). Variants in periodical reprintings and in the Galignani edition (Paris, 1828) and American editions, which follow English printed versions, have been disregarded.

The *apparatus criticus* uses the following abbreviations:

B & C	WW to Biggs and Cottle, mid-July 1800 (manuscript, Yale University Library; see *EY*, 287).
1800	*Lyrical Ballads* (2 vols.; London, 1800).
Taylor	WW to Anne Taylor, 9 April 1801 (manuscript, Harvard University Library; see *EY*, 328–329).
1802	*Lyrical Ballads* (2 vols.; London, 1802).
1805	*Lyrical Ballads* (2 vols.; London, 1805).
1815	*Poems* (2 vols.; London, 1815).
1820	*The Miscellaneous Poems* (4 vols.; London, 1820).
1827	*The Poetical Works* (5 vols.; London, 1827).
1831	*Selections from the Poems of William Wordsworth, Esq.*, ed. Joseph Hine (London, 1831).
1832	*The Poetical Works* (4 vols.; London, 1832).
1834	*Selections from the Poems of William Wordsworth, Esq.*, ed. Joseph Hine (London, 1834).
1836	*The Poetical Works* (6 vols.; London, 1836).
1840	*The Poetical Works* (6 vols.; London, 1840).

1841   *The Poetical Works* (6 vols.; London, 1841). Reissued 1843 with no *FV* variants.

1843B   *Select Pieces from the Poems of William Wordsworth* (London: James Burns, 1843).

1847M   *Select Pieces from the Poems of William Wordsworth* (London: Edward Moxon, 1847). 1847M* denotes a variant in 1847M originally appearing in the Female Vagrant's story in *Guilt and Sorrow*, 1842 (ll. 199–306, 343–350). Despite the publication date, the readings in Burns's *Select Pieces* antedate those in the Female Vagrant's story in the 1842 publication of *Guilt and Sorrow*. See *LY*, III, 1188–1193, for evidence that Burns's edition, which was certainly not authorized by WW, was printed from copy obtained from the Reverend Mr. Gough, which WW had authorized. The *Select Pieces* printings of *The Female Vagrant* are the only instances of manuscript or authorized printed versions of any stanzas of *SP* in which the concluding alexandrine is consistently set to the left of the preceding lines of the stanza.

Adventures on Salisbury Plain

Part First

1

A Traveller on the skirt of Sarum's Plain
O'ertook an aged Man with feet half bare;
Propp'd on a trembling staff he crept with pain,
His legs from slow disease distended were;
His temples just betrayed their silver hair   5
Beneath a kerchief's edge, that wrapp'd his head
To fence from off his face the breathing air.
Stuck miserably o'er with patch and shred
His ragged coat scarce showed the Soldier's faded red.

2

"And dost thou hope across this Plain to trail   10
That frame o'ercome with years and malady,
Those feet that scarcely can outcrawl the snail,
These withered arms of thine, that faltering knee?
Come, I am strong and stout, come lean on me."
The old man's eyes a wintry lustre dart,   15
And so sustained he faced the open lea.
But short the joy that touched his melting heart,
For ere a mile be gone his friend and he must part.

3

Nor of long absence failed he soon to tell
And how he with the Soldier's life had striven   20
And Soldier's wrongs; but one who knew him well
A house to his old age had lately given.
Thence he had limp'd to meet a daughter driven
By circumstance which did all faith exceed
From every stay but him: his heart was riven   25
At the bare thought: the creature that had need
Of any aid from him most wretched was indeed.

---

9 Cf. *RC*, MS. B, 713 (*PW*, V, 399), where Margaret looks hopefully for "A Man whose garments shewed the Soldier's red."

4

He said that on his comrade's road there lay
One lonely inn upon the wilder moor.
But entrance none was there for such as they,   30
No board inscribed the needy to allure,
The grapes hung glittering at the gilded door.
But now their short-lived fellowship must end.
Down sate with pain the Soldier sick and poor,
Nor can the younger quit his helpless friend   35
Where thus the bare white roads their dreary line extend.

5

Ere long a post-boy's scarlet vest he spied
On the wide down, at distance flashing bright,
And when the wheels approached, he rose and cried,
"Have mercy on this broken Soldier's plight;   40
Deed of such sort shall well itself requite."
The old man then was on the cushion placed
And all his body trembled with delight.
Forthwith, self-satisfied, his comrade faced,
And yet the sun was high, the far-extended waste.   45

6 ·

The evening came with clouds and stormy fire;
That inn he long had pass'd and wearily
Measured his lonesome way; the distant spire
That fix'd at every turn his backward eye
Was lost, though still he turn'd, in the blank sky.   50
By thirst and hunger press'd he gaz'd around
And scarce could any trace of man descry,
Save dreary corn-fields stretch'd as without bound;
But where the sower dwelt was nowhere to be found.

7

No tree was there, no meadow's pleasant green,   55
No brook to wet his lips or soothe his ear.
Vast piles of corn-stack here and there were seen,
But thence no smoke upwreathed his sight to cheer.
He mark'd a homeward shepherd disappear
Far off and sent a feeble shout, in vain;   60
No sound replies but winds that whistling near
Sweep the thin grass and passing wildly plain,
Or desart lark that pours on high a wasted strain.

8

Long had he fancied each successive slope
Conceal'd some cottage, whither he might turn   65
And rest; but now, along heaven's darkening cope
He watch'd the crows in eddies homeward borne,
Then sought in vain some shepherd's ragged thorn
Or hovel, from the storm to shield his head.
For as he onward pass'd, more wild, forlorn,   70
And vacant, the huge plain around him spread;
Ah me! the wet cold ground must be his only bed.

9

And be it so—for to the chill night shower
And the sharp wind his head he oft has bared;
And he has counted many a wretched hour.   75
—A Sailor he, the sailor's evils shared,
For when from two full years of labour hard
Home he return'd, enflamed with long desire,
Even while in thought he took his rich reward
From his wife's lips, the ruffian press gang dire   80
Hurried him far away to rouze the battle's fire.

10

For years the work of carnage did not cease,
And Death's worst aspect daily he survey'd
Death's minister: then came his glad release,
And Hope returned and pleasure fondly made   85
Her dwelling in his dreams. By thought betray'd,
He seems to feel his wife around him throw
Her arms and she, this bloody prize of victory laid
In her full lap, forgets her years of woe
In the long joy and comfort from that wealth to flow. 90

11

He urged his claim; the slaves of Office spurn'd
The unfriended claimant; at their door he stood
In vain, and now towards his home return'd,
Bearing to those he loved nor warmth nor food,
In sight of his own house, in such a mood   95
That from his view his children might have run,
He met a traveller, robb'd him, shed his blood;
And when the miserable work was done
He fled, a vagrant since, the murderer's fate to shun.

12

Yet oft when Fear her withering grasp foregoes,   100
Such tendency to pleasure loved before
Do life and nature shew, that common cares
Might to his bosom hours of joy restore.
Affliction's least complaints his heart explore
Even yet, though danger round his path be sown.   105
And fear defend the weak, the best not more.
And wer't not so, the hardest might bemoan
The pangs, the sleepless nights, the miseries he has known.

13

The proud man might relent and weep to find
That now, in this wild waste, so keen a pang   110
Could pierce a heart to life's best ends inclined.
For as he plodded on, with sudden clang
A sound of chains along the desart rang:
He looked, and saw on a bare gibbet nigh
A human body that in irons swang,   115
Uplifted by the tempest sweeping by,
And hovering round it often did a raven fly.

14

It was a spectacle which none might view
In spot so savage but with shuddering pain
Nor only did for him at once renew   120
All he had feared from man, but rouzed a train
Of the mind's phantoms, horrible as vain.
The stones, as if to sweep him from the day,
Roll'd at his back along the living plain;
He fell and without sense or motion lay,   125
And when the trance was gone, feebly pursued his way.

15

As doth befall to them whom frenzy fires,
His soul, which in such anguish had been toss'd,

---

100   foregoes] So in the manuscript, but the rhyme scheme demands the reading "forbears," which is found in the drafts in MS. 1, 38ᵛ. See above, p. 115.

117   WW's note to this line in *Poems, Chiefly of Early and Late Years* (1842) reads: "From a short MS. poem read to me when an under-graduate, by my schoolfellow and friend Charles Farish, long since deceased. The verses were by a brother of his, a man of promising genius, who died young." (From 1846, "schoolfellow" read "school-fellow".) For a text of the poem *The Heath* and a discussion of Charles and John Bernard Farish, see T. W. Thompson, *Wordsworth's Hawkshead*, ed. Robert Woof (London, 1970), 311–321.

Sank into deepest calm; for now retires
Fear; a terrific dream in darkness lost   130
The dire phantasma which his sense had cross'd.
His mind was still as a deep evening stream;
Nor, if accosted now, in thought engross'd,
Moody, or inly-troubled, would he seem
To traveller who might talk of any casual theme.   135

16

But all was chearless to the horizon's bound;
His weary eye—which, whereso'er it strays
Marks nothing but the red sun setting round,
Or on the earth strange lines, in former days
Left by gigantic arms—at length surveys   140
What seems an antique castle spreading wide;
Hoary and naked are its walls and raise
Their brow sublime: in shelter there to bide
He ran; the pouring rain smoked thick as on he hied.

17

Hurtle the clouds by deeper darkness piled,   145
Gone is the raven timely rest to seek;
He seem'd the only creature in the wild
On whom the elements their rage might wreak;
Save that the bustard, of those limits bleak
Shy tenant, seeing by the uncertain light   150
A man there wandring gave a mournful shriek,
And half upon the ground, with strange affright
Forc'd hard against the wind a thick unwieldy flight.

18

Thou hoary Pile! thou child of darkness deep
And unknown days, that lovest to stand and hear   155
The desart sounding to the whirlwind's sweep,
Inmate of lonesome Nature's endless year;
Even since thou sawest the giant Wicker rear
Its dismal chambers hung with living men,
Before thy face did ever wretch appear,   160
Who in his heart had groan'd with deadlier pain
Than he who travels now along thy bleak domain?

---

149   bustard] See note to l. 68 of *SP*, above.
158–159   See note to ll. 424–427 of *SP*, above.

19

Beneath that fabric scarce of earthly form
More dreadful was the whirlwind's rage extreme.
All track quite lost, through rain and blinding storm   165
Three hours he wilder'd on, no moon to stream
From gulf of parting clouds one friendly beam,
Or any friendly sound his footsteps led.
Once did the lightning's faint disastrous gleam
Disclose a naked guide-post's double head,   170
Sight which, though lost at once, some glimpse of pleasure shed.

20

No swinging sign creak'd from its cottage elm
To bid his weary limbs new force assume;
'Twas dark and void as ocean's watry realm
Roaring with storms beneath night's starless gloom;   175
No gypsey cowr'd o'er fire of furze or broom;
No labourer watch'd his red kiln glaring bright,
Nor taper glimmer'd dim from sick man's room;
Along the heath no line of mournful light
From lamp of lonely toll-gate stream'd athwart the night.   180

21

At length, though hid in clouds, the moon arose;
The downs were visible: and now revealed
A structure stands which two bare slopes enclose.
It was a spot where, ancient vows fulfill'd,
Kind pious hands did to the Virgin build   185
A lonely Spital, the belated swain
From the night-terrors of that waste to shield.
But there no human being could remain;
And now the Walls are named the dead house of the Plain.

163–165   In revision these lines became:
    Within that fabric, scarce of earthly form
    Winds met in conflict each by turns supreme
    In power.
Cf. *Prelude*, VI, 559–560:
                every where along the hollow rent
    Winds thwarting winds, bewilder'd and forlorn.
    176–177   WW often returns to the same kind of landscape in the poems of this period. See,
for example, the *SP* poems, *RC*, and the fragments from DC MS. 2 in Appendix I, below. For
the "gipsey" and the lime-kiln cf. *RC*, MS. B, 32–36 (*PW*, V, 380).
    180   See note to l. 117 of *SP*, above.

22

Though he had little cause to love the abode   190
Of man, or covet sight of mortal face,
Yet when the ambiguous gloom that ruin shew'd,
How glad he was at length to find a place
That bore of human hands the chearing trace.
Till to the moor the early shepherd goes,   195
Here shall sweet sleep his senseless limbs embrace.
In a dry nook where fern the floor bestrews
He lays his stiffen'd limbs: his eyes began to close.

23

When hearing a deep sigh, that seem'd forth sent
From one who mourn'd in sleep, he raised his head,   200
And saw a woman on the pediment
Outstretched and turning from uneasy bed;
The moon a wan dead light around her spread.
He waked her and at once her spirits fail
From fear by instant recollection bred;   205
For of that ruin she had heard a tale
Which now with freezing thoughts did all her powers assail.

24

Had heard of one who, forced from storms to shroud,
Felt the loose walls of this decayed retreat
Rock to his horse's neighings shrill and loud,   210
While his horse paw'd the floor with furious heat;
Till on a stone that sparkled to his feet
Struck, and still struck again, the troubled horse.
The man half-raised the stone with pain and sweat,
Half-raised, for well his arm might lose its force   215
Disclosing the grim head of a new-murder'd corse.

25

Such tales of this lone mansion she had learn'd,
And when that shape, with eyes in sleep half drown'd
By the moon's sullen lamp she first discern'd,
Cold stony horror all her senses bound.   220
He spoke and in low words of chearing sound.
Him further to allure to purpose kind,
Quickly she conversed of that desart ground,
Which seem'd to those of other worlds consign'd,
Whose voices she had heard as paused the hollow wind.   225

26

She said as through a bottom bare and deep
That day she journey'd on the houseless moor,
An old man, beckoning from the chalky steep,
Came tott'ring sidelong down to ask the hour;
There never clock was heard from steeple tow'r.   230
From the wide corn the plundering crows to scare
A rusty gun he held; in sun and shower,
Old as he was alone he lingered there,
His hungry meal too scant for dog that meal to share.

27

Much of the wonders of that boundless heath   235
She spoke and of a Swain who far astray
Reached unawares a height and saw beneath
Gigantic beings ranged in dread array;
Such beings, thwarting oft the traveller's way,
With shield and stone-ax [stride across the wold,   240
Or, throned on that dread circle's summit gray
Of mountains hung in air, their state unfold,
And like a thousand Gods mysterious council hold].

28

Much more of dreams from antient ages fetch'd,
And spectral sights that fill the shadowy plain,   245
And of wild sounds that mock the shepherd stretch'd
On the round barrow 'mid his fleecy train
She told, delighted that her fears were vain;
Nor of that corse there found did mention make,
And well it was, for surely once again   250
The fit had made his bones with horror quake:
She knew not what a hell such spot had power to wake.

29

But soon her heart on other thoughts was bent
So friendly was his voice, and now the wind
In feeble murmurs told his rage was spent.   255
Meanwhile discourse ensued of various kind
Which by degrees a confidence of mind

240–243 Words in brackets are supplied from MS. 1. They are wanting in MS. 2, but as the photograph shows, a pencil jotting indicates that ll. 177–180 of *SP* were to fit here.

And mutual interest fail'd not to create.
And now to natural sympathy resign'd,
In that forsaken building where they sate   260
The woman thus began her story to relate.

30

"By Derwent's side my Father's cottage stood,"
(The Woman thus her artless story told)
"One field, a flock, and what the neighbouring flood
Supplied, to him were more than mines of gold.   265
Light was my sleep; my days in transport roll'd:
With thoughtless joy I stretch'd along the shore
My father's nets, or watched, when from the fold
High o'er the cliffs I led my fleecy store,
A dizzy depth below! his boat and twinkling oar.   270

31

"My father was a good and pious man,
An honest man by honest parents bred,
And I believe that, soon as I began
To lisp, he made me kneel beside my bed,
And in his hearing there my prayers I said: 275
And afterwards, by my good father taught,

262–270 *omitted Taylor–*
268–270 My Father's nets, or from the mountain fold
        Saw on the distant Lake his twinkling oar,
        Or watch'd his lazy boat still less'ning more and more. *B & C-1800 but*
[1] Father's] father's *1800*   [2] lake . . . oar *1800*
271–391 *omitted 1815*
271 father] Father *1802–1805, 1820–1841*
271–272 By Derwent's side my father dwelt—a man
         Of virtuous life, by pious parents bred; *1847M**
272 bred,] bred; *1802–1805, 1832, 1836–1843B*
273 believe that,] believe, that, *1802–1805*
276 And afterwards] And, afterwards *1802*   father] Father *1802–1805*

262–396 The reader is reminded that these lines, and lines 424–558, were published sepa-
rately with many variants, 1798–1847, as *The Female Vagrant*. They are presented here, although
not part of MS. 2, for reasons explained in the Introduction, pp. 9–10, and the Prefatory Note,
above. The Fenwick note to *The Female Vagrant* reads: "I find the date of this is placed in 1792
in contradiction, by mistake, to what I have asserted in 'Guilt and Sorrow.' The correct date is
1793–4. The chief incident of it, more particularly her description of her feelings on the Atlantic
are taken from life." In the only surviving manuscript of the notes the date "1793–4" has been
added in pencil by a second hand in a space left by the copyist, Edward Quillinan. When *The
Female Vagrant* was published as a separate poem, there were no stanza numbers, the woman's
words were not introduced with quotation marks, and there was no break at l. 396 and no close-
quote in l. 555.

I read, and loved the books in which I read;
For books in every neighbouring house I sought,
And nothing to my mind a sweeter pleasure brought.

32

"Can I forget what charms did once adorn   280
My garden, stored with pease, and mint, and thyme,
And rose and lilly for the sabbath morn?
The sabbath bells, and their delightful chime;
The gambols and wild freaks at shearing time;
My hen's rich nest through long grass scarce espied;   285
The cowslip-gathering at May's dewy prime;
The swans, that, when I sought the water-side,
From far to meet me came, spreading their snowy pride.

33

"The staff I yet remember which upbore
The bending body of my active sire;   290
His seat beneath the honeyed sycamore
When the bees hummed, and chair by winter fire;
When market-morning came, the neat attire
With which, though bent on haste, myself I deck'd;

280–297 *omitted Taylor–1805*
280 charms] charm *1820*   Can I forget our croft and plot of corn; *1836–1843B*   A little croft we owned—a plot of corn, *1847M**
281 My] Our *1836–1843B* A *1847M**   pease] peas *1832–*   thyme,] thyme; *1836–1841*
282 rose and lilly] rose, and lily, *1820–1834* rose, and lily— *1836–1841* rose and lily, *1843B* sabbath] Sabbath *1831, 1834* Sabbath- *1843B*   morn?] morn; *1843B*
282–284 And flowers for posies, oft on Sunday morn
      Plucked while the church bells rang their earliest chime.
      Can I forget our freaks at shearing time! *1847M**
283 sabbath] Sabbath *1831, 1834* Sunday- *1843B*
284 shearing time] shearing-time *1836–1843B*
285 nest] nest, *1843B*
286 at May's] in June's *1820–*
287–288 The swans, that with white chests upheaved in pride,
      Rushing and racing came to meet me at the waterside. *1836– but* swans, that] swans that, *1840–1841* swans, that, *1843B* swans that *1847M**   upheaved] upreared *1847M* pride,] pride *1847M**   racing] racing, *1843B*   waterside.] waterside? *1840–1841* waterside? *1843B* water-side! *1847M**
288 pride.] pride? *1820–1834*
289 yet] well *1847M**
290 sire] Sire *1820–1841*
291 honeyed] honey'd *1827–1831, 1834* honied *1836–*
292 When] Where *1820–*   hummed] humm'd *1827–1831, 1834*   winter] winter- *1843B*
293 market-morning] market morning *1831, 1834–1836*
294 deck'd] decked *1820, 1832, 1836–*

My watchful dog, whose starts of furious ire,   295
When stranger passed, so often I have check'd;
The red-breast known for years, which at my casement peck'd.

34

"The suns of twenty summers danced along,—
Ah! little marked, how fast they rolled away:
Then rose a mansion proud our woods among,   300
And cottage after cottage owned its sway,
No joy to see a neighbouring house, or stray
Through pastures not his own, the master took;
My Father dared his greedy wish gainsay;
He loved his old hereditary nook,   305
And ill could I the thought of such sad parting brook.

35

"But, when he had refused the proffered gold,
To cruel injuries he became a prey,
Sore traversed in whate'er he bought and sold:
His troubles grew upon him day by day,   310
Till all his substance fell into decay.

295–296 Our watchful house-dog, that would tease and tire
The stranger, till its barking-fit I checked; *1836– but* stranger, till] stranger till
1847M *

296 passed] pass'd *1827–1831, 1834*   check'd] checked *1820, 1832*

297 red-breast] redbreast *1831, 1834* red-breast, *1832, 1836– but* redbreast, *1843B*   peck'd]
pecked *1820, 1832, 1836–*

299 Ah!] Too *1847M* * marked,] marked *1802–1805, 1820– but* mark'd *1827–1831, 1834*
rolled] roll'd *1827–1831, 1834*   away:] away; *1831–1834* away! *1843B*

300–306 But, through severe mischance, and cruel wrong,
My father's substance fell into decay;
We toiled, and struggled—hoping for a day   [3]
When Fortune should put on a kinder look;
But vain were wishes—efforts vain as they: [5]
He from his old hereditary nook
Must part,—the summons came,—our final leave we took. *1820– but*
[1] mischance,] mischance *1843B–* [2] decay;] decay: *1832, 1836–* [3] toiled,] toil'd, *1827–
1831, 1834* toiled *1843B–*   struggled—] struggled, *1836–* [4] Fortune] fortune *1843B*
should] might *1847M (first so in G & S 1845)* [5] wishes—] wishes, *1836–1841, 1847M*   they:]
they; *1832, 1836–* [7] part,—] part; *1836–1841, 1847M* part— *1843B*   came,—] came—
1843B came;— *1847M* *

300 mansion proud] stately hall *1800*   stately Hall *B & C, 1802–1805*

301 sway,] sway. *1800, 1802–1805*

302 house] House *1802–1805*

307 But, when] But when *1800*

307–315 *omitted 1820–*

311 Till] And *1802–1805*

His little range of water was denied;
All but the bed where his old body lay,
All, all was seized, and weeping, side by side,
We sought a home where we uninjured might abide.   315

36

"Can I forget that miserable hour,
When from the last hill-top, my sire surveyed,
Peering above the trees, the steeple tower,
That on his marriage-day sweet music made?
Till then he hoped his bones might there be laid,   320
Close by my mother in their native bowers:
Bidding me trust in God, he stood and prayed,—
I could not pray:—through tears that fell in showers,
Glimmer'd our dear-loved home, alas! no longer ours!

37

"There was a youth whom I had loved so long,   325
That when I loved him not I cannot say.
'Mid the green mountains many and many a song
We two had sung, like little birds in May.
When we began to tire of childish play

312–314 They dealt most hardly with him, and he tried
          To move their hearts—but it was vain—for they
          Seized all he had; and, weeping side by side, *1802–1805*
   WW wrote to Miss Taylor 9 April 1801 that l. 312 "must have another substituted for it which
I have not written."
     316 It was in truth a lamentable hour *1802–1805 but* hour] hour, *1805*   It was indeed a
miserable hour *1820–*
     317 When] When, *1802–1805, 1832, 1836–*   sire] Sire *1802–1805*   surveyed] survey'd
1827–1831, 1834
     318 steeple tower,] steeple tower *1800–1805, 1820– but* steeple-tower *1843B*
     319 marriage-day] marriage day *1800, 1820–1834, 1847M*   made?] made. *1802–1805*
made! *1820–*
     320 then] then, *1820–1841, 1847M*   laid,] laid *1843B–*
     321 mother] Mother, *1802–1805* mother, *1843B*   bowers:] bowers; *1802–1805, 1820–
1831, 1834*
     322 prayed,—] pray'd,—   *1827–1831, 1834* prayed—   *1843B* prayed;—   *1847M**
     323 pray:—] pray *followed by double space 1843B*   showers,] showers *1805, 1834, 1847M*
     324 I saw our own dear home, that was no longer ours. *1802–1805*   Glimmer'd] Glimmered
1820, 1832, 1836–   home, alas!] home—alas, *1843B*
     325 youth] Youth, *1802–1805* Youth *1832, 1836–1841, 1847M*
     326 say.] say: *1832, 1836–*
     327 'Mid] Mid *1827–1831, 1834*   and many a] a thoughtless *1827–*
     328 little] gladsome *B & C–*   May.] May; *1832, 1836–*
     329 play] play, *1827–*

---

     312   See note to l. 258 of *SP*, above.

We seemed still more and more to prize each other: 330
We talked of marriage and our marriage day;
And I in truth did love him like a brother,
For never could I hope to meet with such another.

38

"His father said, that to a distant town
He must repair, to ply the artist's trade.   335
What tears of bitter grief till then unknown!
What tender vows our last sad kiss delayed!
To him we turned:—we had no other aid.
Like one revived, upon his neck I wept,
And her whom he had loved in joy, he said   340
He well could love in grief: his faith he kept;
And in a quiet home once more my father slept.

39

"Four years each day with daily bread was blest,
By constant toil and constant prayer supplied.
Three lovely infants lay upon my breast;   345
And often, viewing their sweet smiles, I sighed,
And knew not why. My happy father died
When sad distress reduced the children's meal:
Thrice happy! that from him the grave did hide

---

330 seemed] seem'd *1827–1831, 1834*   other:] other; *1800, 1802–*
331 talked] talk'd *1827–1831, 1834*   marriage day] marriage-day *1836–1843B*
332 I in truth] I, in truth, *1843B*   brother,] brother; *1802–1805*
334–335 Two years were pass'd, since to a distant Town
       He had repair'd to ply the artist's trade. *1802– but* pass'd,] passed, *1820* pass'd *1827–1831, 1834* passed *1832, 1836–*   Town] town *1820–*   repair'd] repaired *1820, 1832, 1836–* the artist's] a gainful *1836–*   trade.] trade, *1832, 1836* trade: *1840– but* trade; *1843B*
336 grief] grief, *1832, 1836–*   unknown!] unknown? *1800* unknown, *1843B*
337 delayed] delay'd *1827–1831, 1834*
338 turned:—] turn'd:— *1827–1831, 1834* turned— *1843B*   aid.] aid: *1832, 1836–*
339 wept,] wept: *1802–1805* wept; *1843B–*
340 said] said, *1827–1841, 1847M*
341 grief:] grief; *1832, 1836–*   kept;] kept: *1831, 1834*
342 father] Father *1802–1805*
343–344 We lived in peace and comfort; and were blest
       With daily bread, by constant toil supplied. *1802– but* comfort;] comfort, *1843B*
345 infants] Infants *1802–1805*   Three lovely babes had lain upon my breast; *1836–*
346 sighed] sigh'd *1827–1831, 1834*
347 father] Father *1802–1834*   died] died, *1832, 1836–*
348 sad distress] threatened war *1847M** children's] childrens' *1800* Children's *1802–1805*
349 happy!] happy, *1843B*   from] for *1820–*   did] could *1836–*

The empty loom, cold hearth, and silent wheel,   350
And tears that flowed for ills which patience could not heal.

40

"'Twas a hard change, an evil time was come;
We had no hope, and no relief could gain.
But soon, with proud parade, the noisy drum
Beat round, to sweep the streets of want and pain.   355
My husband's arms now only served to strain
Me and his children hungering in his view:
In such dismay my prayers and tears were vain:
To join those miserable men he flew;
And now to the sea-coast, with numbers more, we drew.   360

41

"There foul neglect for months and months we bore,
Nor yet the crowded fleet its anchor stirred.
Green fields before us and our native shore,
By fever, from polluted air incurred,
Ravage was made, for which no knell was heard.   365
Fondly we wished, and wished away, nor knew,
'Mid that long sickness, and those hopes deferr'd,

---

351 that] which *1820*   flowed] flow'd *1827–1831, 1834*   could] might *1836–*   heal.]
heal! *1843B*
352 change,] change— *1843B* change; *1847M**
353 gain.] gain: *1847M**
354 with proud parade] day after day *Taylor–1805*
355 round,] round *1847M**   to sweep] and clear'd *Taylor* to clear *1836–*
356 arms] arms, *1831, 1834*
357 view:] view; *1832, 1836–*
359 flew;] flew: *1802–1805* flew, *1843B–*
360 sea-coast,] sea-coast *1843B*   more, we] more we *1820* more I *1843B*
361–362 There, long were we neglected, and we bore
        Much sorrow ere the fleet its anchor weigh'd; *Taylor–1805, 1820– but* There,] There
Taylor, 1820–   long were we] were we long *1836–*   neglected,] neglected; *Taylor*   sor-
row] sorrow, *1820–1841*   weigh'd;] weigh'd. *Taylor* weighed; *1820, 1832, 1836– but* weighed:
1843B
363 us] us, *Taylor, 1820–41, 1847M*   and] & *Taylor*
364–366 We breath'd a pestilential air that made
        Ravage for which no knell was heard. We pray'd
        For our departure; wish'd and wish'd—nor knew *Taylor–1805, 1820–but*
[1] breath'd . . . air] breathed . . . air, *1820–* [2] pray'd] prayed *1820, 1832, 1836–*   heard.]
heard— *Taylor* [3] departure;] departure— *1843B*   wish'd and wish'd—nor] wish'd and
wish'd, nor *Taylor* wished and wished—nor *1820, 1832, 1836– but* wished and wished, nor *1843B*
knew] knew, *1843B–*
367 sickness,] sickness *1843B–*   deferr'd] delay'd *Taylor–1805, 1827–1831, 1834* delayed
1820, 1832, 1836–

That happier days we never more must view:
The parting signal streamed, at last the land withdrew,

42

"But from delay the summer calms were past.   370
On as we drove, the equinoctial deep
Ran mountains-high before the howling blast.
We gazed with terror on the gloomy sleep
Of them that perished in the whirlwind's sweep,
Untaught that soon such anguish must ensue,   375
Our hopes such harvest of affliction reap,
That we the mercy of the waves should rue.
We reached the western world, a poor, devoted crew.

43

"Oh! dreadful price of being to resign
All that is dear *in* being! better far   380
In Want's most lonely cave till death to pine,
Unseen, unheard, unwatched by any star;
Or in the streets and walks where proud men are,
Better our dying bodies to obtrude,
Than dog-like, wading at the heels of war,   385
Protract a curst existence, with the brood
That lap (their very nourishment!) their brother's blood.

44

"The pains and plagues that on our heads came down,
Disease and famine, agony and fear,
In wood or wilderness, in camp or town,   390

---

368 view:] view. *1847M**
369 streamed,] stream'd, *1827–1831, 1834* streamed; *1836–1841* streamed—*1843B–*
withdrew,] withdrew. *1800, 1802–*
370 But the calm summer season now was past. *1802–*
371 deep] Deep *1802–1805*
372 mountains-high] mountains high *1843B–*   blast.] blast; *1802–1841* blast, *1843B–*
373–374 And many perish'd in the whirlwind's sweep.
         We gazed with terror on their gloomy sleep, *1802– but* perish'd] perished *1805, 1820,*
1832, 1836–
375 ensue,] ensue *1834*
377 rue.] rue: *1820– but* sue, *1834*
378 reached] reach'd *1802–1805, 1827–1831, 1834*   western world] Western World *1802–*
1805   poor,] poor *1843B–*   devoted] devoted, *1820*
379–387 *omitted Taylor–*

---

378   See note to l. 306 of *SP*, above.

It would thy brain unsettle even to hear.
All perished—all, in one remorseless year,
Husband and children! one by one, by sword
And ravenous plague, all perished: every tear
Dried up, despairing, desolate, on board   395
A British ship I waked, as from a trance restored."

45

She paused—or by excess of grief oppress'd,
Or that some sign of mortal anguish broke
In strong convulsion from her comrade's breast—
She paused and shivering wrapp'd her in her cloak   400
Once more a horrid trance his limbs did lock.
Him through the gloom she could not then discern
And after a short while again she spoke;
But he was stretch'd upon the wither'd fern,
Nor to her friendly summons answer could return.   405

Part Second

46

Now dim and dreary was the Plain around;
The ghosts were up on nightly roam intent;
And many a gleam of grey light swept the ground
Where high and low those ghostly wanderers went,
And whereso'er their rustling course they bent   410
The startled earth-worms to their holes did slink,
The whilst the crimson moon, her lustre spent,
With orb half-visible, was seen to sink
Leading the storm's remains along the horizon brink.

47

The Sailor now awoke and, on his side   415
Upraised, inquir'd if she had nothing seen;

391 unsettle] unsettle, *1802–1805*   It would unman the firmest heart to hear. *1847M**
392 *In 1815 "The Female Vagrant" was introduced*: Having described her own Situation with her Husband, serving in America during the War, she proceeds, *whereupon follows the poem from l. 392.*
perished—] perish'd— *1827–1831, 1834* perished, *1843B*   all, in] all in *1843B–*
393 children] Children *1802–1827, 1832*
394 perished] perish'd *1827–1831, 1834*

413   sink] First written "slink," probably picked up by mistake from l. 411.

And when the Maiden answered, "No," he cried,
"'Tis well. I am a wretched man I ween.
Your tale has moved me much and I have been
I know not where." Quoth she, "Your heart is kind,   420
And if no wish of sleep should intervene,
Till we by morning light some track can find,
I will relate the rest, 'twill ease my burden'd mind.

48

"Peaceful as some immeasurable plain
By the first beams of dawning light impress'd,   425
In the calm sunshine slept the glittering main.
The very ocean has its hour of rest,
That comes not to the human mourner's breast.
Remote from man, and storms of mortal care,
A heavenly silence did the waves invest;   430
I looked and looked along the silent air,
Until it seemed to bring a joy to my despair.

49

"Ah! how unlike those late terrific sleeps!
And groans, that rage of racking famine spoke,
Where looks inhuman dwelt on festering heaps!   435
The breathing pestilence that rose like smoke!

424 some] this *1847M*
425 impress'd] imprest *1815–1843B*   Is now, by beams of dawning light imprest, *1847M*
426 sunshine] sun-shine *1802*   main.] main; *1843B–*
427 has] hath *1827–*   rest,] rest. *1802–*
428–430 I too was calm, though heavily distress'd!
     Oh me, how quiet sky and ocean were!
     My heart was healed within me, I was bless'd *Taylor–but*
[1] calm,] calm— *Taylor*   distress'd] distrest *1815–1820*   I too forgot the heavings of my breast. *1827–* [2] Oh me,] O me! *Taylor* O me, *1843B*   How quiet, round me ship and ocean were! *1847M*** [3] healed] heal'd *Taylor* hushed *1815–1820*   bless'd] blest, *1815–1820*   As quiet all within me. I was blest! *1827–but* blest!] blest, *1843B–*
430 invest;] invest: *1800*
431 I looked and looked] And look'd, & look'd *Taylor* And look'd, and look'd *1827–1831, 1834* And looked, and looked *1802–1820, 1832, 1836–1841* And looked and looked *1843B* And looked, and fed *1847M*** along] upon *1847M***   air,] air *1832, 1836–1841, 1847M*
432 seemed] seem'd *1827–1831, 1834*
433 Ah!] Ah, *1843B*   sleeps!] sleeps, *1820–*
434 groans,] groans *1847M***   spoke,] spoke: *B & C, 1800, 1802* spoke! *1805–1843B* spoke; *1847M***
435 Th'unburied Dead that lay in festering Heaps! *B & C*   The unburied dead that lay in festering heaps! *1800, 1802– but* heaps!] heaps, *1847M***
436 smoke!] smoke, *1847M***

The shriek that from the distant battle broke!
The mine's dire earthquake, and the pallid host
Driven by the bomb's incessant thunder-stroke
To loathsome vaults, where heart-sick anguish toss'd,   440
Hope died, and fear itself in agony was lost!

50

"Yet does that burst of woe congeal my frame,
When the dark streets appeared to heave and gape,
While like a sea the storming army came,
And Fire from Hell reared his gigantic shape,   445
And Murder, by the ghastly gleam, and Rape
Seized their joint prey, the mother and the child!
But from these crazing thoughts my brain, escape!
—For weeks the balmy air breathed soft and mild,
And on the gliding vessel Heaven and Ocean smiled.   450

51

"Some mighty gulph of separation past,
I seemed transported to another world:—
A thought resigned with pain, when from the mast
The impatient mariner the sail unfurl'd,
And whistling, called the wind that hardly curled   455

---

437 broke!] broke, *1847M**
440 toss'd] tossed *1832, 1836–*
441 lost!] lost.! *1820*
442–449 At midnight once the storming Army came,
        Yet do I see the miserable sight,
        The Bayonet, the Soldier, and the Flame
        That followed us and faced us in our flight:
        When Rape and Murder by the ghastly light   [5]
        Seized their joint prey, the Mother and the Child!
        But I must leave these thoughts.—From night to night,
        From day to day, the air breathed soft and mild; *Taylor–1805 but*
[1] Army came,] army came: *Taylor* [3] Bayonet . . . Flame] bayonet . . . flame *Taylor* [4] followed us and faced us] follow'd us and fac'd us, *Taylor*   flight:] flight; *1805* [6] Seized . . . and the Child] Seiz'd . . . & the child *Taylor* [7] thoughts.— . . . night,] thoughts— . . . night *Taylor* [8] to day, . . . breathed soft and] to day . . . breath'd soft & *Taylor*   mild;] mild *Taylor* mild: *1805*
442–450 *omitted 1815–*
445 Hell] hell *B & C, 1800*
450 Heaven . . . Ocean smiled.] heaven . . . ocean smil'd *Taylor*
451 gulph] gulf *1815–*
452 seemed] seem'd *1827–1831, 1834*   world:—] world: *1836–1841* world,— *1843B* world; *1847M**
453 resigned] resign'd *1827–1831, 1834*
454 unfurl'd] unfurled *1820, 1832, 1836–*
455 And] And, *1805–*   called . . . curled] call'd . . . curl'd *1827–1831, 1834*

The silent sea. From the sweet thoughts of home,
And from all hope I was forever hurled.
For me—farthest from earthly port to roam
Was best, could I but shun the spot where man might come.

52

"And oft, robb'd of my perfect mind, I thought   460
At last my feet a resting-place had found:
Here will I weep in peace, (so fancy wrought,)
Roaming the illimitable waters round;
Here watch, of every human friend disowned,
All day, my ready tomb the ocean-flood—   465
To break my dream the vessel reached its bound:
And homeless near a thousand homes I stood,
And near a thousand tables pined, and wanted food.

53

"By grief enfeebled was I turned adrift,
Helpless as sailor cast on desart rock;   470
Nor morsel to my mouth that day did lift,
Nor dared my hand at any door to knock.
I lay, where with his drowsy mates, the cock

---

456 home,] home *1805–1841, 1847M*
457 hope] hope, *1843B*   forever] for ever *1802–*   hurled] hurl'd *1827–1831, 1834*
458 me—] me, *1843B*
460–462 And oft I thought (my fancy was so strong)
        Here will I dwell, said I, my whole life-long, *Taylor–but*   [3]
[1] thought] thought, *Taylor* [2] I at last] I, at last, *Taylor, 1820–*   found;] found: *Taylor,*
1843B [3] dwell,] dwell *Taylor*   Here will I dwell, said I, my] "Here will I dwell," said I,
"my *1805– but single quotes in 1847M*   life-long,] life long *Taylor* life long, *1815–*
        463 round;] round: *1802–1841*
        464 Here will I live:—of every friend disown'd, *Taylor–* but live:—] live: *Taylor* live,— *1832*
live, *1836–*   every friend] all but heaven *1847M**   disown'd,] disowned, *1820, 1836–*
disown'd *1827–1831, 1834* disowned,— *1832*
        465 Here will I roam about the ocean flood.— *Taylor–1805 but* ocean flood.—] ocean-flood—
Taylor flood.—] flood." *1805*   And end my days upon the ocean flood."—*1815– but*
ocean flood."—] ocean-flood." *1843B* peaceful flood.'— *1847M**
        466 dream] dream, *1843B*   reached] reach'd *1827–1834*   bound:] bound; *1843B–*
        467 And homeless . . . I] Homeless, . . . they *Postscript to Yarrow Revisited, 1835–1850*
        468 pined,] pin'd, *1802–1805* pined *1836–*
        469 enfeebled] enfeebled, *1820–1834, 1843B* turned] turn'd *1827–1831, 1834*
        469–470 No help I sought, in sorrow turned adrift
                Was hopeless, as if cast on some bare rock; *1847M**
        470 desart] desert *1805–1834* some bare *1836–*
        472 dared] raised *1847M**
        473 lay, where] lay where, *1805–*   mates . . . cock] Mates . . . Cock *1802–1834*   with
his drowsy] with drowsy *1831 but corrected in errata sheet*

From the cross timber of an out-house hung;
How dismal tolled, that night, the city clock!   475
At morn my sick heart hunger scarcely stung,
Nor to the beggar's language could I frame my tongue.

54

"So passed another day, and so the third:
Then did I try, in vain, the crowd's resort,
In deep despair by frightful wishes stirr'd,   480
Near the sea-side I reached a ruined fort:
There, pains which nature could no more support,
With blindness linked, did on my vitals fall;
Dizzy my brain, with interruption short
Of hideous sense; I sunk, nor step could crawl,   485
And thence was borne away to neighbouring hospital.

55

"Recovery came with food: but still, my brain
Was weak, nor of the past had memory.
I heard my neighbours, in their beds, complain

---

474 cross timber] cross-timber *1836*–   out-house] outhouse *1843B*   hung;] hung: *1820*–*1841, 1847M*
475 How dismal] Dismally *Taylor*–   tolled] toll'd *Taylor, 1827*–*1831, 1834*   tolled, that night,] tolled that night *1843B*   city clock] city-clock *1843B*
476 morn] morn, *1843B*
477 frame] fit *1832, 1836*–
478 passed] pass'd *1802*–*1815, 1827*–*1831, 1834*   third:] third; *1802*–
478–479 So passed a second day, and when the third
   Was come, I tried in vain the crowd's resort. *1836*– *but* day,] day; *1843B*–   and] and, *1847M**
479 try, in vain,] try in vain *1802*–*1834*   resort,] resort. *1802*–
480 In] —In *1802*–*1841, 1847M*   despair] despair, *1820*–   stirr'd] stirred *1820, 1832, 1836*–
481 reached . . . ruined] reach'd . . . ruin'd *1827*–*1831, 1834*   fort:] Fort: *1802*–*1831, 1834* Fort; *1832* fort; *1836*–
482 There,] There *1843B*
483 linked] link'd *1802*–*1831, 1834*   fall;] fall, *1802*–*1843B*
484–485 And I had many interruptions short
   Of hideous sense; I sank, nor step could crawl, *1802*– *but*
[1] And] And, *1847M**   I had] after *1827*– [2] sense;] sense, *1827*–   crawl,] crawl *1815* crawl; *1827*–*1834, 1843B* crawl: *1836*–*1841, 1847M*
486 borne away to . . . hospital] carried to a . . . Hospital *1802*–*1820*   Unsought for was the help that did my life recall. *1827*– *but* recall] recal *1836*–*1841, 1847M*
487 still,] still *1815*–*1820*
487–488 Borne to an hospital, I lay with brain
   Drowsy and weak, and shatter'd memory; *1827*– *but* an] a *1847M**   shatter'd] shattered *1832, 1836*–
489 neighbours, . . . beds,] neighbours . . . beds *1843B*–

Of many things which never troubled me;   490
Of feet still bustling round with busy glee,
Of looks where common kindness had no part,
Of service done with careless cruelty,
Fretting the fever round the languid heart,
And groans, which, as they said, would make a   495
    dead man start.

56

"These things just served to stir the torpid sense,
Nor pain nor pity in my bosom raised.
Memory, though slow, returned with strength; and thence
Dismissed, again on open day I gazed,
At houses, men, and common light, amazed.   500
The lanes I sought, and as the sun retired,
Came, where beneath the trees a faggot blazed;
The wild brood saw me weep, my fate enquired,
And gave me food, and rest, more welcome, more desired.

57

"My heart is touched to think that men like these,   505
The rude earth's tenants, were my first relief:
How kindly did they paint their vagrant ease!
And their long holiday that feared not grief,
For all belonged to all, and each was chief.
No plough their sinews strained; on grating road   510

---

490 me;] me— *1847M* *
491 glee,] glee; *1802–1843B*
492 part,] part; *1802–1843B*
493 careless cruelty] cold formality *1847M* *
494 heart,] heart; *1802–1843B*
495 groans,] groans *1827, 1832, 1836–*   would] might *1815–*
496 torpid] slumbering *1836–*
498 My memory and my strength returned; and thence *1802–1820 but* and thence] and, thence
1820   With strength did memory return; and, thence *1827–*
499 Dismissed] Dismiss'd *1827*
500 light,] light *1832, 1836–1843B*
501 and] and, *1805–*
502 Came,] Came *1805–*
503 wild brood] Travellers *1802–1834* travellers *1836–*   enquired] inquired *1805–1831,
1834–*
504 food,] food,— *1805–1841* food— *1843B–*   more desired] mor edesired *1815*
505–513 *omitted 1815–*
506 The rude earth's tenants] Wild houseless Wanderers *1802–1805*
507 ease!] ease, *1805*
508 grief,] grief! *1802–1805*

No wain they drove, and yet, the yellow sheaf
In every vale for their delight was stowed:
For them, in nature's meads, the milky udder flowed.

58

"Semblance, with straw and panniered ass, they made
Of potters wandering on from door to door: 515
But life of happier sort to me pourtrayed,
And other joys my fancy to allure;
The bag-pipe dinning on the midnight moor
In barn uplighted, and companions boon
Well met from far with revelry secure,   520
In depth of forest glade, when jocund June
Rolled fast along the sky his warm and genial moon.

59

"But ill it suited me, in journey dark
O'er moor and mountain, midnight theft to hatch;
To charm the surly house-dog's faithful bark,   525
Or hang on tiptoe at the lifted latch;
The gloomy lantern, and the dim blue match,
The black disguise, the warning whistle shrill,
And ear still busy on its nightly watch,

---

511 drove, . . . yet,] drove; . . . yet *1802–1805*
512 stowed:] stow'd; *1802–1805*
513 In every field, with milk their dairy overflow'd. *1802–1805*
514 They with their pannier'd Asses semblance made *1802–1834 but* They . . . Asses] They,
. . . Asses, *1832* pannier'd] panniered *1820, 1832*
514–516 Rough potters seemed they, trading soberly
          With panniered asses driven from door to door;
          But life of happier sort set forth to me, *1836– but* [1] soberly] soberly, *1843B*
515 potters] Potters *1802–1834*   door:] door; *1831–*
516 pourtrayed] pourtray'd *1802–1805, 1827–1831, 1834* portrayed *1832*
517 allure;] allure— *1847M**
518 bag-pipe] bag-pipe, *1820–1841* bagpipe *1843B*   moor] moor, *1820–1841*
519 uplighted,] uplighted; *1827–1841, 1847M*   companions] Companions *1802–1815*
Companion's *1820*   boon] boon, *1847M**
520 secure,] secure *1847M**
521 In depth of . . . glade] Among the . . . glades *1802–*   when] while *1836–*
522 Rolled] Roll'd *1827–1831, 1834*
523 But ill they suited me; those journies dark *1802– but* me;] me— *1827– but* me, *1843B*
journies] journeys *1805–*
524 hatch;] hatch! *1802–*
525 house-dog's] House-dog's *1802–1834*
526 tiptoe] tip-toe *1802–1831, 1834, 1847M*   latch;] latch. *1815– but* latch: *1843B*

Were not for me, brought up in nothing ill;   530
Besides, on griefs so fresh my thoughts were brooding still.

60

"What could I do, unaided and unblest?
Poor Father! gone was every friend of thine:
And kindred of dead husband are at best
Small help, and, after marriage such as mine,   535
With little kindness would to me incline.
Ill was I then for toil or service fit:
With tears whose course no effort could confine,
By high-way side forgetful would I sit
Whole hours, my idle arms in moping sorrow knit.   540

61

"I lived upon the mercy of the fields,
And oft of cruelty the sky accused;
On hazard, or what general bounty yields,
Now coldly given, now utterly refused.
The fields I for my bed have often used: 545
But, what afflicts my peace with keenest ruth
Is, that I have my inner self abused,
Foregone the home delight of constant truth,
And clear and open soul, so prized in fearless youth.

---

530 ill;] ill: *1802–1841, 1847M*
531 still.] still *1832*
533 Poor] My *1802–*   Father!] father!—*1843B–*   gone] —gone *1843B*   thine:] thine; *1843B*
535 help,] help; *1802–1827, 1832, 1836–* help: *1831, 1834*
537 Ill . . . fit:] Nor . . . fit; *1847M**
538 My deep-drawn sighs no effort could confine; *1836–*
539 By high-way side] By the road-side *1802–1834* In the open air *1836–1843B* In open air *1847M**
540 hours,] hours *1843B*   my] with *1836–*
541–558 *printed as one 18-line stanza 1834*
541–543 I led a wandering life among the fields;
        Contentedly, yet sometimes self-accused,
        I liv'd upon what casual bounty yields, *1802– but*   [3]
[1] fields;] fields *1831, 1834*   The roads I paced, I loitered through the fields; *1836– but* fields;] fields, *1843B* [2] self-accused,] self-accused; *1843B* [3] liv'd] lived *1805–1834*   Trusted my life to what chance-bounty yields, *1836–but* chance-bounty] chance bounty *1843B–* yields,] yields,— *1843B*
545 fields] ground *1802–*   used:] used; *1843B*
546 But,] But *1843B–*   ruth] ruth, *1847M**
547 Is,] Is *1847M**
548 Foregone] Forgone *1802–1834*   home delight] home-delight *1843B*
549 youth.] youth *1827* youth; *1831, 1834*

62

"Three years a wanderer, often have I view'd,   550
In tears, the sun towards that country tend
Where my poor heart lost all its fortitude:
And now across this moor my steps I bend—
Oh! tell me whither—for no earthly friend
Have I."—She ceased, and weeping turned away,   555
As if because her tale was at an end
She wept;—because she had no more to say
Of that perpetual weight which on her spirit lay.

63

She ended, of all present thought forlorn,
Nor voice nor sound that moment's pang express'd   560
Till nature, with excess of grief o'erborne,
From her full eyes their watry load releas'd.
He sate and spake not, ere her weeping ceased.
She rose and to the ruin's portal wont,
And saw the dawn salute the silvering east.   565
Meanwhile her sorrow failed not to relent;
And now with crimson fire kindled the firmament.

64

"But come," she cried, "come after weary night
Of such rough storm the breaking day to view."
So forth he came and eastward look'd: the sight   570
Into his heart a [   ] anguish threw;

550 a wanderer] thus wandering *1802–1834*   view'd] viewed *1820, 1832*
550–551 Through tears the rising sun I oft have viewed;
        Through tears have seen him towards that world descend *1836– but* [1] viewed;]
viewed, *1843B–*
552 fortitude:] fortitude; *1832, 1843B*
553 Three years a wanderer now my course I bend—   *1836– but* bend—] bend,—   *1843B*
554 Oh! . . . whither—] Oh, . . . whither! *1843B*
555 *close-quote 1802–1834 only*   ceased] ceas'd *1834*   turned] turn'd *1827–1831, 1834*
away,] away;— *1820–1841* away; *1843B–*   turned away] *printed as one word 1847M*
556 end] end, *1847M**
557 wept;—] wept; *1843B–*
The date 1792 appeared at the end of the text of "The Female Vagrant," 1840–1841

559 forlorn] See note to l. 325 of *SP*, above.
568 she] Written "he" by mistake.
571 The line is a later addition.

His wither'd cheek was ting'd with ashy hue.
He stood and trembled both with grief and fear,
But she felt new delight and solace new,
And, from the opening east, a pensive chear   575
Came to her weary thoughts while the lark warbled near.

65

They look'd and saw a lengthening road and wain
That rang down a bare slope not far remote;
The downs all glister'd dropp'd with freshening rain;
Whistled the waggoner with joyous note.   580
The cock, scarce heard, at distance sounds his throat;
But town or farm or hamlet none they view'd;
Only were told there stood a lonely cot
Thence three long miles. Together they renewed
Their journey and the road towards that cot pursued.   585

66

The woman from the ruin'd tenement
Did with a light and chearful step depart,
But deep into his vitals she had sent
Anguish that rankled like a fiery dart.
She with affectionate and homely art   590
His peace of mind endeavour'd to restore:
"Come let us be," she said, "of better heart."
Thus oftentimes the Woman did implore,
And still the more he griev'd, she loved him still the more.

67

On themes indifferent often she began   595
To hold discourse, but nothing could beguile
His thoughts, still cleaving to the murder'd man.
When they had travelled thus a full half mile,
"Why should you grieve," she said, "a little while
And we shall meet in heaven." But now they hear   600
The mail come rattling on in scamp'ring file.
And when the coachman gave the morning chear,
The Sailor's face was pale with momentary fear.

---

576   weary] Written over an illegible word.
579   rain] Written "rains" by mistake.
580   joyous] Written over an erased word.

68

But now they view upon the darker heath
Small hillocks smoking in the early beam.   605
One volume mingles every various wreath
And steals along the waste its silver gleam.
To them the sight was pleasant, but a scream
Thence bursting shrill did all remark prevent;
They paused and heard a hoarser voice blaspheme,   610
And female cries. Their course they thither bent,
And met a man who foamed with anger vehement.

69

A woman stood with quivering lips and wan,
Near an old mat with broken bread bestrown;
And pointing to a child her tale began.   615
Trembling the infant hid his face; the clown
Meanwhile, in monster mood, with ugly frown
Cursing the very hour that gave her birth,
Strove, as she spake, her voice to drown,
Yet still she told that on the cover'd earth   620
At breakfast they were set, the child their joy and mirth.

70

Her husband for that pitcher rose; his place
The infant took—as true as heaven the tale—
And when desired to move, with smiling face
For a short while did in obedience fail.   625
He was not five years old, and him to trail
And bruise, as if each blow had been his last,
She knew not what for life his brain might ail.
Shuddering the soldier's widow stood aghast
And stern looks on the man her grey-hair'd comrade cast. 630

71

And with firm voice and indignation high
Such further deed in manhood's name forbad.
He, confident in passion, made reply
With bitter insult and revilings sad,
Calling him vagabond, and knave, and mad,   635
And ask'd what plunder he was hunting now;
The gallows would one day of him be glad.

Here cold sweat started from the sailor's brow,
Yet calm he seem'd, as thoughts so poignant would allow;

72

Nor answer made, but stroked the child, outstretch'd   640
His face to earth, and as the boy turn'd round
His batter'd head, a groan the Sailor fetch'd.
The head with streaming blood had dy'd the ground,
Flow'd from the spot where he that deadly wound
Had fix'd on him he murder'd. Through his brain   645
At once the griding iron passage found;
Deluge of tender thoughts then rush'd amain
Nor could his aged eyes from very tears abstain.

73

Within himself he said, "What hearts have we!
The blessing this the father gives his child!   650
Yet happy thou, poor boy! compared with me,
Suffering not doing ill, fate far more mild."
Such sight the father of his wrath beguil'd;
Relenting thoughts and self-reproach awoke;
He kiss'd the boy, so all was reconcil'd.   655
Then with a voice which inward trouble broke
In the full swelling throat, the Sailor them bespoke.

74

"'Tis a bad world, and hard is the world's law;
Each prowls to strip his brother of his fleece;
Much need have ye that time more closely draw   660
The bond of nature, all unkindness cease,
And that among so few there still be peace:
Else can ye hope but with such num'rous foes
Your pains shall ever with your years increase."
While his pale lips these homely truths disclose,   665
A correspondent calm stole gently on his woes.

75

And passing onward, down at length they look
Where through a narrow valley's pleasant scene

645–646 Cf. Spenser's "That through his thigh the mortall steele did gryde" (*FQ*, II, viii, xxxvi, 5). De Selincourt notes also Milton's "The griding sword with discontinuous wound / Passd through him" (*Paradise Lost*, VI, 329–330).

A wreath of vapour track'd a winding brook,
That babbled on through groves and meads of green;   670
A single cottage smoked the trees between;
The dripping groves resound with chearful lays,
And melancholy lowings intervene
Of scatter'd herds, that in the meadows graze,
While through the furrow'd grass the merry   675
    milk-maid strays.

76

[   ] the prospect shew'd;
Down the thick woods they dropp'd into the vale.
Comfort by prouder mansions unbestow'd
Their wearied frames, she hoped, would soon regale.
Erelong they reach'd the cottage in the dale;   680
It was a rustic Inn; the board was spread,
The milk-maid followed with her brimming pail,
And lustily the master carved the bread,
Kindly the housewife press'd, and they in comfort fed.

77

But breakfast done, she learn'd they now must part.   685
He had resolved to turn toward the seas
Since he that tale had heard, and while her heart
Struggled with tears, nor could its sorrow ease,
She left him there; for, clustering round his knees,
With his oak staff the cottage children play'd;   690
And soon she reach'd a spot o'erhung with trees
And banks of ragged earth; beneath the shade
Across the pebbly road a little runner stray'd.

78

A cart and horse beside the rivulet stood;
Chequering the canvass roof the sunbeams shone.   695
She saw the carman bend to scoop the flood,
And now approach'd the wain, wherein was one,
A single woman, lying spent and gone;
The carman wet her lips as well behoved;

---

686   seas] First written "sea" by mistake.
693   runner] Lake District term for a small hillside stream which feeds the lakes and rivers.
See also note to l. 540 of *G & S*, below.

Bed under her lean [?shadow] there was none;   700
Though even to die near one she most had loved
She could not of herself those wasted limbs have moved.

79

The Soldier's widow learn'd with honest pain
And homefelt force of sympathy sincere,
Why thus that worn-out wretch must there sustain   705
The jolting road and morning air severe.
And crying, "Would, my friend, thy aid were here,
Or yours, good cottagers," her steps retraced
To that same house, the wain still following.
She found her comrade there and cried in haste,   710
"Come, come, my friends, and see what object here is placed."

80

As to the door with eager speed they ran,
From her bare straw the woman half uprais'd
Her bony visage, gaunt and deadly wan.
No pity asking, on the group she gazed,   715
As if with eye by blank suffusion glazed,
Then sunk upon her straw with feeble moan.
Fervently cried the housewife, "God be prais'd,
I have a house that I can call my own;
Nor shall she perish there, untended and alone!"   720

81

So in they bear her to the chimney-seat,
And busily, though yet with fear, untie
Her garments, and, to warm her icy feet
With death's numb waters swoln, their hands apply,
And chafe her pulseless temples cold and dry.   725
At last she strove her languid head to rear,
And said, "I thank you all; if I must die,
The God in heaven my prayers for you will hear;
Today I did not think my end had been so near.

82

"Barr'd every comfort labour could procure,   730
Suffering what no endurance could asswage
I was compell'd to seek my father's door,
But sickness stopp'd me in my pilgrimage;

I feared to be a burthen to his age;
The overseers placed me in this wain,   735
Thus to be carried back from stage to stage,
Unwilling that I should with them remain;
And I had hopes that I my home might yet regain.

83

"And thus far on my journey I am come;
Oh God, as I have meekly suffered, meek   740
Shall be my end. My lips will soon be dumb;
If child of mine e'er wander hither, speak
Of me, say that the worm is on my cheek.
In a lone house beside the sea we dwelt,
Near Portland Light-house, in a lonesome creek.   745
I have a father too and he will melt
In tears to learn the end of woes so largely dealt.

84

"Long in that house I knew a widow's cares,
Yet still two children did partake my bed,
And strange hopes trembled through my dreams and   750
    prayers.
Strong was I then and labour gave us bread,
Till one was found by stroke of violence dead
And near my door the Stranger chanced to lie;
And soon suspicion drove us from our shed.
In vain to find a friendly face we try,   755
Nor could we live together those poor boys and I.

85

"For one had seen, he said, in vest of blue,
That day my husband in the neighbourhood;
Now he had fled, and whither no one knew,
And he had done the deed in the dark wood   760
Near his own home!—but he was kind and good;

735–737 For a description of the indifference of parish overseers (in details which con-
temporary accounts confirm), see John Langhorne's *The Country Justice* (1774–1777), Part II,
where a pregnant woman is driven out:
    The Ruffian Officer oppos'd her Stay,
    And, cruel, bore her in her Pangs away:
    So far beyond the Town's last Limits drove,
    That to return were hopeless, had She strove.
    743 See *RC*, MS. B, 353–354 (*PW*, V, 390), where the Pedlar uses the same image for
Margaret: "She is dead / The worm is on her cheek."

Never on earth was milder creature seen;
He'd not have robb'd the raven of its food.
Oh had my husband 'mong the living been
I could not have beheld the hours of anguish keen." 765

86

But when he heard her thus with labouring breath
And pain and weakness tell the wretchedness
His hand had wrought, and, in the hour of death,
Saw her lips move his name and deeds to bless,
At such a sight he could no more suppress 770
The feelings which did in his heart revive;
And, weeping loud, in this extreme distress
He cried, "O bless me now, that thou should'st live
I do not wish or ask: forgive me, now forgive."

87

To speak the change that voice within her wrought 775
Nature by sign or sound made no essay;
A sudden joy surprized expiring thought,
And every mortal pang dissolved away.
Borne gently to a bed, there dead she lay;
Silently o'er her face the husband bent. 780
A look was on her lips which seem'd to say,
"Comfort to thee my dying thoughts have sent."
But not to him, it seem'd, on other things intent.

88

For him alternate throbbed his pulse and stopp'd;
And when at table placed the bread he took 785
To break it, from his faltering hands it dropp'd,
While on those hands he cast a rueful look.
His ears were never silent, sleep forsook
His nerveless eyelids stiffen'd even as lead;
All through the night the floor beneath him shook 790
And chamber trembled to his shuddering bed;
And oft he groan'd aloud, "Oh God that I were dead!"

89

Nor, bred in solitude, unus'd to haunt
The throngs of men, did this good cottage pair
Repine mortality's last claim to grant; 795
And in due time with due observance bear

Her body to the distant church, their care
The husband thank'd, nor one hour more remain'd
Under their roof, but to the open air
And fields, a burden not to be sustain'd   800
He carried, in his breast a dreadful quiet reign'd.

90

But they, alone and tranquil, call'd to mind
Events so various; recollection ran
Through each occurrence and the links combin'd,
And while his silence, looks, and voice they scan,   805
And trembling hands, they cried, "He is the man!"
Nought did those looks of silent woe avail.
"Though we deplore it much as any can,
The law," they cried, "must weigh him in her scale;
Most fit it is that we unfold this woful tale."   810

91

Confirm'd of purpose, fearless and prepared,
Not without pleasure, to the city strait
He went and all which he had done declar'd:
"And from your hands," he added, "now I wait,
Nor let them linger long, the murderer's fate."   815
Nor ineffectual was that piteous claim.
Blest be for once the stroke which ends, tho' late,
The pangs which from thy halls of terror came,
Thou who of Justice bear'st the violated name!

92

They left him hung on high in iron case,   820
And dissolute men, unthinking and untaught,
Planted their festive booths beneath his face;
And to that spot, which idle thousands sought,
Women and children were by fathers brought;
And now some kindred sufferer driven, perchance,   825
That way when into storm the sky is wrought,
Upon his swinging corpse his eye may glance
And drop, as he once dropp'd, in miserable trance.

811–819   Cf. Joseph Fawcett's *The Art of War* (London, 1795), pp. 44–45, in which a mur-
derer is driven to confess by the pangs of his own conscience. Parallels in details of the story are
striking, but the attitudes of the two poets toward the guilty man are very different.

Adventures on Salisbury Plain (1795–c. 1799)

Photographic Reproductions and Transcriptions

In interpreting the transcription of MS. 2 which follows, it is important to note that the process of revision has taken place at two widely spaced intervals. The fair copy of the poem is in the hand of DW, as are also some additional stanzas and small local corrections. WW has made a few corrections too, either as the fair copy was being made or shortly after. The bulk of the revision, however, is in the hand of MW and is the work of 1841, when *Adventures on Salisbury Plain* was once again being considered for publication. MW's is the bold, dark hand which dominates many of the photographs. In considering levels of correction, it must be borne in mind that the deletion marks on the stanzas may have been made at different times, even though a photograph may reveal little distinction in their appearance. In general DW and WW make neat deletions horizontally through the words to be replaced. MW, on the other hand, slashes out whole stanzas with bold cross-strokes. In the first part of the poem she has renumbered the stanzas to take account of her deletions.

Adventures on Salisbury Plain

Part First

A Traveller on the skirt of Sarum's Plain
Pursued his way ~~a~~ old Man with feet half bare
Propp'd on a trembling Staff he crept with pain
~~feeble with age~~ ~~on state decease~~ ~~twenty~~
~~His legs~~ ~~worn meagre with~~
His temples just betrayed their silver hair

Beneath a kerchief's edge that wrapp'd his head
To fence from off his face the breathing air
Much miserably o'er with patch & shred
His ragged coat scarce shewed the Soldier's red
~~He himself~~ ~~of~~ ~~a m~~

And dost thou hope across this Plain to trail
~~That~~ ~~years & malady~~
~~These withered arms of thine that~~
Come, I am strong & stout, come lean on me.
~~The old~~
And, so supported ~~he faced the cheery len~~
But short the joy that touched his melting heart
~~Scarce~~ a mile begone his friend and he
must part

'Tis a long way for me who like a snail
Must crawl on ~~while they~~
While they ~~his~~ began to talk
That he he had ~~a shadow~~ they have ~~even~~
~~themselves to~~ ~~I was long to~~

Adventures on Salisbury Plain

Part First

I

1   *A Traveller on the skirt of Sarum's Plain*
    Pursued his way a
2   ~~*O'ertook an aged*~~ *Man with feet half bare*
                       walked
                    [?walked]
3   *Propp'd on a trembling staff he crept with pain*
    ~~*Feeble with age*~~   *& scanty fare*
4   ~~*His legs from slow disease distended were*~~
    With labor worn megre with
5   *His temples just betrayed their silver hair*
6   *Beneath a kerchief's edge that wrapp'd his head*
7   *To fence from off his face the breathing air*
8   *Stuck miserably o'er with patch & shred*
                     faded
9   *His ragged coat scarce shewed the Soldiers red*

          thee
  ~~*Ill help*~~ [*?*] ~~*If I can*~~ [?for] ~~*weak*~~ *thine*
                    arm
10 *And dost thou hope across this Plain to trail*
    [?on] ~~*limbs so weak*~~
    body weak with
11 *That ~~frame oercome with years~~ & malady*
    limbs
12 ~~*These feet that scarcely can outcrawl the snail*~~
13 ~~*These withered arms of thine, that faltering knee*~~
14 *Come, I am strong & stout come lean on me :*
    soldier   *thankd him with a* [?painful]
15 *The ~~old man's eyes a wintry lustre dart,~~*   [?kind]
    [?pported]   *faced*
         pported
16 *And, so sustained he faced the open lea.*
                the old mans heart
17 *But short the joy that touched his melting heart*
18 *For ere a mile be gone his friend and he*
               must part

  Tis a long way for one who like a snail
  Must crawl in whatsoever road he
                 be
           t *y*
  While thus he travell'd he began to tell
  That he he had been a solider—they have given
  A pension to me I was living well

---

1   The fair copy is by DW throughout. The stanza numbering was added later, probably by
MW in 1841.
2   Unless otherwise noted, all revisions not in the hand of WW may be taken to be by MW.
See Editorial Procedure, above.
  9/10   The oblique mark above "thee" may be a deletion stroke.

Meanwhile his eyes men begry into tale
Nor of long absence failed he soon to tell
~~That he had been the~~ soldier ~~often~~ had striven
~~~~ Cold as dead lot
~~~~ ~~~~ ~~~~ before who knew him well
~~~~ ~~~~ had lately ~~~~
Thence he had limp'd to meet a daughter driven
By circumstance which ~~~~ faith exceed
From every stay but him; his heart was worn
At the bare thought: the ~~~~ had need
Of ~~~~ ~~~~ him most wretched ~~was~~ indeed
~~~~ ~~~~ ~~~~ had been by this too ~~~~
~~That your ~~ he chanced ere long to see
~~~~ that as his comrade ~~~~ ~~~~
An inn, that stood upon the ~~~~ moor
But entrance none was there for such as ~~they~~ he
~~~~ ~~~~ the needy to allure;
~~~~ No bush proclaimed peace you will find
~~~~ ~~~~ ~~~~ ~~~~ ~~~~
But now their short-lived fellowship must end
Down sate ~~~~ ~~~~ the soldier sick and poor
Nor can the younger quit his helpless friend
Where thus the bare white roads their dreary
                    line extend

Ere long a post-boy's scarlet vest he spied
On the wide ~~~~ of distance flashing bright
And when the wheels approached he rose & cried
"Have mercy on this broken soldier's plight
Deed of such sort shall well itself requite"
The old man then was on the cushion placed
~~And~~ all his body trembled with delight
Forthwith, self-satisfied his comrade faced,
And yet the sun was high, the far extended
                    waste

Then while the ~~~~ now ~~~~ begun to tell ~~~~
~~~~ had been a soldier & had striven
with a ~~~~

      Meanwhile this aged man began to tell
19 *Nor of long absence failed he soon to tell*
      That he had been a   and
20 *And how he with the Soldier's life had striven*
                    h ⌉
      With a [?w]⌠ard lot
21 *And soldiers wrongs : but one who knew him well*
      kind good man to him a house had given
22 *A house to his old age had lately given*
23 *Thence he had limp'd to meet a daughter driven*
                does ⌉
24 *By circumstance which did ⌠all faith exceed*
25 *From every stay but him : his heart was riven*
                              had need⌉
      but [?sure ?as] she [? ?] ⌠
26 *At the bare thought : the creature that had need*
27 *Of any aid from him most wretched was indeed*
      Ill cherish her with kindness both in word
                      and Deed

      Thus journeying⌉ on he chanced ere long to see
      [? ? ?told] his⌠
28 *He said that on his comrade's road there lay*
      An inn that stood   open
29 *One lonely inn upon the wilder moor*
                                          he
30 *But entrance none was there for such as they,*
  in Small show [?as ?had]
31 *No board inscribed the needy to allure :*
      gilded No bush proclaimed here you will find a frien
32 *The grapes hung glittering at the gilded door.*
      [?no]
33 *But now their short-lived fellowship must end*
                  weary old man
34 *Down sate with pain the Soldier sick and poor*
35 *Nor can the younger quit his helpless friend*
36 *Where thus the bare white roads their dreary*
                              line extend

37 *Ere long a post-boy's scarlet vest he spied*
                plain
38 *On the wide down at distance flashing bright*
39 *And when the wheels approached he rose & cried :*
40 *"Have mercy on this broken Soldier's plight*
41 *Deed of such sort shall well itself requite"*
42 *The old man then was on the cushion placed*
                o⌉   b ⌉
43 *And all his bd⌠dy trem[?t] ⌠led with delight*
      with a light heart
44 *Forthwith, self-satisfied his comrade faced,*
45 *And yet the sun was high, the far-extended*
                                    waste

            [?began]
      Meanwhile the aged man began to tell [?pleas'd ?him]
      That he had been a soldier & had striven
      With a hard lot

---

22 What appears to be punctuation is blotting from the facing page.
28 *"Thus journeying"* is written over the first revision.
31 *in*] Apparently an editorial direction.

3   The gathering clouds grow red with ~~stormy fire~~
That ~~way~~ he long had pass'd and weary
Measured his lonesome way ~~to~~ the distant spire
~~Still~~ ~~at every turn~~ deye
Was lost, though still he ~~stood~~ in the blank sky
By thirst and hunger press'd he gaz'd around
And scarce could any trace of man descry,
Save dreary corn-fields stretch'd ~~without a bound~~
But where the tower dwelt was no where to be found

          4

No tree was there, no meadow's pleasant green,
No brook to wet his lips or soothe his ear
Vast piles of corn-stack here & there were seen
But ~~not one~~ dwelling ~~place~~
~~the weary~~
And so he ~~saw~~ a feeble shout
~~voice made~~
No ~~sound~~
~~long~~ The thin grass ~~on the plain~~
Or desart ~~earth that~~
~~that~~ on his ear ~~grain~~

          5

Long had he fancied each successive slope
Conceal'd some cottage whither he might turn
And rest;— but now, along heaven's darkening cope
The crows ~~sweeping~~
~~some shepherd~~
Or hovel, from the storm to shield his head
~~But sought in vain~~ ever
more wild, forlorn
And vacant the huge plain around him spread
Ah me! the wet cold ground must be his only bed

                3   *gathering clouds grow red with*
46   The ~~evening came with clouds and~~ stormy fire
47   That inn he long had pass'd and wearily
                   ~~And [?he ?pursues] his way~~
48   Measured his lonesome way: the distant spire
                      looks ⎱ back ⎰
                   Which oft as he [?turn'd] ⎰ *round* ⎱ *had fix'd his*
49   ~~That fix'd at every turn his backward~~ eye
                                        lookd
50   Was lost, though still he ~~turn'~~d, in the blank sky
51   By thirst and hunger press'd he gaz'd around
52   And scarce could any trace of man descry
53   Save dreary corn-fields stretch'd as without bound
54   But where the sower dwelt was no where to be found

                          4

55   No tree was there, no meadow's pleasant green,
56   No brook to wet his lips or soothe his ear
57   Vast piles of corn-stack here & there were seen
                                       h ⎱
              not one dwelling place his [?] ⎰*eart to chear*
58   But ~~thence no smoke upwreathed his sight to~~
                                       ~~cheer~~
              Some Labourer thought he may perchance be near
59   ~~He mark'd a homeward shepherd disappear~~
              And so he sent a
60   ~~Far off, and sent a~~ feeble shout, in vain
              voice made answer he could only hear
61   No ~~sound replies but winds that whistling near~~
                   T ⎱   *whistling near him on the plain*
62   ~~Sweep t~~ ⎰*he* thin grass ~~and passing wildly plain~~
63   ~~Or desart lark that pours on high a wasted~~
                                   ~~strain~~
                   that on his ears wasted its ~~wasted~~
                           s ⎱   *merry*
              Or lark~~s above his head S~~⎰*inging a* ~~lonesome~~
                                              ~~strain~~

                          5

64   Long had he fancied each successive slope
65   Conceal'd some cottage whither he might turn
66   And rest;— but now, along heaven's darkening cope
                                          by ⎱
                   T ⎱   [——?——] ~~pass~~ [——?——]⎰⎰ *swept by*
67   ~~He watch'd t~~ ⎰*he* crows‸ in eddies homeward borne
                                   T ⎱
              ~~And now~~ *Meanwhile* [?]⎰*hus warned he sought*
68   ~~Then sought in vain~~ some shepherd's ~~ragged~~ thorn,
                                   guardian
69   Or hovel, from the storm to shield his head
              ~~But~~   *as he [?went]*   *But sought in vain ever—*
70   For ~~as he onward pass'd~~ more wild, forlorn
71   And vacant the huge plain around him spread
72   Ah me! the wet cold ground must be his only
                                   bed

              ~~In my own home whence I ha~~ve [?walk]
                                   limpd & [?slow]
              With ~~three days walk~~

---

62   Not strictly an overwriting, though treated as one here and in similar instances elsewhere: the "t" has been capitalized by adding a horizontal top stroke.

And be it so— for to the chill night shower
And the sharp wind his head he oft has bared
And he has counted many a wretched hour.
A suitor tending after labour heard
Three years endured what found he for reward
He to an armed fleet was forc'd away
By seamen who perhaps themselves had shared
Like fate, was hurried to the stairs & lay
In spite of all that in his heart, or theirs said nay
see loose sheet for middle of this   2

        6th stan

Ten years the work of carnage did not cease
And Death's dire aspect daily he survey'd
Death's minister; then came his glass to clean
And Hope returned & Pleasure fondly made
Her dwelling in his dreams   said
His happy arms already   he throw
Round her slender neck, the   of victory laid
In her full lap   he sees her joy or flow
As if thenceforth nor rain her wrinkle
                                    she could flow
                                              show
By fraud he lost what fairly he had earned
Even on the deserts head that he returned
Hears not   he love their needful food

                                 in such a mood
That from his   his children might have
He met a traveller robb'd him, shed his blood
And when the miserable work was done
He fled, a vagrant since, the murderer's fate
Alas   my spot so lonely is   to shun
But it   a deadly pang
Brought from without to inward miseries

6

73   *And be it so—   for to the chill night shower*
74   *And the sharp wind his head he oft has bared*
75   *And he has counted many a wretched hour.*
      ~~He is~~ a Mariner has and ill hath fared
76   ~~*A Sailor he the sailor's evils shared*~~*:*
                    h }
      A Sailer landing after labour [?] } *ard*
77   ~~*For when from two full years of labour hard*~~
      Three years endured what found he for reward
78   ~~*Home he return'd enflamed with long desire*~~
                   away }
      He to an armed fleet was forced [?] }
79   ~~*Even while in thought he took his rich reward*~~
      By Seamen who perhaps themselves had shared
80   ~~*From his wifes lips the ruffian press gang dire*~~
      Like fate was hurried to be slain & slay
81   ~~*Hurried him far away to rouze the battle's fire*~~
      In spite of all that in his heart, or theirs said nay
        See loose sheet for middle of this
            6th Stan

82   *For years the work of carnage did not cease*
             dire
83   *And Death's ~~worst~~ aspect daily he survey'd*
84   *Death's minister, then came his glad release*
                P }
85   *And Hope returned &* p } *leasure fondly made*
                  by fancy's }
                 [? ?] } *aid*
86   *Her dwelling in his dreams*—~~*by thought betray'd*~~
      His happy arms already did he throw }
      [? ? ? ? ? ?] }
87   ~~*He seems to feel his wife around him throw*~~
      Round his Wife's } *neck the*
        [?*while?*] }
88   ~~*Her arms and she this bloody prize of victory laid*~~
              l }
      In her full } [?] } *ap he sees her joy oerflow*
      [? ?*her* ?*she*] }
89   ~~*In her full lap forgets her years of woe*~~
      As if thenceforth nor pain nor trouble
         [?]
90   ~~*In the long joy & comfort from that wealth*~~ *to*
                           flow
      she could know

76/77 MW has entered extensive work for this revision at the back of the notebook. See
Additions to MS. 2, 79ᵛ, below.
81/82 The loose sheet has not survived.

```
                    u  ⎱              fa⎱irly
        By fra[w]⎰d he lost what he⎰     he had earned
91     He urged his claim the slaves of Office spurn'd
             Lion ⎱
         The [  ? ] ⎰ roams & gluts his tawny brood
92     The unfriended claimant at their door he stood
          Even in the desarts heart but he returned
                                              he
93     In vain & now towards his home return'd
                 not ⎱
          Bears [?] ⎰ to those he loves their needful food
94     Bearing to those he loved nor warmth nor food
          His home approaching but
                                home
95     In Sight of his own house in such a mood
                      sight
96     That from his view his children might have
                                               run
97     He met a traveller robb'd him, shed his blood
98     And when the miserable work was done
99     He fled, a vagrant since, the murderer's fate
                                         to shun


                            7

          Alas for alas no spot so lonely is
                        with one
          But it salutes him a deadly pang
          Brought from without to inward miseries
```

91–108   For early composition on the sailor see additions to MS. 1, Section B, above.

93   Before the line was deleted, "return'd" was converted to "turn'd."

99/100; 110   MW's fair copy of the revision is a new opening for the stanza beginning l. 109, as indicated by the number 7 in margin at l. 110.

Yet oft when Fear her withering grasp foregoes   21

Such tendency to pleasure loved before

Do life & nature shew that common care

Might to his bosom hours of joy restore

Affliction's least complaints his heart explore

Even yet, though danger round his path be sown

And fear defend the break the best not move

And were't not so the hardest might bemoan

The pangs the sleepless nights, the miseries he has known

7   ~~The~~ from that moment ~~of~~ all peace of mind

      The ~~proud~~ man might relent and weep to find

      ~~No~~ saw in this wild waste ~~so~~ a dreary pang

      ~~No~~ scarce a heart to ~~life~~

in   ~~Now as~~ he plodded on with sullen

      ~~A sound of brieus along the wild waste~~ ran

      He looked, & saw ~~upon a~~ a gibbet near

      A human body that in irons swang

      Uplifted by the tempest ~~whirling rushing~~ by

      And hovering round it often did a raven fly

8

      It was a spectacle which none might view

      In spot so savage but with shuddering pain

      Nor only did for him at once renew

      All he had feared from man but seized a brain

      Of the mind's phantoms horrible as vain

      The stones, as if to sweep him from the day

      Roll'd at his back along the living plain

      He fell, and without sense or motion lay

      And when the trance was gone again pursued

      now ~~feeble~~ his way

And ~~really~~ ~~feeble~~ forlorn

~~come into his heart ~~ a pang

was felt by one of woman born

100 *Yet oft when Fear her withering grasp foregoes*
101 *Such tendency to pleasure loved before*
102 *Do life & nature shew that common cares*
103 *Might to his bosom hours of joy restore*
104 *Affliction's least complaints his heart explore*
105 *Even yet, though danger round his path be sown*
106 *And fear defend the weak the best not more*
107 *And wer't not so the hardest might bemoan*
108 *The pangs the sleepless nights, the miseries he has*
                                    known

      He from that moment lost all peace of mind
109 *The proud man might relent and weep to find*
    7   and   a deadly
110 ~~*That* now in this wild waste *so keen* a pang~~
    ~~did~~
111 ~~*Could pierce a heart to life's best ends inclined*~~
    Now As [?on] }   *with sullen* }
    [?] }   ~~*he heard a*~~ }
112 *For, ~~as~~ he plodded on ~~with sullen~~ clang*
    As oft [?it ? ?of] ~~chains that near~~ him
  in   rang
                   wild waste
113 ~~*A sound of chains along the desart rang*~~
          upon a   high
114 *He looked, & saw ~~on a bare~~ gibbet ~~nigh~~*
115 *A human body that in irons swang*
        whirling   ~~rushing~~
116 *Uplifted by the tempest ~~sweeping~~ by*
117 *And hovering round it often did a raven fly*

                  8

118 *It was a spectacle which none might view*
119 *In spot so savage but with shuddering pain*
120 *Nor only did for him at once renew*
121 *All he had feared from man but rouzed a train*
122 *Of the minds phantoms horrible as vain*
123 *The stones, as if to sweep him from the day*
124 *Roll'd at his back along the living plain*
125 *He fell, and without sense or motion lay*
               again
126 *And when the trance was gone ~~feebly~~ pursued*
                   his way

                was } in } this }
     now while he [?] [?] }[?] }[?] }
    And ~~travelling now along this~~ spot forlorn
    There came into his heart as keen a pang
    As ere was felt by man of woman born

---

113 *in*] See note to l. 31, above.

As The whose brain 9 demoniac frenzy
When with severest joy the soul hath toss'd
Sinks into quiet, when the mood
To when to all but memory was lost
The mere phantasma which his sense had eyed
His mind was still as a deep evening stream
Nor if accosted now, in thought engross'd
Moody or only troubled would he seem
To traveller who might talk of any casual theme

10

But all was chearless to the horizon's bound
His weary eye which wheresoe'er it strays
Marks nothing but the red sun setting
Or, on the earth strange lines in former days
Left by gigantic arms, at length, surveys
What seems an antique castle spreading wide
Hoary and naked are its walls, & raise
Their brow sublime: in shelter there to bide
He turned the prowling rain smokes thick on every
                                              side

11
                in
Hurtle the clouds by deeper darkness piled.
Gone is the raven timely rest to seek:
He seem'd the only creature in the wild
On whom the elements their rage might wreak
Save that the bustard, of those limits bleak
Shy tenant seeing by the uncertain light
A man there wandring gave a mournful shriek
And half upon the ground with strange affright
Force'd hard against the wind a thick unwieldy
                                              flight

9

        one whose brain demoniac frenzy
127 As ~~doth befal to them whom frenzy~~ fires
        W⎫
      [?T]⎰*hen with severest fit the Soul hath*
128 ~~His soul which in such anguish had been~~ toss'd
      i⎱ s⎱   quiet⎫ *when the mood*
129 Sa⎰nk ⎰into ~~deepest~~ calm ⎰, ~~for~~ now retires
      ~~So when in darkness~~
130 ~~Fear a terrific dream in darkness lost~~
      So when to all but memory was lost
131 The dire phantasma which his sense had cross'd
132 His mind was still as a deep evening stream
133 Nor if accosted now, in thought engross'd
134 Moody or inly-troubled would he seem
135 To traveller who might talk of any casual theme

10

                      s⎫
136 But all was chearless to the horizon ⎰ bound
137 His weary eye which wheresoe'er it strays
138 Marks nothing but the red sun setting round
139 Or on the earth strange lines in former days
140 Left by gigantic arms, at length surveys
141 What seems an antique castle spreading wide
142 Hoary and naked are its walls, & raise
143 Their brow sublime : in shelter there to bide
       turned   *on every*
144 He ~~ran~~; the pouring rain smoked thick ~~as on he~~
                          ~~hied~~
                    side

11

        in
145 Hurtle the clouds ~~by~~ deeper darkness piled
146 Gone is the raven timely rest to seek :
147 He seem'd the only creature in the wild
148 On whom the elements their rage might wreak
149 Save that the bustard, of those limits bleak
150 Shy tenant seeing by the uncertain light
151 A man there wandring gave a *mournful shriek*
152 And half upon the ground with strange affright
153 Forc'd hard against the wind a thick unwieldy
                        flight

~~The~~ ~~lonely~~ Pile of ¹³ ~~Stone-henge~~ of darkness deep
And unknown days — that lovest to stand & hear
The desart sounding to the whirlwinds' sweep
Inmate of lonesome Nature's endless year
Even since thou sawest the giant Wicker rear
So dismal chambers thronged with living men
Before thy face did ever wretch appear
Who in his heart had groan'd with deadlier pain
Than he who travels now along thy bleak domain

¹³   on the lonesome
~~Within~~ ~~Beneath~~ that fabric reared of earthly form
~~No~~ ~~winds~~ ~~not~~ ~~reflected~~ ~~each~~ ~~by~~ ~~turns~~
~~Its~~ ~~power~~ all ~~quite~~ ~~lost~~ through ~~battering~~
Two hours he wilder'd on, no moon to stream
From gulf of parting clouds one friendly beam
Nor any friendly sound his footsteps led.
Once did the lightning's faint disastrous gleam
Disclose a naked guide-posts double head
Sight which, though lost at once some glimpse
                        of pleasure shed

¹⁴ toward
No swinging sign creak'd from ~~a~~ cottage elm
To bid his weary limbs new force assume
'Twas dark and void as ocean's watry realm
Roaring with storms beneath nights starless gloom
No gypsey cowr'd oer fire of furze or broom
No labourer watch'd his red kiln glaring bright
Nor taper glimmer'd dim from sick man's room
Along the heath no line of mournful light
From lamp of lonely toll-gate stream'd athwart
                        the night

1 2

          P⎱   ou⎱
154   ~~*Thou hoary*~~ *p* ⎰*ile!—the* ⎰*child of darkness deep*
            of Stone henge
155   *And unknown days—that lovest to stand & hear*
156   *The desart sounding to the whirlwind's sweep*
157   *Inmate of lonesome Nature's endless year*
158   *Even since thou sawest the giant Wicker rear*
           t⎱ ro⎱   ed⎱
159   *Its dismal chambers* ⎰*hu*⎰*ng* ⎰ *with living men*
160   *Before thy face did ever wretch appear*
161   *Who in his heart had groan'd with deadlier pain*
162   *Than he who travels now along thy bleak domain*

1 3
                           [?]⎱
                 on the lonesome [?]⎰

     Within
163   ~~*Beneath*~~ *that fabric, scarce of earthly form*
     Winds met in conflict each by turns supreme
164   ~~*More dreadful was the whirlwind's rage extreme*~~
     In power all   battering
165   ~~*All*~~ ₐ*track quite lost, through* ~~*rain*~~ *& ~~blinding~~ storm*
     wo⎱
166   *Three* ⎰ *hours he wilder'd on, no moon to stream*
167   *From gulf of parting clouds one friendly beam*
  N⎱
168   ⎰*Or any friendly sound his footsteps led.*
169   *Once did the lightning's faint disastrous gleam*
170   *Disclose a naked guide-post's double head*
171   *Sight which, though lost at once some glimpse*
                          of pleasure shed

1 4
     board
172   *No swinging sign*ₐ*creak d from ~~its~~ cottage elm*
173   *To bid his weary limbs new force assume*
174   *'Twas dark and void as ocean's watry realm*
175   *Roaring with storms beneath night's starless gloom*
176   *No gypsey cowr'd o'er fire of furze or broom*
177   *No labourer watch'd his red kiln glaring bright*
178   *Nor taper glimmer'd dim from sick man's room*
179   *Along the heath no line of mournful light*
180   *From lamp of lonely toll-gate stream'd athwart*
                      the night [?]

---

159   *hung*] Converted to "thronged" by adding letters and overwriting "n" with "ro."
162/163   The revision is probably intended for l. 162.

15

At length though hid in clouds the moon arose
The downs were visible: and now revealed
A structure stands which two bare slopes incon.
'Twas a spot, where, ancient sons fulfill'd
Their pious hands did the virgin build
A lonely Spital, the belated swain
From the night terrors of that waste to shield
But there no human being could remain,
And now the walls are named the dead house
                              of the Plain

16

Though he had little cause to love the abode
Of man or court sight of mortal face
Yet when the ~~doubtful~~ gloom that oun shew'd
                                        some trace
Hey glad he was of length to find a ~~place~~
~~Of human shelter~~ in thy lone come here
Till to the moor the early shepherd goes
Here shall sweet sleep his senseless limb embrace
In a cry roth where fern the floor bestrews
He lays his stiffen'd limbs. his eyes began to close

17   to come
When hearing a deep sigh that seem'd ~~forth~~
From one who mourn'd in sleep, he raised his head
And saw a Woman ~~in the middle~~ that naked room
Out stretched & turning ~~from an unary~~ bed
The moon a wan dead light around her shed,
He waked her, & at once her spirits fail
From fear by instant recollection bred;
For of that ruin she had heard a tale
Which now with freezing thoughts did all her
                              powers assail

15

181   *At length though hid in clouds, the moon arose*
182   *The downs were visible: and now revealed*
183   *A structure stands which two bare slopes enclose.*
184   *It was a spot, where, ancient vows fulfill'd,*
185   *Kind pious hands did to the Virgin build*
186   *A lonely Spital; the belated swain*
187   *From the night terrors of that waste to shield*
188   *But there no human being could remain;*
                  W⎱
189   *And now the w ⎰alls are named the dead house*
                                   of the Plain

16

190   *Though he had little cause to love the abode*
191   *Of man or covet sight of mortal face*
                     doubtful
192   *Yet when the* ~~ambiguous~~ *gloom that ruin shew'd*
                                some trace
193   *How glad he was at length to find* ~~a place~~
            Of human shelter in this lonesome place
194   ~~*That bore of human hands the chearing trace*~~
195   *Till to the moor the early shepherd goes*
196   *Here shall sweet sleep his senseless limbs embrace*
197   *In a dry nook where fern the floor bestrews*
198   *He lays his stiffen'd limbs: his eyes began to close*

17

                           to come
199   *When hearing a deep sigh that seem'd* ~~forth sent~~
200   *From one who mourn'd in sleep, he raised his head*
              W⎱   in that naked room
201   *And saw a w ⎰oman* ~~on the pediment~~
                     on a restless
202   *Outstretched & turning* ~~from uneasy~~ *bed*
                              shed,
203   *The moon a wan dead light around her* ~~spread~~
204   *He waked her, & at once her spirits fail*
205   *From fear by instant recollection bred;*
206   *For of that ruin she had heard a tale*
207   *Which now with freezing thoughts did all her*
                                   powers assail

18   25

Had heard of one who forced from storms to shroud
Felt the loose walls of this decayed retreat
Rock to ~~his horse~~ neighings shrill & loud
While his horse paw'd the floor with furious heat
Till on a stone that sparkled to his feet
Rock & still struck again the troubled horse
The man half raised the stone with pain & sweat
Remained, for well his arm might lose its force
Deeming the grim head of a new murder'd corse

19

Such tales of this lone mansion she had learn'd
And when that shape with eyes in sleep half drown'd
By the moon's sullen lamp she first discern'd
Cold stony horror all her senses bound.
~~he address'd in~~ words of cheering sound.
~~Recovering heart take~~ answer did she make
~~her to allure to purpose kind~~
And well it was that if the corse there found
~~convenced that devout ground~~
In converse that ensued she nothing spake.
~~She knew not what dire peril~~
                                                     road

She saw as through a bottom bare & deep
That day she journey'd on the houseless moor
An old man beckoning from the shelving ouse
came tottering sidelong down to ask the hour
There never clock was heard from steeple tow'r
From the wide copse the plundering crows to scare
A rusty gun he held in sun & shower,
Old as he was alone he lingered there
This hungry meal too scant for dog that meal
So scantly was his meal   to share

18

208 *Had heard of one who forced from storms to shroud*
209 *Felt the loose walls of this decayed retreat*
      incessant
210 *Rock to ~~his horse's~~ neighings shrill & loud*
211 *While his horse paw'd the floor with furious heat*
212 *Till on a stone that sparkled to his feet*
213 *Struck, & still struck again the troubled horse*
214 *The man half-raised the stone with pain & sweat*
215 *Half-raised, for well his arm might lose its force*
216 *Disclosing the grim head of a new-murder'd corse*

19

217 *Such tales of this lone mansion she had learn'd*
218 *And when that shape with eyes in sleep half drown'd*
219 *By the moon's sullen lamp she first discern'd*
220 *Cold stony horror all her senses bound.*
        r⟩ he addressed in
221 *He ⟨ ~~spoke, and in low~~ words of chearing sound.*
        Recovering heart like answer did she make
222 *~~Him further to allure to purpose kind~~*
        And well it was that of the corse there found
223 *~~Quickly she conversed of that desart ground~~*
        In converse that ensued she nothing spake.
224 *~~Which seem'd to those of other worlds consign'd~~*
        She knew not what dire pangs had power to wake
225 *~~Whose voices she had heard as paused the hollow~~*
                                    ~~wind~~

226 *She said as through a bottom bare & deep*
                                    or ⟩
227 *That day she journey'd on the houseless mo[?re]⟩*
228 *An old man beckoning from the chalky steep*
229 *Came tott'ring sidelong down to ask the hour*
230 *There never clock was heard from steeple tow'r*
231 *From the wide corn the plundering crows to scare*
232 *A rusty gun he held: in sun & shower,*
233 *Old as he was alone he linger'd there*
234 *His hungry meal too scant for dog that meal*
                                    to share
        Too scanty was his meal ∧

Much of the wonders of that boundless heath
She spoke & of a swain who far astray
Reached unawares a height & saw beneath
Gigantic beings ranged in dread array
Such beings, thwarting oft the traveller's...
With shield and stone——

                    Strictly —— the trouble

Much more of dream... from antient ages fetch'd
And special sights that... fill the shadowy...
And of wild sounds that... the shepherd...
On the round... 'mid his fleecy train
She told delighted that her fears were vain
Nor of that... did mention make
And well it was for surely... again
The fit had made his... with horror quake
She knew not what a hell such spot had power
                                    to make

                    20.

But soon her mind on other thoughts was bent
So friendly was his voice & now the...
In feeble murmurs told his rage was spent
Meanwhile discourse ensued of various kind
Which by degrees a confidence of mind
And mutual interest fail'd not to create
And now to natural sympathy resign'd
In that forsaken building where they sate
The woman thus began her story to relate.

235 *Much of the wonders of that boundless heath*
    old man spoke of one
236 *She spoke & of a Swain who far astray*
237 *Reached unawares a height, & saw beneath*
238 *Gigantic beings ranged in dread array*
239 *Such beings, thwarting oft the traveller's way*
240 *With shield and stone-ax*
    striding oer the wold
[241] -
[242] -
[243] -
244 *Much more of dream[?s] from antient ages fetch'd*
245 *And spectal sights that fill the shadowy plain*
246 *And of wild sounds that mock the shepherd stretch'd*
247 *On the round barrow, 'mid his fleecy train*
248 *She told, delighted that her fears were vain*
249 *Nor of that corse there found did mention make*
250 *And well it was for surely once again*
251 *The fit had made his bones with horror quake*
252 *She knew not what a hell such spot had power*
    to wake

20

    mind
253 *But soon her* ~~heart~~ *on other thoughts was bent*
254 *So friendly was his voice, & now the wind*
    its
255 *In feeble murmurs told* ~~his~~ *rage was spent*
256 *Meanwhile discourse ensued of various kind*
257 *Which of degrees a confidence of mind*
    u⎰
258 *And mutt⎱al interest fail'd not to create*
259 *And now to natural sympathy resign'd*
260 *In that forsaken building. where they sate*
    thus
261 *The woman* ~~thus~~ *began her story to relate.*

[241–243] Although DW omitted these lines in the fair copy, she indicated by dots that substitute lines were to be inserted. WW has shown by inserting in pencil a portion of l. 241 that ll. 177–180 of MS. 1 were still thought to fit.

245 spectal] "spectral" must have been intended.

261 MS. 2 contains no story for the woman. In Part First there is no indication even that a story is to be inserted, but in Part Second, at l. 423, a row of asterisks marks the beginning of the second part of the woman's narrative.

27

Or that some sign of mortal anguish broke

~~By strong convulsion from her comrade's breast~~

Once more a horrid trance his limbs did lock

Him through the gloom she could not then discern

And after a short while again she spoke

But he was stretch'd upon the wither'd fern

Nor to her friendly summons answer could return.

A man ~~&c~~ it to bare small

Rose up from the cool seat which he had ~~found~~

Beneath the seemly shade of a stone-wall:

He bore a scythe of which the blade was bound

With twisted straw and on the grassy ground

That edged the road like one who would inquire

He ~~round~~ he saunter'd slowly, looking round.

He seem'd a travelling ~~voyager~~ & in attire

Bound to some distant ~~field~~ to earn the mowers

hire.

         Here paus'd she either by her
397 *She paused or by excess of grief oppress'd*
398 *Or that some sign of mortal anguish broke*
399 *In strong convulsion from her comrade's breast*
         Shivering she wrapped her body
400 *She paused & shivering wrapp'd her in her cloak*
401 *Once more a horrid trance his limbs did lock*
402 *Him through the gloom she could not then discern*
403 *And after a short while again she spoke*
404 *But he was stretch'd upon the wither'd fern*
405 *Nor to her friendly summons answer could return.*

---

       with wither [?frame] of
A man of knotty joints, and stature small
Rose up from the cool seat which he had found
Beneath the scanty shade of a stone-wall:
He bore a scythe of which the blade was bound
With twisted straw and on the grassy ground
That edged the road like one who would inquire
His road he saunter'd slowly, looking round.
He seem'd a travelling peasant in attire
            [?spot]
Bound to some distant land to earn the mowers
                  hire.

    One who had left his home to
    Who from his home had come
    Thus sauntering on the skirt of Sarum
    Erelong [?twas ?on]
    He over took a man with feet
          he was & walked with
                half bare
    An aged man who crept alone with [?pain]
    He was an [?aged]
    So forth he came into the open light
    And look'd one look towards the east
               but do
    Whateer he will he must the woman
         view

405/406 It is not certain what relation the stanza that follows the end of Part First bears to *ASP.* For comment see the Introduction, pp. 9–10, above. In l. 2, "seat" is written over "grass," which is erased; the erased words in ll. 4–6 cannot be recovered.

33

Adventures on Salisbury Plain

Part second

Now dim and dreary was the Plain around
The ghosts were up on nightly roam intent
And many a gleam of grey light swept the ground
Where high & low those ghostly wanderers went
And whereso'er their rustling course they bent
The rattled earth worms to their hollow did lend
The whilst the crimson moon her lustre spent
With orb half visible was seen to sink
Leading the starry remains along the horizon

The Woman seemed to wish her story to relate
My Father, thus did she begin her tale
Lived many years in plenty ease and rest
Our house stood in a corner of the vale
Of Taunton Dean far distant in the west
Three fields we had as fruitful as the best
We were untroubled and our thoughts were gay
Our farm was the dearest like a little nest
No greener fields than ours could eye survey
And happily indeed we lived from day to day

Adventures on Salisbury Plain

Part second

406 *Now dim and dreary was the Plain around*
407 *The ghosts were up on nightly roam intent*
408 *And many a gleam of grey ligh swept the*
                                       ground
409 *Where high & low those ghostly wanderers went*
410 *And wheresoe'er their rustling course they bent*
411 *The startled earth-worms to their holes did slink*
412 *The whilst the crimson moon her lustre spent*
                                          sink
413 *With orb half visible was seen to* ~~slink~~
414 *Leading the storm's remains along the horizon*
                                             brink

            beg that she
The Woman seem d to wish her story to relate
               the
My Father, thus did she begin her tale
Liv'd many years in plenty ease and rest
          was
Our house ~~stood~~ in a corner of the vale
Of Taunton-Dean far distant in the west
Three fields we had as fruitful as the best
We were untroubled and our thoughts were
              gay
Our farm was shelter'd like a little nest

No greener fields than ours could eye survey
And happily indeed we liv'd from day to
            day.

414/415   For no obvious reason DW left a gap in which WW entered a new version of *ASP*,
261–270.

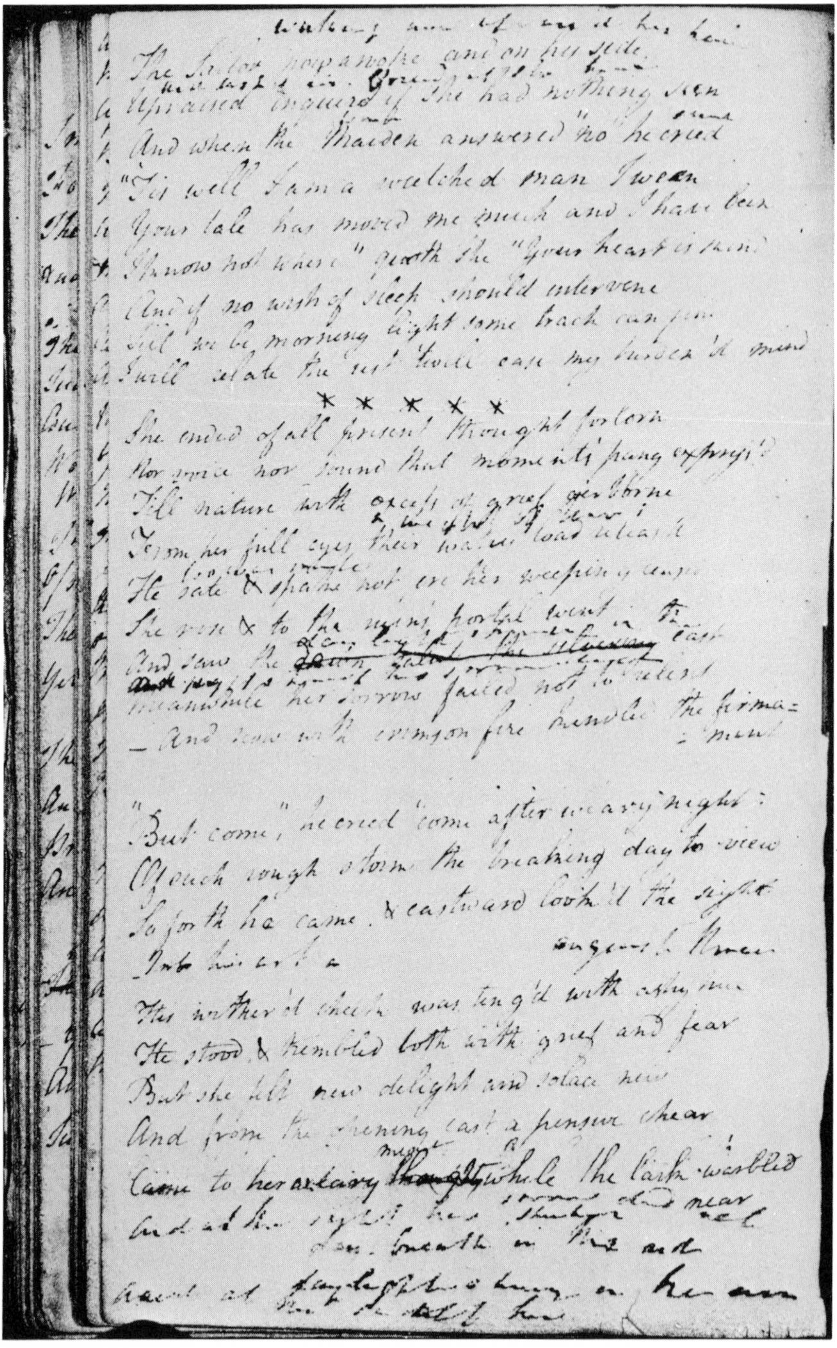
The Sailor now awoke and on his side
Upraised inquired if she had nothing seen
And when the Maiden answered "No" he cried
"Tis well I am a wretched man I ween
Your tale has moved me much and I have been
I know not where" quoth she "Your heart is kind
And of no wish of sleep should intervene
Till we by morning light some track can find
I will relate the rest twill ease my burden'd mind
* * * * *
She ended of all present thought forlorn
Nor voice nor sound that moment's pang express'd
Till nature with excess of grief o'erborne
From her full eyes their watry load releas'd
He sate & spake not, ere her weeping ceas'd
She rose & to the ruin'd portal went
And saw the dawn salute the silvery east
Meanwhile her sorrows failed not to relent
— And now with crimson fire kindled the firmament

"But come," he cried "come after weary night
Of such rough storm the breaking day to view
So forth he came & eastward look'd the sight
His wither'd cheek was ting'd with ashy hue
He stood & trembled both with grief and fear
But she felt new delight and solace new
And from the opening east a pensive cheer
Came to her ... while the lark warbled near

415
         waking now uprais'd his head
The Sailor now awoke and on his side
       And ask'd his Friend if she had
416 *Upraised inquir'd if she had nothing seen*
        Woman   said
417 *And when the Maiden answered "no" he cried*
                e
418 *"'Tis well I am a wretched man I we[?a]ʃn*
419 *Your tale has moved me much and I have been*
420 *I know not where" quoth she "Your heart is kind*
421 *And if no wish of sleep should intervene*
422 *Till we be morning light some track can find*
423 *I will relate the rest 'twill ease my burden'd mind*

       *   *   *   *   *

559 *She ended of all present thought forlorn*
560 *Nor voice, nor sound that moment's pang express'd*
561 *Till nature with excess of grief o'erborne*
               a weight of tears;
562 *From her full eyes their watry load releas'd*
       too was mute
563 *He sate & spake not, ere her weeping ceased*
564 *She rose & to the ruin's portal went*
         day light [?spreading] in the
565 *And saw the* ~~dawn salute the silvering~~ *east*
   [?At]
   [?And] } sight whereof her sorrow [?did]
566 *Meanwhile her sorrow failed not to relent*
567 *—And now with crimson fire kindled the firma =*
              = ment

568 *"But come," he cried "come after weary night:*
569 *Of such rough storm the breaking day to view*
570 *So forth he came, & eastward look'd the sight*
[571]   Into his art a   anguish threw
572 *His wither'd cheek was ting'd with ashy hue*
573 *He stood, & trembled both with grief and fear*
574 *But she felt new delight and solace new*
575 *And from the opening cast a pensive chear*
           mind
     weary ~~thoughts~~
576 *Came to her* [? ?] *while the lark warbled*
            near
       sorrow did [?rel]
   And at the sight [?her ?]
       day-break in the [?]
       daylight [?shining] on her [?]
   And at the [?sight] her

---

422 *be*] An obvious miswriting for "by."
423/559 The asterisks indicate where the second part of the woman's narrative should be inserted.
[571] Line omitted in fair copy.

They look'd & saw a lengthening road & wain   35
That wane down a bare slope not far remote
The downs all ~~dropp'd~~ with ~~glittering~~ ... rains
Whistled the waggoner with joyous note
The cock scarce heard, at distance sounds his throat
— But town or farm, or hamlet none they view'd
Only were told there stood a lonely cot
Thence three long miles. Together they renewed
Their journey, and the road towards that cot pursued

The woman from the rude tenement
Did with a sigh and mournful step depart
But deep into his entrails one and one
Anguish that rankled like a fiery dart
She with affectionate and homely art
The peace of mind endeavoured to restore
Come it ... be the sudden ... heart
Thus oftentimes the woman ... implore
And still the more he grieved she loved him still the more

And now or ... indifferent ...
... indifferent ... he ...
To note discourse but nothing could require
His thoughts still recurring to the murdered man
When they had travell'd thus a full half mile
Why should you grieve she said a little while
And we shall meet in heaven but now they
The mail come rattling on in scamp'ring file
And when the watchman gave the morning ...
The Sailor's face was pale with momentary fear

Not on the sand the ship it ...
... ...

She

577 ~~They~~ look'd & saw a lengthening road & wain
578 That rang down a bare slope not far remote
were glistering all bedropp'd with
579 The downs ~~all glister'd dropp'd with~~ freshening
rains
580 Whistled the waggoner with joyous note
581 The cock, scarce heard, at distance sounds his
throat
582 —But town or farm, or hamlet none they view'd
583 Only were told there stood a lonely cot
584 Thence three long miles. Together they renewed
585 Their journey, and the road towards that cot
pursued
586 The woman from the ruin'd tenement
587 Did with a light and chearful step depart
through her Comrades vitals
588 But deep into his vitals she had sent
589 Anguish that rankled like a fiery dart
out
590 She with affectionate and homely art
591 His peace of mind endeavour'd to restore
592 Come let us be she said of better heart
593 Thus oftentimes the Woman did implore
594 And still the more he griev'd she loved him
still the more
And now on themes indifferent
595 On themes indifferent often she began
596 To hold discourse but nothing could beguile
597 His thoughts still cleaving to the murder'd ma
598 When they had travell'd thus a full half mile
599 Why should you grieve she said a little while
600 And we shall meet in heaven but now they
hear
601 The mail come rattling on in scamp'ring file
602 And when the coachman gave the morning chear
603 The Sailor's face was pale with momentary fear

clear & [?fair]
But come she said the sky is ~~fair the light~~
And   we our journey
~~Our journey~~ safely∧we may [?pur]

---

586 *the*] The "e" is written over "at," erased.
590 out] See note to l. 31.
595 *On*] The "n" is written over "f," erased.

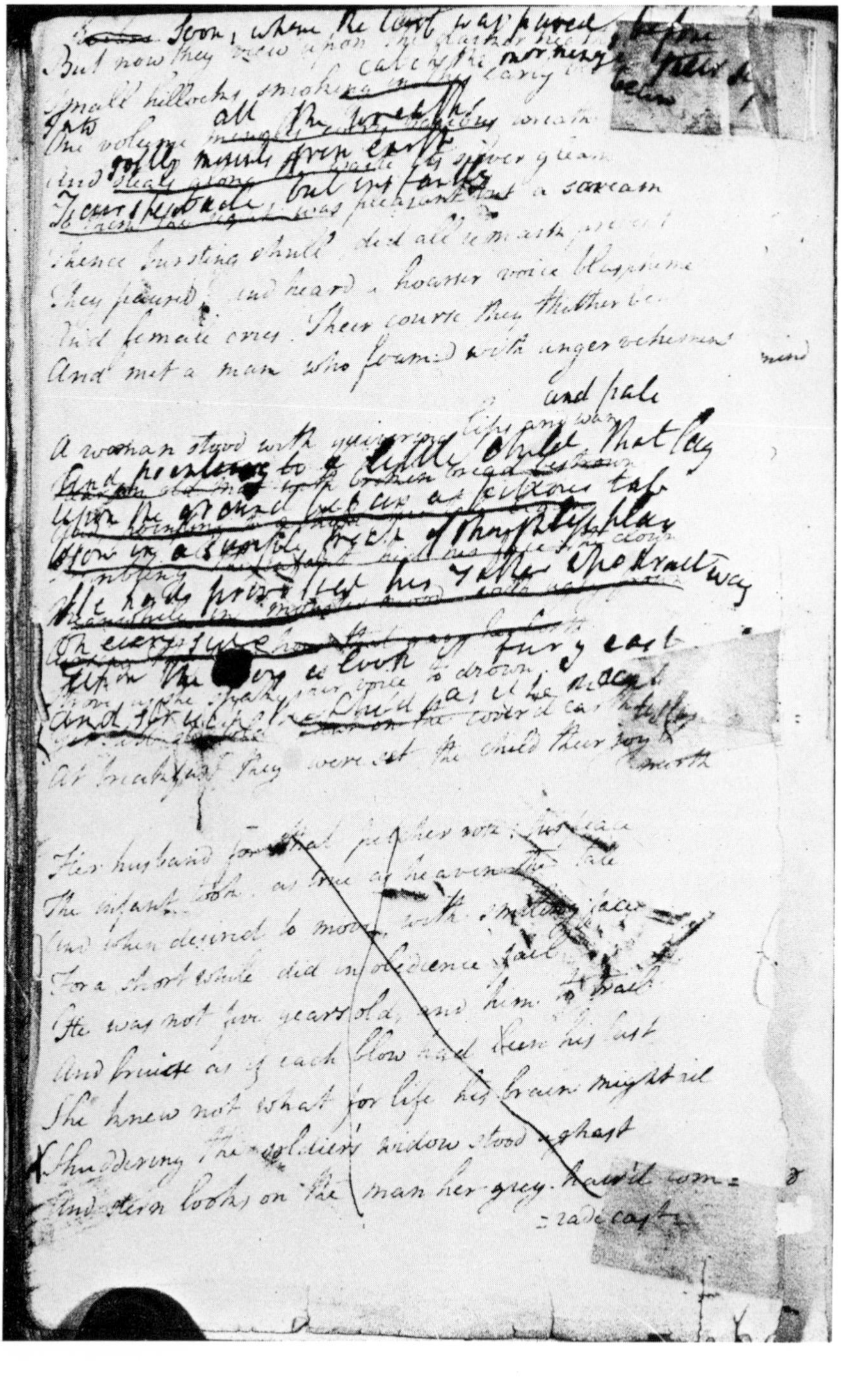

But n   Soon, where the Cart was passed, before
604   *But now they view upon the darker heath*   their sight
                        catch the mornings beam
605   *Small hillocks smoking* ~~in~~ *the early beam*
        Into   all the wreaths
606   *One volume* ~~mingles every various~~ *wreath*
              softly mounts from earth
607   *And* ~~steals along the waste~~ *its silver gleam*
        Fair spectacle but instantly   scream ⎫
608   ~~To them the sight was~~ *pleasant but a* [?] ⎬
609   *Thence bursting shrill, did all remark prevent*
610   *They paused, and heard a hoarser voice blaspheme*
611   *And female cries. Their course they thither bent*
612   *And met a man who foamed with anger vehement*

                                 and pale
613   *A woman stood with quivering lips and wan*
        And pointing to a little child that lay
614   ~~Near an old mat with broken bread bestrown~~
        Upon the ground began a piteous tale
615   ~~And pointing to a child her tale began~~
        How in a simple freak of thoughtless play
616   ~~Trembling the infant hid his face ;~~ *the clown*
        He had provoked his Father who straitway
617   ~~Meanwhile in monster mood with ugly frown~~
        On every side
618   ~~Cursing the very hour that gave her birth~~
        Upon the Boy a look of fury cast
619   *Strove as she spake her voice to drown.*
        And struck the Child as if he meant
                              to slay
620 ✗ ~~Yet still she told, That on the cover~~'*d earth*
621   *At breakfast they were set, the child their joy &*
                                      mirth

622   *Her husband for that pitcher rose ; his place*
623   *The infant took, as true as heaven the tale*
624   *And when desired to move, with smiling face*
625   *For a short while did in obedience fail*
626   *He was not five years old, and him to trail*
          se ⎫
627   *And brui*[?] ⎬ *as if each blow had been his last*
628   *She knew not what for life his brain might ail*
629 ✗ *Shuddering the soldier's widow stood aghast*
630   *And stern looks on the man her grey-hair'd com =*
                                = rade cast.

---

629   The meaning of the X and of a partially visible X at l. 620 is unclear.

And with firm voice & indignation high
Such further deed in manhood's name forbad
confident in passion, made reply
to the bitter insult and revilings ~~A new~~
~~castrof~~ ~~when with~~ what meaning here
~~vagrant~~ he had
And ask'd what plunder he was hunting now
~~what~~ ~~stroud~~ the gallows would one day of him beglad.
Here cold sweat started from the Sailor's brow
yet calm he seem'd as thoughts so poignant
would allow
Softly he stroked the child whom
No answer made but stroked the child on the ~~child's~~
~~work~~ face to earth; and as the boy turn'd round
His gather'd head a groan ~~the~~ ~~child's~~
~~Urch he saw~~ ~~when~~ the groan
~~he~~ ~~ready to the~~ ground
~~to reply to cry~~ ~~ly wound~~
~~from~~ though his soul
~~He had~~ ~~in the dare~~
At once the yielding iron passage found
~~of tender thoughts then~~ ~~again~~
~~sunken~~
He would his ~~eyes~~ eyes from ~~very~~

To turn himself he said "what hearts have we
The blessing his the father gives his child
Yet happy thou poor boy compared ~~with~~ me
Suffering not doing ill fate ~~more mild~~"
The Sailor ~~only~~ looked ~~be quiet~~
~~The father~~ ~~relenting~~ ~~troupe~~
He ~~his boy~~ all was reconcil'd awok
Then with a voice which inward trouble broke
~~In the full swelling~~ troake the ~~lad~~ them be=
~~The~~ spoke

·DOVE·COTTAGE·TRUST·

631　*And with firm voice & indignation high,*
632　*Such further deed in manhood's name forbad*
633　*He confident in passion, made reply*
634　*With bitter insult and revilings sad*　　　　*Amen*

　　　　　　　im⎱
　　　Asked her⎰ *with taunts what business here*
635　*Calling him vagabond, & knave, & mad*
　　　　　　　　　　　　　he had
636　*And ask'd what plunder he was hunting now*
　　　　What kind of
637　*The gallows would one day of him be glad.*
638　*Here cold sweat started from the sailor's brow*
639　*Yet calm he seem'd as thoughts so poignant*
　　　　　　　　　　　　　would allow
　　　Softly he stroked the child who lay
640　*Nor answer made but stroked the child outstretch'd*
　　　With
641　*His face to earth ; and, as the boy turn'd round*
642　*His batter'd head a groan the Sailor fetch'd.*
　　　As if he saw then, and upon that ground
643　*The head with streaming blood had dy'd the*

　　　　　　　　　　　　ground

　　　A　repetition of the
644　*Flow'd from the spot where he that*ₐ*deadly wound*
645　*Had fixed on him he murder'd. Through his brain*
　　　He had himself inflicted
646　*At once the griding iron passage found*
647　*Deluge of tender thoughts then rush'd amain*
　　　　　　　sunken
648　*Nor could his aged eyes from very tears abstain*

649　*Within himself he said "what hearts have we*
650　*The blessing this the father gives his child*
651　*Yet happy thou poor boy! compared with me*
652　*Suffering not doing ill, fate far more mild"*
　　　The strangers pitying looks of
653　*Such sight the father of his wrath beguil'd*
　　　The Father and relenting thoughts
654　*Relenting thoughts & self-reproach awoke*
　　　　　　　　　　　　awoke

　　　　his Son
655　*He kiss'd the boy, so all was reconcil'd*
656　*Then with a voice which inward trouble broke*
657　*In the full swelling throat the Sailor them be=*
　　　　　　　　　　　= spoke

634　*Amen*] This pious ejaculation, almost certainly used for breaking in a new pen, is found on many Wordsworthian MSS.

and as this world's law

Each proud to [...] his brother or his peer
Much need have ye that time more closely [...]
The bond of nature & brotherkindness can
And that among so few there still be peace
Else can ye hope but with such numerous foes
Your pains shall [...] with your years increase"
While his [...] lips these homely truths disclose
A correspondent calm stole gently on his way.

And halting [...] down at length they look
Where through a narrow valley's pleasant scene
A wreath of vapour track'd a winding brook
That babbled on through groves & meadows green
A single cottage smok'd the trees between
The dripping groves [...] with cheerful lays
And melancholy lowings intervene
Of scatter'd herds that in the meadows graze
While through the furrowed grass the [...] milk-maid strays

Down the thick woods they dropp'd into the vale
Comfort by prouder mansions unbestow'd
Their wearied frames she hoped would soon regale
Ere long they reach'd that cottage in the dale
It was a rustic Inn the board was spread
The milk-maid followed with her brimming pail
And lustily the master carved the bread
Kindly the housewife press'd & they in comfort fed

658   "} ' *Tis a bad world and hard is the world's law*
       Even for the man who wears the warmest
659   *Each prowls to strip his brother of his fleece*
                                    fleec
660   *Much need have ye that time more closely draw*
             all }
661   *The bond of nature; cease}* *unkindness cease*
662   *And that among so few there still be peace*
663   *Else can ye hope but with such num'rous foes*
664   *Your pains shall ever with your years increase"*
        wan   e}
665   *While his ~~pale~~ lips tho}se homely truths disclose*
666   *A correspondent calm stole gently on his woes.*

667   *And passing onward down at length they look*
668   *Where through a narrow valley's pleasant scene*
669   *A wreath of vapour track'd a winding brook*
                              ows
670   *That babbled on through groves & meads‸of green*
671   *A single cottage smoked the trees between*
672   *The dripping groves resound with chearful lays*
673   *And melancholy lowings intervene*
674   *Of scatter'd herds that in the meadows graze*
                             lonely
675   *While through the furrow'd grass the ~~merry~~*
                       milk-maid strays

676   *the prospect shew'd*
677   *Down the thick woods they dropp'd into the vale*
678   *Comfort by prouder mansions unbestow'd*
679   *Their wearied frames she hoped would soon regale*
             at }
680   *Erelong they reach'd the }* *cottage in the dale*
681   *It was a rustic Inn the board was spread*
682   *The milk-maid followed with her brimming pail*
683   *And lustily the master carved the bread*
684   *Kindly the housewife press'd & they in comfort*
                             fed

---

661   "cea" was converted to "all," leaving the "se" of "cease"; the "e" was used to begin the "u" of the following word.

676   The opening of the line is omitted in the fair copy.

But breakfast done she learn'd they now must part
He had resolved to turn towards the sea
Since he that tale had heard & while his heart
Struggled with tears nor could its sorrow ease
She left him there: for clustering round his knees
With his oak staff the cottage children play'd
And soon she reach'd a spot o'erhung with trees
And banks of rugged earth. Beneath the shade
Across the pebbly road a little runner stray'd.

A cart and horse beside the rivulet stood.
Chequering the canvass roof the sunbeams shone.
By it the carman bending to scoop the flood
~~as the wan~~ wherein lay one
~~A pale-faced woman in~~
The carman wet her lips ~~body~~ there was none
Though even to die near one she most had loved
She could not of herself there would have moved

The soldiers indeed learn'd with honest pain
And heartfelt love of sympathy sincere
Why this that worn out wretch must here
The jolting road & morning air severe
~~The wain pursued its way~~
In pure compassion, she her
~~Back to the~~
~~the horse~~

Far as the village — a sad sight to
She enter alone — & forth in haste
The friends whom she had left but a few
minutes past

685　　But breakfast done, she learn'd they now must part
　　　　　　　　　　　　　　　　　　　　　as ⎫
686　　He had resolved to turn towards the se[?]⎰
687　　Since he that tale had heard, & while her heart
688　　Struggled with tears nor could its sorrow ease
689　　She left him there : for clustering round his knees
690　　With his oak staff the cottage children play'd
691　　And soon she reach'd a spot o'erhung with trees
692　　And banks of ragged earth : beneath the shade
693　　Across the pebbly road a little runner stray'd.

694　　A cart and horse beside the rivulet stood :
695　　Chequering the canvass roof the sunbeams shone.
696　　She saw the carman bend to scoop the flood,
　　　　As the Wain fronted her   lay ⎫
697　　And now approach'd the wain; wherein was ⎰ one
　　　　A pale-faced ⎫ Woman in disease far gone
　　　　　wretched ⎰
698　　A single woman lying spent & gone
　　　　[?lying ?alone, ?and ?]
699　　The carman wet her lips as well behoved
　　　　　　　　　　　body [?figu]
700　　Bed under her lean shadow there was none
701　　Though even to die near one she most had loved
702　　She could not, of herself those wasted limbs
　　　　　　　　　　　　　　　have moved

703　　The Soldier's widow learn'd with honest pain
704　　And homefelt force of sympathy sincere
　　　　　　　　　　　　　　ch ⎫
705　　Why thus that worn-out wrett ⎰must there
　　　　　　　　　　　　　　　　sustain
706　　The jolting road & morning air severe
　　　　The wain pursued its way & following near
707　　And crying would my friend thy aid were here
　　　　　　　　　　　　　　s   re ⎫
　　　　In pure compassion, she her step[? now] ⎰ traced
708　　Or yours good cottagers her steps retraced
　　　　Back to the The Far as the cottage house
709　　To that same house the wain still following
　　　　　　　　　　　　　　　near
　　　　Far as the house—finding her comrade there
710　　She found her comrade there, & cried in haste
711　　Come, come, my friends, & see what object here
　　　　　　　　　　　　　　　is placed

　　　　Far as the Cottage—a sad sight is here
　　　　　　　　　　　　ran ⎫ out
　　　　She cried aloud—& forth [?sh] ⎰ in haste
　　　　The friends whom she had left but a few
　　　　　　　　　　　　minutes past

709–711　The final readings are copied at page foot.

Up to the door with eager speed they ran
From her bare straw the woman half upraised
Her bony visage gaunt & deadly wan
No pity asking on the ground she gazed
~~With a wan eye distracted & amazed~~
~~with eye~~

Then sunk upon her straw with feeble moan
Fervently cried the housewife "God be praised
I have a house that I can call my own
Nor shall she perish there untended & alone

So in they bear her to the chimney-seat
And busily though yet with fear unlie
Her garments & to warm her icy feet
With death's numb waters swoln her heavy
And chafe her pulseless temples cold & dry
At last she shrove her languid head to rear
And said "I thank you all if I must die
The God in heaven my prayers for you will hear
Today I did not think my end had been so near —
Bodily care comfort labour could procure
Suffering what no endurance could assuage
I was compelled to seek my father's door
But sickness stopp'd me in my pilgrimage;
I feared to be a burthen to his age;

The miser's peace me in this icain
I must be carried back from stage to stage
Unwilling that I should with them remain
And shew hopes that I my home might get again

712   *As to the door with eager speed they ran*
713   *From her bare straw the woman half uprais'd*
714   *Her bony visage, gaunt & deadly wan*
715   *No pity asking, on the group she gazed*
       With a dim eye distracted & amazed
716   *As if with eye by blank suffusion glazed*
       Like,
717   *Then sunk upon her straw with feeble moan*
718   *Fervently cried the housewife "God be prais'd*
719   *I have a house that I can call my own*
720   *Nor shall she perish there untended & alone*

721   *So, in they bear her to the chimney-seat*
722   *And busily though yet with fear untie*
723   *Her garments & to warm her icy feet*
724   *With death's numb waters swoln, their hands*
                                  apply
725   *And chafe her pulseless temples cold & dry*
726   *At last she strove her languid head to rear—*
727   *And said— "I thank you all—if I must die*
728   *The God in heaven my prayers for you will hear*
729   *Today, I did not think my end had been so near—*
730   *Barr'd every comfort labour could procure*
731   *Suffering what no endurance could asswage*
732   *I was compell'd to seek my father's door*
733   *But sickness stopp'd me in my pilgrimage.*
734   *I feared to be a burthen to his age;*

735   *The overseers placed me in this wain*
736   *Thus to be carried back from stage to stage*
737   *Unwilling that I should with them remain*
738   *And I had hopes that I my home might yet regain*

729/730   Because of the reformation of the stanzas over extensive erasure, there is no longer a space visible in the MS. between the stanzas.

My lot for life has long been burthensome
~~And there far on my journey I am come~~   41

Oh God ~~If I have~~ meekly suffer'd meek
~~If~~ ~~there may~~ my end ~~the~~
~~can~~ my life will soon be done.

~~Then if~~ if mine e'er wander hither speak
~~and say this~~ a worm is one my cheek
In a lone ~~hut~~ house beside   the ~~sea we dwelt~~
Near Portland Light-house in a ~~lonesome~~ creek   O Shellens
~~There~~ my father too ~~the good~~ old ~~man~~
~~if she~~ ~~wolled me to~~ hear of all that I have felt
~~& there   learn the end   of woes~~

within   ~~that~~ ~~hut~~
~~&~~ that ~~that~~ I never a widows cares
~~I still~~ wedd   two children did partake my bed
And strange ropes trembled through   my way
    & prayers
Strong was I then, and labour gave us bread.

Until   a man was found by ~~to the~~ ~~evidence~~ said
~~Whose~~ body ~~neep~~   ~~our colliers~~ chanced to lie
~~dead   from~~ suspicion arose us from our shed
In vain to find a friendly face we try
Nor could we live together those poor boys &

~~throw to us to pull to them~~
Nor one had seen ~~he said it twice the~~
~~that he~~ my husband in the   neighbourhood   lurking
Now he had fled, & whither no one knew
And he had done the deed in the lush wood
"Near his own home! _____ but he was kind &
    good
Never on earth was milder creature, see
He'd not have robb'd the raven of its food
Oh had my husband 'mong the living been
~~I could not have beheld those~~
    buried
My days had ~~first~~   secure from misery keen
    To keen

<pre>
        A ⎱   My lot in life has long been burdensome
739   T ⎰nd thus far on my journey I am come

               if ⎱
740   Oh God! as ⎰ I have meekly suffered meek
          Meek may my end be
741   Shall be my end—my lips will soon be dumb—⎱

          Should   e'r ⎱
742   If child of mine e[?r] ⎰ wander hither speak

                              n
743   Of me say that the worm is o[?n] ⎱ my cheek

                 hut ⎱
744   In a lone house ⎰ beside   the sea we dwelt
                                    sheltering
745   Near Portland Light-house in a lonesome creek
                              the good old man
          My ⎱   , ⎱   ould ⎱
746   I have a ⎰ father too—, ⎰ & he will ⎰ melt
                    if he sh. hear of all that I have felt
747   In tears to learn the end of woes so largely
                                                  dealt

                        o ⎱ use hut
          Within   hut ⎰
748   Long in that house I knew a widow's cares
                        little
749   Yet still two ∧children did partake my bed
750   And strange hopes trembled through my dreams
                                              & prayers,
751   Strong was I then, and labour gave us bread.
          Until
            A man
752   Till one was found by stroke of violence dead
          Whose body near our cottage
                 our ⎱
753   And near my ⎰ door the Stranger chanced to lie
          A dire ⎱
          [? ?] ⎰
754   And soon suspicion drove us from our shed
755   In vain to find a friendly face we try
756   Nor could we live together those poor boys & I

                 that day, as well he knew
                        he said & swore it too
757   For one ∧had seen he said in vest of blue
                 M ⎱   lurking
758   That day, m ⎰y husband ∧in the neighbourhood
759   Now he had fled, & whither no one knew

760   And he had done the deed in the dark wood ' ⎱
761   "Near his own home!—but he was kind &
                                              good
762   Never on earth was milder creature see
763   He'd not have robb'd the raven of its food

764   Oh! had my husband ' ⎰ mong the living been
                        ose ⎱   s ⎱
765   I could not have beheld the ⎰ hour ⎰ of anguish
                                              keen

                 passed
                 been
                 [?been] ⎱ ⎱   d ⎱
          My days had [?passe ⎰d] secure ⎰ from misery
                 [?]   so keen
</pre>

But when he heard her thus with blamings greater
And own'd weakness all the way ?
His hand had wrought & in the hour
Saw her lips move his name & deeds to bless
At such a sight he could no more suppress
The feelings that did within his bosom
And weeping loud, in this extreme distress
He cried "Oh bless thee now that thou shouldst be in
I do not wish — forgive me. now forgive

To speak the change that once within her wrongs
Nature by sign or sound made no essay
At sudden joy surprized expiring thought
And every mortal pang dissolved away
Borne gently to a bed there dead she lay
Her pale while over her husband bent
A look was in her face that seem'd to say
By sight I praying touch'd my sight
Peace to my parting soul the ——
But not to him —— burn'd on other ——tent
* Meanwhile — She slept in peace
Which——
For him ——— his pulse ——— slept
And when at table placed the bread he took
To break it from his falt'ring hands it dropp'd
While on those hands he cast a mournful look
His tears were never silent, sleep forsook
His eyelids
All through the night the floor beneath his chamber trembled to his shuddering bed
And oft he groan'd aloud "oh God that I were dead
* Turn to the beginning
2 Turn to the end

766 But when he heard her thus with labouring breath
767 And pain & weakness tell the wretchedness
768 His hand had wrought & in the hour of death
769 Saw her lips move his name & deeds to bless
770 At such a sight he could no more suppress
   F⟩ that ⟩ within his bosom strive
771 ~~The f~~⟨eelings which ⟩ did ~~in his heart revive~~
772 And, weeping loud, in this extreme distress
      !⟩
773 He cried Oh bless me now ⟩ that thou should'st live
774 I do not wish or ask, forgive me, now forgive

775 To speak the change that voice within her wrought
776 Nature by sign or sound made no essay
777 A sudden joy surprized expiring thought
778 And every mortal pang dissolved away
  These bore her to a couch where dead she
779 Borne gently to a bed there dead she lay
  Yet still while over her
780 ~~Silently o'er her face~~ the husband bent
   in face that ⟩
781 A look was ~~on~~ her ~~lips~~ which ⟩ seem'd to say
    t⟩
 Be bless⟨ed by sight of ~~parting soul~~ thee by heaven is
        s ⟩
782 Comfort to thee my ~~dying thoughts have~~ ⟩ sent
       [?]⟩
 Peace to my parting soul the fullness [?of]⟩ content
783 But not to him it seem'd on other things in=
         = tent
 * Meanwhile She slept in peace
 Which seeing [?it] his very hands did drop
       s ⟩
784 ~~For him alternate throbbed~~ his pulse ⟩ & ~~stopp'd~~
      throbb'd⟩
     [?] ⟩& stopt
785 And when at table placed the bread he took
786 To break it, from his faltering hands it dropp'd
 And Then
787 ~~While~~ on those hands he cast a rueful look
788 His ears were never silent, sleep forsook
  burning that were stiff as lead
789 His ~~nerveless~~ eyelids ~~stiffen'd even as lead~~
790 All through the night the floor beneath him shook
791 And chamber trembled to his shuddering bed
792 And oft he groan'd aloud "oh God that I were
         dead!"—2
 * Turn to the beginning   shuddering in his bed
 2 Turn to the end   that were stiff as [?lead]

782 sent] Retained for use as the last word in the revised line.
783/784 The asterisk directs to DW's pointer at page foot: "*Turn to the beginning"; the word "Meanwhile" indicates that the stanza beginning "Meanwhile the aged soldier o'er the Plain," which is copied opposite the opening stanzas of ASP, Part Second, should be inserted here. See additions to MS. 2, 39ᵛ, below. The words "She slept in peace" in MW's hand indicate that the stanza beginning "She slept in peace his pulses throbb'd and stopt" is to be inserted here in future copying. MW has copied this stanza in MS. 3, 51ᵛ. See MS. 4, app. crit. to ll. 630–631. The line beginning "Which seeing" may be a revision of l. 786.
792 DW's figure 2 directs to her pointer at page foot: "2 Turn to the end." There we find the stanza beginning "Thus pass'd for him that lamentable night," which was evidently to be inserted after l. 792. See the lines below l. 828.

63

Nor bred in solitude unus'd to haunt
The throngs of men: did the good cottage pair
Repine, mortal[ity] last claim to grant.
And in due time on the [bier] [others] came bear
Her body to the distant church, their care
The husband think'd nor one hour more remain'd
Under their roof but to the open air
And fields, a but then not to be sustain'd
He carried, in his breast, dreadful quiet [enjoy'd]

But they, alone & tranquil call'd to mend
Events so various recollection ran
Through each occurrence & the [signs] combin'd
And while his [silent] looks & twice they man
And trembling hands they cried "He is the man
Thought did those [loons] of silent woe avail
Though we deplore it much as any can
"He [the] they cried "must weigh him in her [scale]
Most fit it is that we enfold thy [awful] tale.

[Enquirm'd] of purpose, [ceaseless] and prepar'd
[The] worse was [burning]
Not without [pleasure] to the city strait
He went, & all which he had done declar'd
And from your hands he added now I wait
Nor let them linger long, the murderer's fate
Nor ineffectual was that piteous claim
[Roused to the sentence blood that]
which ends the tale.
The pangs which from [thy] a [guilty] came
[How] who of [guilt] bear it the [violated] [name]

[Towards the city feeble & prepar'd]
[they went & their] [to] the magistrate
his crime with full confession he declared

793   Nor bred in solitude unus'd to haunt
794   The throngs of men: did *this good cottage pair*
795   *Repine mortality's last claim to grant*
796   *And in due time with due observance bear*
797   *Her body to the distant church, their care*
798   *The husband thank'd nor one hour more remain'd*
799   *Under their roof but to the open air*
800   *And fields, a burthen not to be sustain'd*
801   *He carried, in his breast a dreadful quiet reign'd*

802   *But they, alone & tranquil call'd to mind*
803   *Events so various, recollection ran*
804   *Through each occurrence & the links combin'd*
805   *And while his silence, looks, & voice they scan*
806   *And trembling hands they cried "He is the man"*
807   *Nought did those looks of silent woe avail*
808   *"Though we deplore it much as any can*
809   *The law" they cried "must weigh him in her scale*
810   *Most fit it is that we unfold this woful tale.*

8 1   *Confirm'd of purpose, fearless and prepared*
      The corse was buried
812   *~~Not without pleasure~~ to the city strait*
813   *He went, & all which he had done declar'd*
814   *And from your hands he added now I wait*
815   *Nor let them linger long, the murderer's fate*
816   *Nor ineffectual was that piteous claim*
        he ⎫
  sed ⎱ *And be* ⎰ *~~the sentence blest that~~*
817   *Blest* ⎰ *~~be for once the stroke which~~ ends tho' late*
        a   *this guilty creature*
818   *The pangs which from ~~thy halls of terror~~ came*

819   *~~Thou who of Justice bear'st the violated name.~~* ⎰

    Towards the City fearless & prepar'd
    He went & there before
    ~~His way he bent and to~~ the magistrate
    His crime with full confession he declared

---

817   *tho'*] The "o" appears to have been reinforced.

They left him hung on high in iron case
~~Warning for~~ the men, unthinking & untaught
~~That~~ ~~~~
~~And such~~ come to gaze upon his face
And to that spot which told ~~~~ sought
Women & children were by fathers wrought
And now some hundred sufferers driven perchance
That way, when into storm the sky is wrought
Upon ~~his~~ swinging corpse his eye may glance
And drop as he once dropp'd in miserable
                                        trance.

~~~~
We ~~~~ The Endeavour ~~~~ ~~~~
Thus pass'd for him that lamentable night.
And Rachel seeing that they vainly tried
To ease his sufferings with the morning light,

Renewed his journey o'er the champaign wide
Yet in the cottage by the sailor's side.
Or by his daughter's bed the old man stay'd
And he and his unhappy son supplied
The little wealth they had & they both pray'd
That in a decent grave the body might be laid
~~Thus pass'd ~~~~ that lamentable night~~
~~And Rachel seeing that this vainly tried~~
~~To ease his sufferings & two days before~~

We had been fellow-travellers I knew
That he was in this neighbourhood and now
Delighted found him here in the cool shade
He lay his pack &c

Confessing him ~~~~ be to the city went
And there declared before the magistrate
His crime & ~~~~ nearing the event
~~~~

820 *They left him hung on high in iron case*
         Warning for
821 ~~*And dissolute*~~ *men, unthinking & untaught*
822 ~~*Planted their festive booths beneath his face*~~
        And such would come to gaze upon his face
823 *And to that spot which idle* ~~*thousands*~~ *sought*
           numbers
824 *Women & children were by fathers brought*
825 *And now some kindred sufferer driven perchance*
826 *That way when into storm the sky is wrought*
        e ⎫
      that ⎭
827 *Upon* ~~*his*~~ *swinging corpse his eye may glance*
828 *And drop as he once dropp'd in miserable*
                 trance.

The End
   Thus passd
   He passd a second lamentable
Thus pass'd for him that lamentable night
And Rachel seeing that they vainly tried
To ease his sufferings with the morning light
       er ⎫
Renewed his ⎭ *journey o'er the champaign wide*
Yet in the cottage by the sailor's side
Or by his daughter's bed the old man stay'd
And he and his unhappy son supplied
The little wealth they had, & they both pray'd
That in a decent grave the body might be
                 laid

   Thus passed fr him that lamentable night
   And Rachel seeing that they vainly tried
   * To ease his sufferings

   Confirm'd in mind he to the city went
   And there declared before the magistrate
   His crime & the whole manner of the event

---

828 See note to l. 792. The lines beginning "two days before," which can be seen in the photograph, belong to work on *The Ruined Cottage*, MS. D, the full copy of which begins on the opposite recto. For an account of that MS see Jonathan Wordsworth, *The Music of Humanity* (London, 1969), esp. 23–28.

Additions to MS. 2

[Inside front cover]
And now she saw a road before them & a wain
He [?lovd] the   [? ?]
But by [?his]   [? ?]
  B ⎫
[?]⎰y loneliness, & goodness & kind deeds
The rigors of [?his ?] oer [?]
His fears & gloomy thoughts & this [?]
That
[?Th]

[11ᵛ]

W ⎫   thus they travelled
[?]⎰hile ~~they were trave~~lling he began to tell
   Erelon this
By this the old man had begun to tell
That he had been a soldier—they have [?given]
A pension to me I was living well
In my own home wherein I have [?] & [?]
[?With][?]

[12ʳ]

Meanwhile this aged man began to tell
   [———?———] Whence he was journeying [?]
         fe ⎫
His means & way of living⎰—God has given
~~Much trouble sorrow to me~~ to [?me]
   My share of sorrow
~~To me much sorrow said~~ he but tis well
     three ⎫
With two ⎰ days [?]

Meanwhile the Soldier had begun to tell
[?Where] he was journeying—God sends
             has given

   Inside front cover   The ink has been washed away from the center of this passage.
   11ᵛ   This draft seems to reverse most of WW's earlier thinking about the relationship between authority and men who had served their country, the soldier and sailor.

<pre>
             A heavy trouble to
                   trouble ⎫   s⎫
My share of [?] ⎬ to me but til ⎬ well [?   ?   ]
                   [?helpl] ⎫
                   [?heartl] ⎬ ess
</pre>
With three days weary journey I have striven
And limp'd thus far to meet—

[39ʳ]

<pre>
                                 fair
</pre>
But come she cried the sky is clear & bright
And safely we our journey may pursue.
So forth he came into the open light
And look'd one look towards the east: but do
<pre>
              [?can] ⎫
</pre>
Whateer he [?] ⎬ he must the woman view
He stood & trembled both with grief & fear

[39ᵛ]

Meanwhile the aged Soldier o'er the Plain
Towards the cottage Inn his steps did bend
And from the man returning with the wain
He learned his daughter's miserable end
When to the house he came and found his friend
And heard the cause for which he linger'd there
Much joy did with the old Man's sorrow blend,
And of his son he begg'd with fervent prayer

Heart-struck had Rachael heard the haven's name
Near which in that lone creek the body lay
But never once into her thoughts it came
That it was he who did her husband slay
And she & the old Soldier all that day
Not knowing how they did their purpose thwart
Strove all they could his anguish to allay
But of the woman he with bursting heart
Entreated evermore that she would thence depart

[79ᵛ]

The Soldiers Widow lingered in the Cot
And when he rose he thanked her pious care
Thro' which his Wife to that kind shelter brought

39ᵛ   The sailor is actually a son-in-law of the soldier in this version of the plot. In the second stanza a complicated plot is envisaged. The sailor has murdered the husband of Rachael, who is now the substitute for the Female Vagrant. WW was trying to compose a new story for her, having published *The Female Vagrant* in *Lyrical Ballads* 1798. See *EY*, 256–257.
79ᵛ   MW's hand, notebook inverted. See MS. 4 transcription, note to ll. 48–50.

Died in his arms he breathed with those thanks a prayer
    He
_∧*Breathed for her, & for that merciful Pair.*
The Corse interred not one hour he remaind
Under their roof but to the open air
And fields a burthen not to be sustaind
He bore ; within his breast a dreadful quiet reigned.

               ly ⎫
Confirmed of purpose fearless & ⎰ prepared
For act & suffring to the city straight
He journeyed

     and
A Sailor he who many a wretchd hour has told
   Has told
For landg after labour hard thro years uncounted
 Thro ⎫
[?]⎰ *years uncounted & for what was his reward*

Incidents upon Salisbury Plain (1841)

Transcription of MS. 4, with variant readings from MS. 3

GUILT AND SORROW;

OR,

INCIDENTS UPON SALISBURY PLAIN

A number of special features make MSS. 3 and 4 difficult to represent in transcription, and the following remarks should therefore be noted carefully. The first problem is the make-up of MS. 4. For some parts of the manuscript it is possible to trace no less than three stages of composition. On nine occasions, where WW corrected lines so heavily that they became illegible, he transferred the revisions to another sheet and then stuck this sheet over the original. Often, however, the poet was not even satisfied with the stuck-on sheets, so corrections were made on these also. In transcription, the stages of composition have been identified as follows, strictly in order of composition:

MS. 4   The basic fair-copy text, chiefly in the hand of MW.
      4a   Fair-copy sheets of scrap letter paper, stuck over heavily corrected sections of MS. 4, found at l. 38 of the Advertisement, and ll. 1, 74, 99, 208, 594, 599, 612, and 621 of the poem.

The situation with the opening lines of the poem, however, is still more complicated. Here one can distinguish:

MS. 4   The basic fair-copy text, chiefly in the hand of MW.
      4a   The fair copy of ll. 1–14 made of scrap paper and stuck over MS. 4.
      4b   A second fair copy, on a separate sheet, sewn in when the manuscript was finally made up.

The entire text of these manuscripts is transcribed below.

The second problem concerns the presentation of MS. 3. MS. 3 is a copy of *Guilt and Sorrow*, ll. 541 to the end, in the hand of MW. MS. 3a is a fair copy of ll. 482–513, in the hand of MW also, preserved on a loose sheet. Neither manuscript warrants transcription, since the variants between them and MS. 4 are for the most part minor. These readings are recorded in an *apparatus criticus*, where readings from MS. 3a are identified as such, and all unlabeled readings are those of MS. 3. MSS. 3 and 3a may be assumed to agree with the fair-copy base text of MS. 4 unless variants are noted. The manuscripts may be assumed to be in MW's hand unless the hand is otherwise identified, and therefore, to avoid needless elaboration, all citations in the *apparatus* are printed in roman type.

Two details may be mentioned about the transcription of MS. 4 itself. First, it will be noted that in contrast to the earlier transcriptions, punctuation marks are shown as deleted or revised. Uncharacteristically Wordsworth himself went over the manuscript at a late date, revising the punctuation and occasionally registering second thoughts about a revision. Second, one symbol used in these transcriptions here is not found in the earlier ones. Square brackets with blank space between [   ] indicate a word obliterated by the sealing wax used to stick on the small pieces of paper described above as MS. 4a. In almost every case the word can be supplied, but it sometimes cannot be seen.

The following abbreviations are used in the *apparatus criticus*:

alt	Alternate reading; the original reading was apparently not deleted.
del	Reading deleted.
del to	Reading changed to another reading. A typical variant in MS. 3 will be recorded thus: 391 tree] bush *del to* stump *del* This means that for "tree" in line 391 of MS. 4, MS. 3 read "bush" which was deleted in favor of "stump" which was then also deleted.
illeg	illegible.
P	Page proof of *Guilt and Sorrow* (1842) at the University of Virginia Library (see Introduction, pp. 14–15).
P2	Second-stage page proof of *Guilt and Sorrow* (1842) at Dove Cottage (see Introduction, pp. 14–15).
del to . . . P	The reading in page proof has been changed to another reading; the hand of the alteration is indicated in parentheses.

Corrections of page proof which merely restore manuscript readings, uncorrected proof variants of readings identical in manuscript and the 1842 text, and queries by the press proofreader are not recorded.

The text of *Guilt and Sorrow* which follows is taken from the 1842 *Poems, Chiefly of Early and Late Years*. All variant readings in the authorized editions up to the final edition of 1849–1850 are recorded in the *apparatus criticus*. A number of typographical errors, especially noticeable in the badly printed edition of 1846 and in the reissue of 1849, have not been recorded. The following abbreviations are used:

1845 *The Poems of William Wordsworth* (1 vol.; London, 1845).
1846 *The Poetical Works of William Wordsworth* (7 vols.; London, 1846).
1849 *The Poetical Works of William Wordsworth* (6 vols.; London, 1849–1850).

(The following editions were reissues and contain no *G & S* variants:
1847 *Poems* [1 vol.], reissue of 1845;
1849 *Poems* [1 vol.], reissue of 1847;
1849 *Poetical Works* [7 vols.], reissue of 1846.)

~~Advertisement~~

              one

1   *Not less than* ~~two~~ *thirds of the following Poem,*

2   *tho' it has from time to time been altered in*

3   *the expression* } *was published so far back as the*

4   *year 1798—*} *under the title of the "Female Vagrant."*

    e }   *an apology seems*

5   *That* } *Extract is of such length that* ~~it seems to~~

    ~~needful~~   *to be required*   *here;*

6   ~~need an~~*apology for reprinting it,but it was*

    ~~fit~~

7   *necessary to restore it* ~~here~~ *to its original position*

    or

    the }

8   *or* } *rest would have been unintelligible. The*

                           1794,

9   *whole was written before the close of the year* ~~1795~~*;*

          detail,

    and I will ~~add~~*, rather as matter of literary*   ~~cannot be of im~~

10   ~~How it came to be so long suppressed is of no im~~

    any importance biography than for any other reason, ~~the~~ *under what*

11   ~~portance to the Reader ; but it may not be impro-~~

    circumstances it was produced.

12   ~~per to mention under what circumstances it was~~

13   ~~composed.~~ [*During the latter part of the summer*

14   *Of 1793 having passed a Month in the Isle of Wight*

15   *in view of the Fleet which was then preparing*

16   *for Sea off Portsmouth, at the commencement of*

17   *the War, I left the place with melancholy forebodings.*

                 r }

            Was }

    T }   *was* }

18   *t* ∫*he American, the* } *then fresh in memory, &* ~~I felt~~

19   ~~that~~ *the struggle which was beginning, & which*

20   *many thought would be brought to a speedy close*

21   *by the irresistible Arms of Great Britain being*

                             , }

22   *added to those of the Allies,* } *I was assured in my*

23   *own mind would be of long continuance, & productive* [1^v]

[Note on fly title of page proof] Mr Bradbury is requested to send a revise of *this* Poem. And in future is desired to send back the MS. Copy along with each proof. *P* (MW)

  16 pendant] *del to* pendent *P* (John Carter)

  23 looks] looked *del to* looked, *P* (WW)

Advertisement] Underlined in MS.

  1   The poem has been copied by MW, save for ll. 199–306 and 335–446 inclusive, which are in an unidentified hand (see Introduction, p. 16). All corrections not by WW are by MW, unless otherwise noted (save for some revisions in the Advertisement in the hand of John Carter).

  13   The bracket is WW's.

ADVERTISEMENT.

Not less than one-third of the following poem, though
it has from time to time been altered in the expression,
was published so far back as the year 1798, under the
title of "The Female Vagrant." The extract is of such
[5]   length that an apology seems to be required for reprinting
it here; but it was necessary to restore it to its original
position, or the rest would have been unintelligible. The
whole was written before the close of the year 1794, and
I will detail, rather as matter of literary biography than for
[10]   any other reason, the circumstances under which it was
produced.

During the latter part of the summer of 1793, having
passed a month in the Isle of Wight, in view of the fleet
which was then preparing for sea off Portsmouth at the
[15]   commencement of the war, I left the place with melancholy
forebodings. The American war was still fresh in memory.
The struggle which was beginning, and which many
thought would be brought to a speedy close by the irresistible
arms of Great Britain being added to those of the allies,
[20]   I was assured in my own mind would be of long continuance,

ADVERTISEMENT.] ADVERTISEMENT, PREFIXED TO THE FIRST EDITION OF THIS POEM, PUB-
LISHED IN 1842. *1845–*
6 here;] here: *1845–*

poss

24 *of distress & misery beyond all* [?calc]} *ible calculation.*
25 *This conviction was the result of the spirit which*
26 *I had witnessed in revolutionary France during a*
27 *long residence in that country. After leaving the*
28 *Isle of Wight I spent two days in wandering on foot*

29 *over Salisbury plain, which,} tho' cultivation was*

rough

30 *then widely spread* [?thro] } *parts of it, had, upon the*

much   ~~desolate and~~

31 *whole a*ʌ*more*ʌ*impressive appearance than it*
32 *wears at present. The monuments & traces*

scattered in abundance over that

33 *of antiquity*ʌ~~*with which that*~~ *region* ~~*abounds*~~*, led*
34 *me unavoidably to compare what we know or guess*
35 *of those remote times, with certain aspects of modern*
36 *society, particularly in what concerns the afflictions*

Of those reflections

37 *& calamaties to which the poor are subject* }ʌ~~*Out of*~~

T}   Stanzas were

38 ~~*those reflections rose*~~ *t* }*he following* ~~*Poem which*~~ [   ]

the result of those reflections, & whatever may be the dem[?erits]

39 ~~*now offered to the Public without any apology,*~~ [?though]

that, in some   that this   of the production, some readers

40 ~~*in many respects it*~~ʌ~~*stands in need of one I am*~~ [?only]

will I hope set a value upon it not [?however to acknowledge]

41 ~~*too conscious. But I may be allowed*~~ʌ~~*to say that as*~~

that I cannot but set some value upon

42 ~~*a memorial of that period of my life the production*~~

not merely for what it is in itself but

were }   early

43 [?] }~~*it merely*~~ *as a memorial of that period of my*

;} nor ~~I cannot~~ I forbear to add that it

44 *life* } ~~*& from a remembrance of its having*~~ *acted*
45 *upon the youthful imagination of my friend Coleridge*
46 *in a way that he used to speak of with much*
47 *delight.*
48 *In conclusion it may be proper to say*
49 *that, of the local features described, two which need not be*

desolate parts

50 *particularised, are taken from other* ~~*desolate parts*~~ *of England.*

38–50 [4a]

refle }

t} ~~Of those produ~~}~~ctions~~

ʌT}he following Stanzas were the result, ~~of those reflections,~~

---

45 my] *del to* [h]is *P* (?WW)
48 he] *del to* he, *P* (?WW)

and productive of distress and misery beyond all possible calculation. This conviction was pressed upon me by having been a witness, during a long residence in revolutionary France, of the spirit which prevailed in that country.

[25] After leaving the Isle of Wight, I spent two days in wandering on foot over Salisbury Plain, which, though cultivation was then widely spread through parts of it, had upon the whole a still more impressive appearance than it now retains.

[30] The monuments and traces of antiquity, scattered in abundance over that region, led me unavoidably to compare what we know or guess of those remote times with certain aspects of modern society, and with calamities, principally those consequent upon war, to which, more than other

[35] classes of men, the poor are subject. In those reflections, joined with some particular facts that had come to my knowledge, the following stanzas originated.

In conclusion, to obviate some distraction in the minds of those who are well acquainted with Salisbury Plain,

[40] it may be proper to say, that of the features described as belonging to it, one or two are taken from other desolate parts of England.

---

36 with some] with *1845–*

26–27 though cultivation was then widely spread through parts of it] In his influential *Stonehenge: A Temple Restor'd to the British Druids* (London, 1740), 1, William Stukeley remarked on the cultivation of the plain: "great encroachments have been made upon it by the plough, which threatens the ruin of this fine champain, and of all the monuments of antiquity thereabouts." For the Wordsworths' reactions to the Plain in 1841 see *MWL*, 246: "cultivation going on in many parts of the Plain takes sadly from the poetical feelings we had so *elaborately* attached to that region."

& whatever may be the demerits of the production, some
readers will, I hope, set a value upon it not merely
for what it is in itself but as a memorial of that

early period of my life ; n *or can I forbear to add*
that it acted upon the youthful mind of my Friend
Coleridge in a way that he used to speak of with delight.
to obviate some distraction in the minds of those who are well acquainted with Salisbury Plain
In conclusion, it may be proper to say, that of the
one or
real features described, two which need not be particularized,
are taken from other desolate parts of England

38–50   [4a] The long line beginning "to obviate" actually ends with "acquainted with," and "Salisbury Plain" is doubled back.

[1ʳ]

1

      lonely   *upon Sarum's Plain*
1 *stet A Traveller on the skirts of Sarum's Plain*
               —[?alone]
    Pursued his lonely way with feet half of figure spare
        : } *lonesome*   *bare*
2 *Pursued his way,— } a Man with feet half bare*
    Stooping his gait yet but not as   *as if to gain*
               limped
3 *Propped on a tremulous staff, he walked͵in pain*
    Help from the staff he bore, for mien and air

                    ; }
4 *With labour worn, meagre with scanty fare, }*
         tho }
    Were hardy, [?] }ugh his cheek seem'd worn with care;
5 *His temples just betrayed their silver hair*
         to }   *and*
    As if of years come} to come or time long fled
6 *Beneath a kerchief's edge that wrapped his head*
            hung }
    Down from his temples [?] } some thin grey hair
7 *To fence from off his face the nipping air*

               ; }
    In straggling locks— } stuck oer with patch and shred
8 *Stuck miserably oer with patch & shred*
    tattered   *retained*
9 *His ragged coat scarce shewed the Soldiers faded red.*

    2

    It cheared him not thus journeying on to see
    Little he rested thus journeying on to see
    A }
    A } stately Inn from mean approach secure
10 *Thus journeying on he chanced an Inn to see*
    That stood alone as mid a dreary moor   *the wildest moor*
11 *In spot as lonesome as the loneliest moor*
    Admittance
12 *But entrance none was there for such as he*
13 *No board inscribed the needy to allure*
14 *No bush proclaimed to aged, sick, or poor*

1–14 [4a]

    1

    A Traveller on the skirt of Sarum's Plain
          vagrant
    Pursued his vagrant way with feet half bare

1–36 See the Prefatory Note for an explanation of the various versions of these lines.
3   *tremulous*] Underlined in MS.

GUILT AND SORROW;

OR,

INCIDENTS UPON SALISBURY PLAIN.

I.

A TRAVELLER on the skirt of Sarum's Plain
Pursued his vagrant way, with feet half bare;
Stooping his gait, but not as if to gain
Help from the staff he bore; for mien and air
Were hardy, though his cheek seemed worn with care   [5]
Both of the time to come, and time long fled:
Down fell in straggling locks his thin grey hair;
A coat he wore of military red
But faded, and stuck o'er with many a patch and shred.

II.

While thus he journeyed, step by step led on,   [10]
He saw and passed a stately inn, full sure
That welcome in such house for him was none.
No board inscribed the needy to allure
Hung there, no bush proclaimed to old and poor

No title between Advertisement and text 1845, 1849. Stanzas unnumbered 1846.

---

1   The Fenwick note to this poem reads: "Unwilling to be unnecessarily particular, I have assigned this Poem to the dates 93 & 94, but in fact much of the 'Female Vagrant's' story was composed at least two years before. All that relates to her sufferings as a Soldier's wife in America & her condition of mind during her voyage home, were faithfully taken from the report made to me of her own case by a friend who had been subjected to the same trials & affected in the same way. Mr. Coleridge, when I first became acquainted with him, was so much impressed with this Poem, that it would have encouraged me to publish the whole as it then stood; but the Mariner's fate appeared to me so tragical as to require a treatment more subdued & yet more strictly applicable in expression than I had at first given to it. This fault was corrected nearly 50 years afterwards when I determined to publish the whole. It may be worth while to remark that tho' the incidents of this attempt do only in a small degree produce each other, & it deviates accordingly from the general rule by which narrative pieces ought to be governed, it is not therefore wanting in continuous hold upon the mind or in unity which is effected by the identity of moral interest that places the two personages upon the same footing in the reader's sympathies. My ramble over many parts of Salisbury plain put me, as mentioned in the preface, upon writing this Poem, & left upon my mind imaginative impressions the force of w^h. I have felt to this day. From that district I proceeded to Bath, Bristol, & so to the banks of the Wye, where I took again to travelling on foot. In remembrance of that part of my journey, which was in 93. I began the verses 'Five years have passed &—'" (DCP, in the hand of Dora Wordsworth).

Stooping his gait, but not as if to gain
Help from the staff he bore, for mien & air
Were hardy, tho' his cheek seemed worn with care
Both of the time to come & time long fled:
   fell in straggling locks his
Down ~~from his temples hung some~~ thin grey hair
 A coat he wore of military red
~~In straggling looks   stuck oer with patch & shred~~
  But faded, & stuck oer with many a patch & shred
~~His tattered coat retained the Soldier's faded red.~~

2

     he journeyed step by step led on
While thus ~~in thoughtful mood he journeyed on~~
    d⎰ *passed a stately Inn*
He saw an ⎱ ~~Inn that cheered him~~ not—full sure
   welcom in such house for him
That ~~entrance there, for such as he~~, was none
No board inscribed the needy to allure
[?Hung]   ~~hung out, proclaimed to poor~~
~~Hung there, nor bush proclaimed to old, or poor~~
   ~~Was~~ Hung there, no bush proclaim to old & poor

1–14 [4b]

Incidents on Salisbury Plain

1

A Traveller on the skirt of Sarum's Plain
Pursued his way, with vagrant feet half bare;
Stooping his gait, but ~~if~~ not as if to gain
Help from the Staff he bore, for mien & air
Were hardy, tho' his cheek seemed worn with care
Both of the time to come, & time long fled:
Down fell in straggling locks his thin grey hair;
A coat he wore of military red
But faded, & stuck oer with many a patch & shred.

2

While thus he journeyed step by step led on

He saw & passed a stately Inn—⎰ full sure
That welcome in such house for him, was none.
No board inscribed the needy to allure
Hung there; no bush proclaimed to old & poor

15–18 [1ʳ]

   ~~Or~~ And   :⎱
15 ~~And~~ desolate, "Here you will find a friend.⎰"
    pendant
16 The ~~gilded~~ grapes glittered above the door—
17 On he must pace, perchance till night descend,
18 Where'er the bare white roads their dreary lines extend.

15–18 [4b]

    will⎱
And desolate, "Here you may⎰ find a friend"!
       :⎱
The pendant grapes glittered above the door,⎰ —

And desolate, "Here you will find a friend!"   [15]
The pendent grapes glittered above the door;—
On he must pace, perchance 'till night descend,
Where'er the dreary roads their bare white lines extend.

On he must pace, perchance till night descend,
                                its
Whe'er the bare white roads dreary lines extend.

[1ᵛ]

3

            e
19   *The gathering clouds grow red with stormy fire*
     ~~To halt were profitless~~
20   ~~*That Inn he long hath past, & wearily*~~
      ~~He kept his onward course:~~
21   ~~*Measures his lonely way: the distant spire*~~
      In streaks diverging wide & mounting high
      That Inn he long had passed the distant spire
                   [e]⎫
22   *Which oft as he looked back had fix[?]*⎰*d his eye*
23   *Was lost, tho' still he looks in the blank sky;*
            ~~from~~⎫
   ~~Whether in hollow or on~~⎰ ~~rising ground~~
24   ~~*By thirst & hunger pressed he gazed around*~~
     Perplexed⎫
   He scarce⎰*& comfortless he gazed around*
25   *And scarce could any trace of man descry*
                  & stretching
26   *Save ~~dreary~~ corn-fields stretched as without bound*
27   *But where the Sower dwelt, was no where to be found.*

4

28   *No tree was there, no meadow's pleasant green*
29   *No brook to wet his lips, or soothe his ear*
30   *Long files of corn-stacks here & there were seen*
31   *But not one dwelling-place his heart to chear*
32   *Some Labourer, thought he, may perchance be near*
33   *And so he sent a feeble shout, in vain;*
34   *No voice made answer, he could only hear*
      Winds rustling over plots of unripe grain
35   ~~*The thin grass whistling round him on the plain*~~
      Or whistling thro' thin grass along the unfurrowed plain
36   ~~*Or Lark that on his ear wasted a joyous strain*~~

19–36 [4b]

3

The gathering clouds grew red with stormy fire
    d⎫
In streaks g⎰*iverging wide & mounting high;*
That Inn he long had passed; the distant spire,
                 is⎫
Which oft as he looked back had fixed her⎰*eye,*
          turn'd
Was lost, tho' still he looks, in the blank sky.
Perplexed & comfortless he gazed around,
And scarce could any trace of Man descry
    corn-⎫
Save dreary⎰*fields stretched & stretching without bound;*
                 n⎫
But where the Sower dwelt was h⎰*o where to be found.*

III.

The gathering clouds grew red with stormy fire,
In streaks diverging wide and mounting high;   [20]
That inn he long had passed; the distant spire,
Which oft as he looked back had fixed his eye,
Was lost, though still he looked, in the blank sky.
Perplexed and comfortless he gazed around,
And scarce could any trace of man descry,   [25]
Save cornfields stretched and stretching without bound;
But where the sower dwelt was nowhere to be found.

IV.

No tree was there, no meadow's pleasant green,
No brook to wet his lip or soothe his ear;
Long files of corn-stacks here and there were seen,   [30]
But not one dwelling-place his heart to cheer.
Some labourer, thought he, may perchance be near;
And so he sent a feeble shout—in vain;
No voice made answer, he could only hear
Winds rustling over plots of unripe grain,   [35]
Or whistling thro' thin grass along the unfurrowed plain.

4

No tree was there, no meadows pleasant green,
         or ⎫
No brook to wet his, [?] ⎬ soothe his ear;
         ⎭
       files
Long of corn-stacks here & there were seen
But not one dwelling-place his heart to chear.
              be ⎫
Some Labourer, thought he, may perchance [?] ⎬ near;
               ⎭
          —⎫
And so he sent a feeble shout , ⎬ in vain;
            ⎭
No voice made answer; he could only hear
           ain,
Winds rustling over plots of unripe ~~green~~
     in ⎫
Or whistling thro' the ⎬ grass along the unfurrowed plain.
        ⎭

5

37   Long had he fancied, each successive slope
38   Concealed some Cottage whither he might turn
39   <u>And rest</u>;—but now along heaven's darkening cope
                           borne;
40   The crows rushed by in eddies, homeward ~~bound~~
                        spreading
41   Thus warned, he sought some shepherds ~~guardian~~ thorn
42   Or hovel from the storm to shield his head [?]
43   But sought in vain; for now all wild, forlorn,
44   And vacant, a huge waste around him spread
         T⎫ *thought he tonight must be my*
45   ~~Ah! me,~~ *t* ⎬*he* ~~wet cold ground~~*must be his only bed*
                         only
     The wet cold ground though he must be ~~tonight~~ my bed.

6

46   And be it so—for to the chill night shower
47   And the sharp wind his head he oft hath bared;
48   A Sailor he, who many a wretched hour
49   Hath told; for landing, after labour hard
50   Three years endured in hope of just reward,
51   He to an armed fleet was forced away
52   By Seamen, who perhaps themselves had shared
             '⎫
53   Like fate— ⎬ was hurried off, a helpless prey,
             ⎭
        G⎫
54   ~~For years ag~~ ⎬ainst all that in <u>his</u> heart, or <u>theirs</u> perhaps, said nay.

[3ᵛ]

7

~~Alas, alas no spot so lonely is~~
~~But it salutes~~

---

42   Punctuation obliterated by ink blot.
45   *Ah! me*] Underlined in MS.
48–50   See Additions to MS. 2, 79ᵛ, above, for work on these lines at the back of that notebook.
54   *For years*] False start to the line by copying beginning of l. 55; underlining in MS.
54/55   False start to Stanza 7 by copying ll. 73–74.

V.

Long had he fancied each successive slope
Concealed some cottage, whither he might turn
And rest; but now along heaven's darkening cope
The crows rushed by in eddies, homeward borne.   [40]
Thus warned he sought some shepherd's spreading thorn
Or hovel from the storm to shield his head,
But sought in vain; for now, all wild, forlorn,
And vacant, a huge waste around him spread;
The wet cold ground, he feared, must be his only bed.   [45]

VI.

And be it so—for to the chill night shower
And the sharp wind his head he oft hath bared;
A Sailor he, who many a wretched hour
Hath told; for, landing after labour hard,
Three years endured in hope of just reward,   [50]
He to an armèd fleet was forced away
By seamen, who perhaps themselves had shared
Like fate; was hurried off, a helpless prey,
'Gainst all that in *his* heart, or theirs perhaps, said nay.

---

50 Three years] Full long *1845–*

55   *For years the work of carnage did not cease*
56   *And death's dire aspect daily he surveyed,*
57   *Death's ministers; then came his glad release,*
58   *And hope returned, & pleasure fondly made*

                    g⎫
59   *Her dwelling*⎰ *in his dreams. By Fancy's aid*

  stet   ~~around his neck~~
    in   *happy*   *his arms*
60   *The ~~happy~~ husband flies ~~his arms~~ to throw*   (stet)
         His arms[?,] and o'er, the and his prize-treasure
61   stet *Round his Wifes neck; ~~the prize of victory~~ laid*
                —the prize of victory laid
62   *In her full lap, he sees such sweet tears flow*
63   *As if thenceforth, nor pain nor trouble she could ~~flow~~ know*

                  8

           for *F*⎫   *that he had*
64   *Vain hope! ~~For,~~f* ⎰*raud took all ~~so hardly~~ earned,*
65   *The Lion roars, & gluts his tawny brood*
                  !⎫
66   *Even in the desart's heart,*⎰ *but he, returned,*
67   *Bears not to those he loves their needful food.*

              so⎫
         ~~in su~~ ⎰~~ch desperate~~
         ~~so fierce a~~
68   *His home approaching, but in such a mood*
69   *That from his sight his children might have run,*
70   *He met a Traveller, robbed him, shed his blood;*
71   *And when the miserable work was done*
72   *He fled, a Vagrant since,*⎱ *the Murderer's fate to shun.*
                ,⎰

[4ʳ]

                9

    ~~Thenceforth no spot of earth to him could be~~
             gave
    ~~So lonely but it brought some deadly pang~~
         7   *of earth*
73   ~~*Alas, alas, no spot so lonely is*~~
       From that day forth no place to him could be
      ~~*So lonely,but that the[ ]nce might come a pang*~~
74   ~~*But it salutes him with some deadly pang*~~
[?So ?–]   *But that thence might come a pang*

73–74 [4a]

                9

    From that day forth no place to him could be
    So lonely, but that thence might come a pang

---

                    y.⎫
75   *Brought from without to inward miseries*⎰
76   *Now, as he plodded on, with sullen clang*
77   *A sound of chains along the desert rang.*
                   t⎫
78   *He looked, & saw upon a gibbed*⎰ *high*

VII.

For years the work of carnage did not cease,   [55]
And death's dire aspect daily he surveyed,
Death's minister; then came his glad release,
And hope returned, and pleasure fondly made
Her dwelling in his dreams. By Fancy's aid
The happy husband flies, his arms to throw   [60]
Round his wife's neck; the prize of victory laid
In her full lap, he sees such sweet tears flow
As if thenceforth nor pain nor trouble she could know.

VIII.

Vain hope! for fraud took all that he had earned.
The lion roars and gluts his tawny brood   [65]
Even in the desert's heart; but he, returned,
Bears not to those he loves their needful food.
His home approaching, but in such a mood
That from his sight his children might have run,
He met a traveller, robbed him, shed his blood;   [70]
And when the miserable work was done
He fled, a vagrant since, the murderer's fate to shun.

IX.

From that day forth no place to him could be
So lonely, but that thence might come a pang
Brought from without to inward misery.   [75]
Now, as he plodded on, with sullen clang
A sound of chains along the desert rang;
He looked, and saw upon a gibbet high

79   *A human body that in irons swang*
80   *Uplifted by the tempest whirling by,*
81   *And hovering round it often did a raven fly.*

10

82   *It was a spectacle which none might view*
83   *In spot so savage, but with shuddering pain;*
84   *Nor only did for him at once renew*
85   *All he had feared from man, but rouzed a train*
86   *Of the mind's phantoms horrible as vain.*
87   *The stones, as if to cover him from day,*
88   *Rolled at his back, along the living plain;*
89   *He fell, & without sense or motion lay;*
          But ⎫
          [?] ⎬   trance was ⎫   ~~rose and~~
90   *And when the* [? ?] ⎬ *gone* ~~once more~~ *pursued his way.*
          ~~And feebly, the trance gone,~~   rose, &

[4ᵛ]

11

                    habitual
91   *As one whose brain demoniac phrensy fires*
          ~~fear trance dread~~
                    fit
92   *Owes to the* ~~fit~~ *in which his Soul hath tossed*
          ~~mood~~
                    fit
          when the ~~mood~~ retires
93   *Profounder quiet* ~~when that fit retires~~
          ~~Even so, the dire phantasm, which had crossed~~
94   ~~So now, in sudden vacancy quite lost~~
          His ⎫   s, ⎫   in sudden
          [–?–] ⎬ sense[?] ⎬ ~~now in vacancy quite lost~~
95   ~~The dire phatasma which his sense had crost~~
          Even so the dire phantasma which had crossed
          His sense, in sudden vacancy quite lost
96   *Left his mind still as a deep evening stream;*
97   *Nor if accosted now, in thought engrossed*
          Possessed, ~~and~~ or
98   ~~Moody or~~ *inly-troubled would he seem*
99   ~~To traveller who might talk of any casual theme~~

91–99 [4a]

                    demoniac
                    ~~habitual~~ ⎫
          As One whose brain [–?–] ⎬ phrensy fires

---

81 hovering] *del to* hovering, *P* (?WW)

---

91   The stuck-on sheet beginning l. 91 is postmarked on the face   RAMSG   OC   15   1841.
Fragments of another postmark are not decipherable. The sheet stuck on ll. 595ff is postmarked
on the reverse side   CAMBRIDGE   OC   12   1841. For sheet stuck on ll. 617ff the postmarks
on the reverse side read   KENDAL   OC   11   1841 and AMBLESIDE   OC   12   1841.
Wordsworth is clearly using any scrap of paper at hand for copying these few lines and tidying
up the manuscript.

A human body that in irons swang,
Uplifted by the tempest whirling by;   [80]
And, hovering, round it often did a raven fly.

X.

It was a spectacle which none might view,
In spot so savage, but with shuddering pain;
Nor only did for him at once renew
All he had feared from man, but roused a train   [85]
Of the mind's phantoms, horrible as vain.
The stones, as if to cover him from day,
Rolled at his back along the living plain;
He fell, and without sense or motion lay;
But, when the trance was gone, rose and pursued his way.   [90]

XI.

As one whose brain demoniac phrensy fires
Owes to the fit in which his soul hath tossed
Profounder quiet, when the fit retires,
Even so the dire phantasma which had crossed
His sense, in sudden vacancy quite lost,   [95]
Left his mind still as a deep evening stream.
Nor, if accosted now, in thought engrossed,
Moody, or inly troubled, would he seem
To traveller who might talk of any casual theme.

90 rose and] feebly *1845–*
91 demoniac] habitual *1845–*   phrensy] frensy *1849*

81   For WW's annotation, see note to l. 117 of *ASP*, above.

th   toss⎫
Owes to the fit in which his Soul ha[? ?]⎬ed
Profounder quiet when the fit retires,
Even so the dire phantasma which had crossed

e⎫
His senses⎬, in sudden vacancy quite lost,

;⎫
Left his mind still as a deep evening stream,⎬
Nor, if accosted now, in thought engrossed,
Moody, or inly troubled would he seem

n⎫
To Traveller who might talk of⎬ any casual theme.

[4ᵛ]

(Here print the stanza marked ~~twe~~ 12 which
follows after the next.)

~~12~~
~~13~~   ~~This Stanza to follow the next—~~

Hurtle &c

All—
100 ~~But~~ *all was cheerless to the horizons bound;*

—⎫
101 *The weary eye* ⎬ *which wheresoe'er it strays*
102 *Marks nothing but the red sun's setting round,*
103 *Or on the earth strange lines, in former days,*
104 *Left by gigantic arms,—at length surveys*
105 *What seems an antique Castle spreading wide;*
106 *Hoary & naked are its walls, & raise*

:+⎫
107 *Their brow sublime* ⎬ *in shelter there to bide*
108 *He turned, while* ~~pouring~~ *rain smoked thick on every side.*
        rain poured down smoking on

[5ʳ]

~~13~~   12
109 *Hurtle the clouds in deeper darkness piled,*

;⎫
110 *Gone is the Raven timely rest to seek:*⎬

W⎫
111 *He seemed the only Creature in the w* ⎬ild
112 *On whom the elements their rage might wreak,*

ose⎫   s⎫
113 *Save that the Bustard, of this* ⎬ *region* ⎬ *bleak*
114 *Shy tenant, seeing by* ~~the~~ *uncertain light*
        M⎫
115 *A m* ⎬an *there wandering, gave a mournful shriek,*
116 *And half upon the ground with strange affright*

y⎫
117 *Forced hard against the wind a thick unwieldl* ⎬y *flight.*
        All, all was cheerless & (as in the Staznza preceding)

110 Raven] *del to* raven *P* (WW)
113 Bustard] *del to* bustard *P* (WW)

108   The corrections are in Dora's hand.

XII.

Hurtle the clouds in deeper darkness piled, [100]
Gone is the raven timely rest to seek;
He seemed the only creature in the wild
On whom the elements their rage might wreak;
Save that the bustard, of those regions bleak
Shy tenant, seeing by the uncertain light [105]
A man there wandering, gave a mournful shriek,
And half upon the ground, with strange affright,
Forced hard against the wind a thick unwieldy flight.

XIII.

All, all was cheerless to the horizon's bound;
The weary eye—which, wheresoe'er it strays, [110]
Marks nothing but the red sun's setting round,
Or on the earth strange lines, in former days
Left by gigantic arms—at length surveys
What seems an antique castle spreading wide;
Hoary and naked are its walls, and raise [115]
Their brow sublime: in shelter there to bide
He turned, while rain poured down smoking on every side.

14

118   *Pile of Stone-henge! so proud to hint, yet keep*

119   *Thy secrets, thou that lov*e*st to stand & hear*

120   *The desert sounding to the whirlwind's sweep,*

121   *Inmate of lonesome Nature's endless year,*

        if [?since]   W
122   *Even*ₐ*if thou saws't the giant w* *ſicker rear*

123   *For sacrifice its throngs of living men,*

        W
124   *Before thy face did ever w* *ſretch appear*

125   *Who in his heart had groaned with deadlier pain*

        wanders wanders
126   ~~*Than he who travels now along thy bleak domain*~~

        y   are
        Than he who now, at night-fall treads this ⎰ bare ⎰ ~~domain~~
                                                               domain

[5ᵛ]

15

127   *Within that Fabric of mysterious form*

128   *Winds met in conflict, each by turns supreme;*

        And from its perilous shelter driven thro' storm
129   ~~*In fearful power — thence driven, thro' battering storm*~~

        And rain h   st
130   ~~*Two hours*~~ *he wildered on, no moon to [?]ſream*

                                           beam,
131   *From gulph of parting clouds, one friendly* ~~*gleam*~~

132   *Nor any friendly sound his footsteps led;*

133   *Once did the lightening's faint disastrous gleam*

            Disclose
            [——?——]   G g   -
134   ~~*Dis*~~[——?——]⎰ *a naked* [?]ſ*uidepost's double head,*
                              a doubtful

135   *Sight which, tho' lost at once,* ~~*some glimpse of*~~ *pleasure shed.*
                                          a doubtful

16

                                                    c
136   *No swinging sign-board creaked from* Ɠ*ottage elm*

                                                :⎱
137   *To stay his steps, with faintness overcome,* ⎰

138   *'Twas dark & void as ocean's watery realm*

139   *Roaring with storms, beneath night's starless gloom*[?,]

140   *No gypsy cowered oer fire of furze or broom,*

141   *No labourer watched his red kiln glaring bright*

---

120 desert sounding] *del to* Plain resounding *P* (WW)
121 year,] *del to* year; *P* (WW)
131 gulph] *del to* gulf *P* (John Carter)

---

134 *guidepost's*] Apparently first written as one word, then hyphenated.
138–143 The punctuation of these lines, save at 140, is not visible because of the stitching of the manuscript.

XIV.

Pile of Stone-henge! so proud to hint yet keep
Thy secrets, thou that lov'st to stand and hear
The Plain resounding to the whirlwind's sweep,   [120]
Inmate of lonesome Nature's endless year;
Even if thou saw'st the giant wicker rear
For sacrifice its throngs of living men,
Before thy face did ever wretch appear,
Who in his heart had groaned with deadlier pain   [125]
Than he who now at night-fall treads thy bare domain!

XV.

Within that fabric of mysterious form,
Winds met in conflict, each by turns supreme;
And, from its perilous shelter driven, through storm
And rain he wildered on, no moon to stream   [130]
From gulf of parting clouds one friendly beam,
Nor any friendly sound his footsteps led;
Once did the lightning's faint disastrous gleam
Disclose a naked guide-post's double head,
Sight which tho' lost at once a gleam of pleasure shed.   [135]

XVI.

No swinging sign-board creaked from cottage elm
To stay his steps with faintness overcome;
'Twas dark and void as ocean's watery realm
Roaring with storms beneath night's starless gloom;
No gipsy cowered o'er fire of furze or broom;   [140]
No labourer watched his red kiln glaring bright,

---

126 Than he who, tempest-driven, thy shelter now would gain. *1845–*
129 its perilous shelter driven] the perilous ground dislodged *1845–*
135 shed.] shed *1845–*
140 cowered] cower'd *1845–*

122–123 See note to ll. 424–427 of *SP*, above. In the slight change of "when" in MS. 2 to
"if" WW expresses uncertainty that Stonehenge was the scene in the ritual murders.
140   See note to ll. 176–177 of *ASP*, above.

142 *Nor* ~~tapered~~ *glimmered dim from sick-man's room*
143 *Along the waste no line of mournful light*
144 *From lamp of lonely toll-gate streamed athwart the night.*

[6ʳ]

17

145 *At length, tho' hid in clouds, the moon arose—* ;⎫

146 *The downs were visible* , ⎬*& now revealed*

 S⎫
147 *A s* ⎰*tructure stands which two bare slopes enclose.*
148 *It was a spot, where, ancient vows fulfilled,*
149 *Kind pious hands did to the Virgin build*

 —⎫
150 *A lonely Spital* , ⎰ *the belated Swain*
151 *From the night-terrors of that Waste to shield;*
152 *But there no human being could remain,*
153 *And now the Walls are named the "Dead House" of the Plain.*

18

154 *Tho' he had little cause to love the abode*
155 *Of man, or covet sight of mortal face;*
   a gleam of light   R⎫
156 *Yet when* ~~the doubtful gloom~~ *that r* ⎰*uin shewed*
157 *How glad he was at length to find some trace*
158 *Of human shelter in this dreary place.*
   his Flock
159 *Till to* ~~the moor~~ *the early Shepherd goes*
160 *Here shall much-needed sleep his frame embrace.*
161 *In a dry nook where fern the floor bestrows*
   :⎫
162 *He lays his stiffened limbs*[?]⎰ *his eyes begin to close.*

19

163 *When, heaving a deep sigh that seemed to come*
   ⎱*he raised his head,*
164 *From one who mourned in sleep* ⎰ ~~that seemed to come~~
165 *And saw a woman in the naked room*
166 *Outstretched, & turning on a restless bed;*
   er⎫
167 *The moon a wan dead light around him* ⎰ *shed.*

 —⎫   ⎫
168 *He waked her—* ⎰*spake in tone that would not fail*⎰
169 *He hoped, to calm her mind, but ill he sped;*
170 *For of that Ruin she had heard a tale*
171 *Which now with freezing thoughts did all her powers assail.*

---

163 heaving] *del to* hearing (John Carter)

---

163 heaving] A mistake for "hearing".

Nor taper glimmered dim from sick man's room;
Along the waste no line of mournful light
From lamp of lonely toll-gate streamed athwart the night.

XVII.

At length, though hid in clouds, the moon arose;   [145]
The downs were visible—and now revealed
A structure stands, which two bare slopes enclose.
It was a spot, where, ancient vows fulfilled,
Kind pious hands did to the Virgin build
A lonely Spital, the belated swain   [150]
From the night terrors of that waste to shield:
But there no human being could remain,
And now the walls are named the "Dead House" of the plain.

XVIII.

Though he had little cause to love the abode
Of man, or covet sight of mortal face,   [155]
Yet when faint beams of light that ruin showed,
How glad he was at length to find some trace
Of human shelter in that dreary place.
Till to his flock the early shepherd goes,
Here shall much-needed sleep his frame embrace.   [160]
In a dry nook where fern the floor bestrows
He lays his stiffened limbs,—his eyes begin to close;

XIX.

When hearing a deep sigh, that seemed to come
From one who mourned in sleep, he raised his head,
And saw a woman in the naked room   [165]
Outstretched, and turning on a restless bed:
The moon a wan dead light around her shed.
He waked her—spake in tone that would not fail,
He hoped, to calm her mind; but ill he sped,
For of that ruin she had heard a tale   [170]
Which now with freezing thoughts did all her powers assail;

---

144   See note to l. 117 of *SP*, above.

20

172   Had heard of One who forced from storms to shroud
173   Felt the loose walls of this decayed ~~abode~~ retreat
174   Rock to incessant neighings shrill & loun $\begin{smallmatrix}d\\\end{smallmatrix}\}$
175   While his horse pawed the floor with furious heat,
176   Till on a stone that sparkled to his feet
177   Struck, & still struck again $\}$ the troubled horse $\}$
178   The man half-raised the stone with pain & sweat $\}$
179   Half-raised, for well his arm might lose its force $\}$
180   Disclosing the grim head of a late-murdered c $\begin{smallmatrix}C\\\end{smallmatrix}\}$orse.

[7ʳ]

21

181   Such of this lone [?place] $\begin{smallmatrix}mans\\\end{smallmatrix}\}$ion she had learned;
182   And when that shape with eyes in sleep half-drowned
183   By the moon's sullen lamp she first de $\begin{smallmatrix}i\\\end{smallmatrix}\}$scerned,
184   Cold stony horror all her senses bound.
185   Her he addressed in words of cheering ~~heart~~
186   Recovering heart, like answer did she make;
187   And well it was that of the c $\begin{smallmatrix}C\\\end{smallmatrix}\}$orse there found
188   In converse that ensued, she nothing spake;
189   She knew not what dire pangs such tale ~~had power to wake~~

22

190   But soon his voice & words of kind intent
191   Banished that dismal thought, $\begin{smallmatrix};\\\end{smallmatrix}\}$ & now the wind
192   In ~~feebler murmurs~~ told its rage was spent;
193   Meanwhile discourse ensued of various kind
194   Which by degrees a confidence of mind
195   And mutual interest failed not to create;
196   And ~~now~~ to natural sympathy resigned
197   In that forsaken building where they sate
198   The Woman thus ~~began her~~ Story ~~to relate~~

---

182 shape] *del to* shape, P (?MW)   drowned] *del to* drowned, P (?MW)

---

192   *rage*] Underlined in MS.

XX.

Had heard of one who, forced from storms to shroud,
Felt the loose walls of this decayed Retreat
Rock to incessant neighings shrill and loud,
While his horse pawed the floor with furious heat;   [175]
Till on a stone, that sparkled to his feet,
Struck, and still struck again, the troubled horse:
The man half raised the stone with pain and sweat,
Half raised, for well his arm might lose its force
Disclosing the grim head of a late-murdered corse.   [180]

XXI.

Such tale of this lone mansion she had learned
And, when that shape, with eyes in sleep half drowned,
By the moon's sullen lamp she first discerned,
Cold stony horror all her senses bound.
Her he addressed in words of cheering sound;   [185]
Recovering heart, like answer did she make;
And well it was that, of the corse there found,
In converse that ensued she nothing spake;
She knew not what dire pangs in him such tale could wake.

XXII.

But soon his voice and words of kind intent   [190]
Banished that dismal thought; and now the wind
In fainter howlings told its *rage* was spent:
Meanwhile discourse ensued of various kind,
Which by degrees a confidence of mind
And mutual interest failed not to create.   [195]
And, to a natural sympathy resigned,
In that forsaken building where they sate
The Woman thus retraced her own untoward fate.

180 late-murdered] late murdered *1845*–
181 learned] learned, *1849*

23

By Derwents side My Father dwelt—a Man
~~Honest and true by pious parents bred,~~

199 ~~*My Father was a good & pious man,*~~
Of virtuous life by pious Parents bred

200 ~~*An honest man by honest parents bred;*~~

201 *And I believe that, soon as I began*

202 *To lisp, he made me kneel beside my bed,*

203 *And in his hearing there my prayers I said:*

204 *And afterwards, by my good father taught,*

205 *I read, and loved the books in which I read;*

206 *For books in every neighbouring house I sought,*

207 *And nothing to my mind a sweeter pleasure brought.*

24

A little croft we owned a

208 ~~*Can I forget our croft and*~~ *plot of corn;*
&

209 ~~*Our*~~ *garden stored with peas, and mint, and thyme;*
And flowers sweet posies

210 *And rose & lily—for the sabbath morn?*
Never shall I forget the pleasant chime.

211 ~~*The sabbath bells and their delightful chime;*~~
ur
O[?] *church-bell made the*

212 ~~*The gambols & wild*~~ *freaks at shearing time;*

213 *My hen's rich nest through long grass scarce espied;*

214 *The cowslip-gathering in June's dewy prime;*

215 *The swans that, with white chests upheaved in pride,*

216 *Rushing and racing came to meet me at the waterside?*

And flowers for posies often pluckd at morn
While the sabbath [   ] were ringing their first chime

oft } on sunday
And flowers for ~~sunday~~ posies [?] } at morn
W Pluckd as the church-bells rang their earliest ch

And flowers, pluckd often on a sabbath morn
[—?—]}
[   ] [—?—]} while the church bells rang their chime
[   ] flowers for posies on the sabbath morn
the church-
[   ]kd while the chearful bells rang their pleasant chime
Can I forget our freaks at shearing time

208–216 [4a]

A little croft we owned—a plot of corn
A garden stored with pease & mint & thyme

---

199 By] *del to* "By *P* (WW)

199–306; 335–446   The Woman's story is entered in an as yet unidentified hand. Corrections on it may be taken to be in the hand of WW or MW.

216/217   The first two lines, "And . . . chime," are written vertically in WW's hand in the left margin. The next two lines, "And . . . ch," are written vertically in WW's hand in the right margin. The five lines, "And flowers . . . time," are written normally, in WW's hand, at the foot of the page.

XXIII.

"By Derwent's side my father dwelt—a man
Of virtuous life, by pious parents bred; [200]
And I believe that, soon as I began
To lisp, he made me kneel beside my bed,
And in his hearing there my prayers I said:
And afterwards, by my good father taught,
I read, and loved the books in which I read; [205]
For books in every neighbouring house I sought,
And nothing to my mind a sweeter pleasure brought.

XXIV.

A little croft we owned—a plot of corn,
A garden stored with peas, and mint, and thyme,
And flowers for posies, oft on Sunday morn [210]
Plucked while the church bells rang their earliest chime.
Can I forget our freaks at shearing time!
My hen's rich nest through long grass scarce espied;
The cowslip-gathering in June's dewy prime;
The swans that with white chests upreared in pride [215]
Rushing and racing came to meet me at the water-side!

> *And flowers for posies, oft on Sunday morn*
> *Plucked while the church bells rang their earliest chime*
> *Can I forget our freaks at shearing-time*
> *My hen's rich nest thro' long grass scarce espied*
> *The cowslip gathering in June's dewy prime;*
> *The Swans that with white chests upheaved in pride*
> *Rushing & racing came to meet me at the water-side*

[8ʳ]

25

                    well
217 *The staff I ~~yet~~ remember which upbore*
218 *The bending body of my active Sire;*
219 *His seat beneath the honied sycamore*
220 *Where the bees hummed, and chair by winter fire;*
221 *When market morning came, the neat attire*
222 *With which, though bent on haste, myself I decked;*
223 *Our watchful house-dog, that would tease and tire*
224 *The stranger, till its barking-fit I checked;*
225 *The red-breast, known for years, which at my casement pecked.*

26

226 *The suns of twenty summers danced along—*
                    Too
227 *Ah! little marked how fast they rolled away:*
228 *But, through severe mischance, and cruel wrong,*
                                            :)
229 *My father's substance fell into decay:)*
230 *We toiled & struggled, hoping for a day*
231 *When Fortune should put on a kinder look;*
232 *But vain were wishes, efforts vain as they;*
233 *He from his old heriditary nook*
234 *Must part; the summons came,—our final leave we took.*

[8ᵛ]

27

235 *It was indeed a miserable hour*
                              S)
236 *When, from the last hill-top, my sire surveyed,*
237 *Peering above the trees, the steeple tower*
238 *That on his marriage-day sweet music made!*
239 *Till then, he hoped his bones might there be laid,*
240 *Close by my mother in their native bowers:*
241 *Bidding me trust in God, he stood and prayed,—*
242 *I could not pray:—through tears that fell in showers,*
243 *Glimmered our dear-loved home, alas! no longer ours!*

---

231 should] *del to* would *P* (WW)

XXV.

The staff I well remember which upbore
The bending body of my active sire;
His seat beneath the honied sycamore
Where the bees hummed, and chair by winter fire; [220]
When market-morning came, the neat attire
With which, though bent on haste, myself I decked;
Our watchful house-dog, that would tease and tire
The stranger till its barking-fit I checked;
The red-breast, known for years, which at my casement [225]
  pecked.

XXVI.

The suns of twenty summers danced along,—
Too little marked how fast they rolled away:
But, through severe mischance and cruel wrong,
My father's substance fell into decay:
We toiled and struggled, hoping for a day [230]
When Fortune would put on a kinder look;
But vain were wishes, efforts vain as they;
He from his old hereditary nook
Must part; the summer came;—our final leave we took.

XXVII.

It was indeed a miserable hour [235]
When, from the last hill-top, my sire surveyed,
Peering above the trees, the steeple tower
That on his marriage day sweet music made!
Till then, he hoped his bones might there be laid
Close by my mother in their native bowers: [240]
Bidding me trust in God, he stood and prayed;—
I could not pray:—through tears that fell in showers
Glimmered our dear-loved home, alas! no longer ours!

---

231 would] might *1845–*
234 summer] summons *1845–*

---

234 summer] Although it makes good sense, "summer" may be an error that passed un-
noticed in 1842. The reading of the last MS. is "summons" and this is the reading from 1845 on.
243 See note to l. 261 of *SP*, above.

28

244 There was a Youth whom I had loved so long,
245 That when I loved him not I cannot say:
246 'Mid the green mountains many a thoughtless song
247 We two had sung, like gladsome birds in May;
248 When we began to tire of childish play,
249 We seemed still more and more to prize each other;
250 We talked of marriage and our marriage-day;
251 And I in truth did love him like a brother,
252 For never could I hope to meet with such another.

[9ʳ]

29

253 Two years were passed since to a distant town
254 He had repaired to ply a gainful trade:
255 What tears of bitter grief, till then unknown!
256 What tender vows our last sad kiss delayed!
257 To him we turned:—we had no other aid:
258 Like one revived, upon his neck I wept,
259 And her whom he had loved in joy, he said,
260 He well could love in grief; his faith he kept;
261 And in a quiet home once more my f $\overset{F}{}$ ather slept.

30

262 We lived in peace and comfort; and were blest
263 With daily bread, by constant toil supplied.
264 Three lovely babes had lain upon my breast;
265 And often, viewing their sweet smiles, I sighed,
266 And knew not why. My happy f $\overset{F}{}$ ather died,
     threatened War
267 When ~~sad distress~~ reduced the children's meal:
268 Thrice happy! that for him the grave could hide
269 The empty loom, cold hearth, and silent wheel,
270 And tears that flowed for ills which patience might not heal.

[9ᵛ]

31

     ~~War was proclaim'd~~
271 stet ~~'Twas a hard change,~~ an evil time was come;
272 We had no hope, and no relief could gain.
273 But soon, with proud parade, the noisy drum
274 Beat round, to clear the streets of want & pain.
275 My h $\overset{H}{}$ usband's arms now only served to strain
276 Me and his c $\overset{C}{}$ hildren hungering in his view;
277 In such dismay my prayers and tears were vain:
278 To join those miserable men he flew;
279 And now to the sea-coast, with numbers more, we drew.

XXVIII.

There was a Youth whom I had loved so long,
That when I loved him not I cannot say: [245]
'Mid the green mountains many a thoughtless song
We two had sung, like gladsome birds in May;
When we began to tire of childish play,
We seemed still more and more to prize each other;
We talked of marriage and our marriage day; [250]
And I in truth did love him like a brother,
For never could I hope to meet with such another.

XXIX.

Two years were passed since to a distant town
He had repaired to ply a gainful trade:
What tears of bitter grief, till then unknown! [255]
What tender vows our last sad kiss delayed!
To him we turned:—we had no other aid:
Like one revived, upon his neck I wept;
And her whom he had loved in joy, he said,
He well could love in grief; his faith he kept; [260]
And in a quiet home once more my father slept.

XXX.

We lived in peace and comfort; and were blest
With daily bread, by constant toil supplied.
Three lovely babes had lain upon my breast;
And often, viewing their sweet smiles, I sighed, [265]
And knew not why. My happy father died,
When threatened war reduced the children's meal:
Thrice happy! that for him the grave could hide
The empty loom, cold hearth, and silent wheel,
And tears that flowed for ills which patience might not heal. [270]

XXXI.

'Twas a hard change; an evil time was come;
We had no hope, and no relief could gain:
But soon, with proud parade, the noisy drum
Beat round to clear the streets of want and pain.
My husband's arms now only served to strain [275]
Me and his children hungering in his view;
In such dismay my prayers and tears were vain:
To join those miserable men he flew,
And now to the sea-coast, with numbers more, we drew.

32

280   *There were we long neglected,* ;⎫ *and we bore*

281   *Much sorrow, ere the fleet its anchor weighed,* ;⎫

282   *Green fields before us, and our native shore,*

283   *We breathed a pestilential air, that made*

284   *Ravage for which no knell was heard. We prayed*

285   *For our departure; wished and wished—nor knew* ⎫

286   *'Mid that long sickness, and those hopes delayed,*

287   *That happier days we never more must view:*

288   *The parting signal streamed,* ;—⎫ *at last the land withdrew.*

[10ʳ]

33

289   *But the calm summer season now was past.*
290   *On as we drove, the equinoctial deep*
291   *Ran mountains-high before the howling blast;*
292   *And many perished in the whirlwind's sweep.*
293   *We gazed with terror on their gloomy sleep,*
294   *Untaught that soon such anguish must ensue,*
295   *Our hopes such harvest of affliction reap,*
296   *That we the mercy of the waves should rue:*
297   *We reached the western world, a poor, devoted crew.*

34

298   *The pains and plagues that on our heads came down,*
299   *Disease and famine, agony and fear,*
300   *In wood or wilderness, in camp or town,*
                        the unman the firmest heart
301   *It would ~~thy brain unsettle even~~ to hear.*
302   *All perished—all, in one remorseless year,*
303   *Husband and children! one by one, by sword*
304   *And ravenous plague, all perished: every tear*
305   *Dried up, despairing, desolate, on board*
306   *A British ship I waked, as from a trance restored.*

[10ᵛ]

35

307   *—Here paused she, of all present thought ~~bereft~~ forlorn;*

308   *No* ⎫ *voice nor sound that moment's pain expressed,*
         Yet
309   *~~Till~~ Nature with excess of grief oerborn*
310   *From her full eyes their watery load released;*

---

306 restored.] *del to* restored." *P* (WW)

---

307   MW takes up the fair copy to 334, inclusive.

XXXII.

There were we long neglected, and we bore [280]
Much sorrow ere the fleet its anchor weighed;
Green fields before us, and our native shore,
We breathed a pestilential air, that made
Ravage for which no knell was heard. We prayed
For our departure; wished and wished—nor knew, [285]
'Mid that long sickness and those hopes delayed,
That happier days we never more must view.
The parting signal streamed—at last the land withdrew.

XXXIII.

But the calm summer season now was past.
On as we drove, the equinoctial deep [290]
Ran mountains high before the howling blast,
And many perished in the whirlwind's sweep.
We gazed with terror on their gloomy sleep,
Untaught that soon such anguish must ensue,
Our hopes such harvest of affliction reap, [295]
That we the mercy of the waves should rue:
We reached the western world, a poor devoted crew.

XXXIV.

The pains and plagues that on our heads came down,
Disease and famine, agony and fear,
In wood or wilderness, in camp or town, [300]
It would unman the firmest heart to hear.
All perished—all in one remorseless year,
Husband and children! one by one, by sword
And ravenous plague, all perished: every tear
Dried up, despairing, desolate, on board [305]
A British ship I waked, as from a trance restored."

XXXV.

Here paused she of all present thought forlorn,
Nor voice, nor sound, that moment's pain expressed,
Yet Nature, with excess of grief o'erborne,
From her full eyes their watery load released. [310]

---

281 weighed;] weighed *1849*

297 See note to l. 306 of *SP*, above.

311   *He too was mute ; & ere her weeping ceased*

312   *He rose, & to the r⎰R⎱uin's portal went,*

313   *And saw the dawn ~~appearing~~ ^opening^ the silvery east*

314   *With rays of promise, north & southward sent ;*

315   *And soon with crimson fire kindled the firmament*

36

316   *"O come, ⎰'⎱" he cried, "come'⎰ after weary night*

317   *"Of such rough storm, this happy change to view!*

318   *So, forth she came, & eastward looked : the sight*

319   *Over her brow <u>like</u> dawn of gladness threw,'⎱*

320   ~~That on~~ ~~Upon~~ ^Upon^ *her cheek, to which its youthful hue*

321   *Seemed to return, dried the last lingering tear*

322   *And from her grateful heart a fresh one drew ;*

323   *The whilst her Comrade* ^to^~~with~~ *her pensive cheer*

324   *Tempered fit words of hope—;⎱ & the lark warbled near.*

[11ʳ]

37

325   *They looked, & saw a lengthening road, & Wain*

326   *That rang down a bare slope not far remote :*

327   *The barrows glistered bright with drops of rain,*

328   *Whist[?les]* ^led^⎱ *the Waggoner with merry note,*

329   *The cock far-off sounded his clarion throat,*

330   *But town, or farm, or hamlet none they viewed,*

331   *Only were told there stood a lonely cot*

332   *A long mile thence. While thither they pursued*

333   *Their way, the Woman thus her* ^mournful^ *tale renewed.*

38

334   *Peaceful as this immeasureable Plain*

335   ^Is now, by^ *~~By the first~~ beams of dawning light imprest,*

336   *In the calm sunshine slept the glittering main.*

---

319 *like*] *del to* like *with note by WW* : [l]ike [n]ot [i]talic
334 Peaceful] *del to* "Peaceful *P* (WW)

---

319   *like*] Underlined in MS.
333/334   A horizontal line apparently marks the resumption of the Woman's story.
334   An unidentified hand completes the Woman's story to 446, inclusive.

He too was mute; and, ere her weeping ceased,
He rose, and to the ruin's portal went,
And saw the dawn opening the silvery east
With rays of promise, north and southward sent;
And soon with crimson fire kindled the firmament.　　[315]

XXXVI.

"O come," he cried, "come, after weary night
Of such rough storm, this happy change to view."
So forth she came, and eastward looked; the sight
Over her brow like dawn of gladness threw;
Upon her cheek, to which its youthful hue　　[320]
Seemed to return, dried the last lingering tear,
And from her grateful heart a fresh one drew:
The whilst her comrade to her pensive cheer
Tempered fit words of hope; and the lark warbled near.

XXXVII.

They looked and saw a lengthening road, and wain　　[325]
That rang down a bare slope not far remote:
The barrows glistered bright with drops of rain,
Whistled the waggoner with merry note,
The cock far off sounded his clarion throat;
But town, or farm, or hamlet, none they viewed,　　[330]
Only were told there stood a lonely cot
A long mile thence. While thither they pursued
Their way, the Woman thus her mournful tale renewed.

XXXVIII.

"Peaceful as this immeasurable plain
Is now, by beams of dawning light imprest,　　[335]
In the calm sunshine slept the glittering main;

---

311 mute;] mute: *1849*

337   *The very ocean hath its hour of rest;*
           ~~Hush'd as if nothing could disturb its~~ rest
338   *I too forgot the heavings of my breast.*
                                round me
                       H⎱   y   ⎱
339   ~~Oh me,~~ h⎰ow quiet ship⎰ *and ocean were!*
340   *As quiet all within me. I was blestt!*⎰
                       fed upon
341   *And looked, and* ~~looked along~~ *the silent air*
342   *Until it seemed to bring a joy to my despair.*

[11ᵛ]

39

343   *Ah! how unlike those late terrific sleeps,*

344   *And groans, that rage of racking famine spoke!*⎰

345   *The unburied dead that lay in festering heaps!*⎰

346   *The breathing pestilence that rose like smoke!*⎰

347   *The shriek fhat from the distant battle broke!*⎰
348   *The mine's dire earthquake, and the pallid host*
349   *Driven by the bomb's incessant thunder-stroke*
350   *To loathsome vaults, where heart-sick anguish tossed,*
351   *Hope died, and fear itself in agony was lost!*

40

352   *Some mighty gulph of seperation past.*
353   *I seemed transported to another world:*
354   *A thought resigned with pain, when from the mast*
355   *The impatient mariner the sail unfurled,*
356   *And, whistling, called the wind that hardly curled*
357   *The silent sea. From the sweet thoughts of home*
358   *And from all hope I was for ever hurled.*
359   *For me—farthest from earthly port to roam*
360   *Was best, could I but shun the spot where man might come.*

[12ʳ]

4
   [?]⎰1

361   *And oft I thought (my fancy was so strong)*
362   *That I, at last, a resting-place had found;*
363   *"Here will I dwell,"* ~~I~~ *said I, "my whole life long,*
364   *Roaming the illimitable waters round:*
                       all but heaven
365   *Here will I live, of* ~~every friend~~ *disowned,*

---

339   *ship*] Altered to "sky" with "h" used as "k."
347   *fhat*] Obviously "that" is intended.
363   The second "I" was probably meant to be deleted, in favor of the third.

The very ocean hath its hour of rest.
I too forgot the heavings of my breast.
How quiet round me ship and ocean were!
As quiet all within me. I was blest,   [340]
And looked, and fed upon the silent air
Until it seemed to bring a joy to my despair.

XXXIX.

Ah! how unlike those late terrific sleeps,
And groans that rage of racking famine spoke;
The unburied dead that lay in festering heaps,   [345]
The breathing pestilence that rose like smoke,
The shriek that from the distant battle broke,
The mine's dire earthquake, and the pallid host
Driven by the bomb's incessant thunder-stroke
To loathsome vaults, where heart-sick anguish tossed,   [350]
Hope died, and fear itself in agony was lost!

XL.

Some mighty gulf of separation past,
I seemed transported to another world;
A thought resigned with pain, when from the mast
The impatient mariner the sail unfurled,   [355]
And, whistling, called the wind that hardly curled
The silent sea. From the sweet thoughts of home
And from all hope I was for ever hurled.
For me—farthest from earthly port to roam
Was best, could I but shun the spot where man might come. [360]

XLI.

And oft I thought (my fancy was so strong)
That I, at last, a resting-place had found;
"Here will I dwell," said I, "my whole life long,
Roaming the illimitable waters round;
Here will I live, of all but heaven disowned,   [365]

---

339 round] 'round *1845–*
341 air] air, *1846*
352 past] passed *1849*
363, 366 *All inverted commas single 1845–.*

ful
peace[—?—]
366   And end my days upon the ~~ocean~~ flood."—
367   To break my dream the vessel reached its bound:
368   And homeless near a thousand homes I stood,
369   And near a thousand tables pined and wanted food.

42

No help I sought ;⎱ by sorrow turn'd adrift—
370   ~~By grief enfeebled was I turned adrift,~~
Was hopeless as if cast on
371   ~~Helpless as sailor cast on~~ some bare rock;
372   Nor morsel to my mouth that day did lift,
raised
373   Nor ~~dared~~ my hand at any door to knock.
374   I lay where, with his drowsy mates, the cock
375   From the cross-timber of an out-house hung:
376   Dismally tolled, that night, the city clock!
377   At morn my sick heart hunger scarcely stung,
378   Nor to the beggar's language could I fit my tongue.

[12ᵛ]

43

379   So passed a second day; and when the third
380   Was come, I tried in vain the crowd's resort.
381   —In deep despair, by frightful wishes stirred,
382   Near the sea-side I reached a ruined fort;
383   There pains which nature could no more support,
384   With blindness linked, did on my vitals fall,
385   And after many interruptions short,
386   Of hideous sense, I sank, nor step could crawl:
387   Unsought for was the help that did my life recall.

44

388   Borne to an hospital, I lay with brain
389   Drowsy and weak, and shattered memory;
390   I heard my neighbours, in their beds, complain
391   Of many things which never troubled me;
392   Of feet still bustling round with busy glee;
393   Of looks where common kindness had no part;
cold formality
394   Of service done with ~~careless cruelty,~~
395   Fretting the fever round the languid heart;
396   And groans which, as they said, might make a dead man start.

---

370 adrift—] adrift *del to* adrift, *P* (?MW)

370–373   Revisions by a second unidentified hand, probably that of Christopher Wordsworth, Jr.

And end my days upon the peaceful flood."—
To break my dream the vessel reached its bound;
And homeless near a thousand homes I stood,
And near a thousand tables pined and wanted food.

XLII.

No help I sought, in sorrow turned adrift   [370]
Was hopeless, as if cast on some bare rock;
Nor morsel to my mouth that day did lift,
Nor raised my hand at any door to knock.
I lay where, with his drowsy mates, the cock
From the cross-timber of an out-house hung: [375]
Dismally tolled, that night, the city clock!
At morn my sick heart hunger scarcely stung,
Nor to the beggar's language could I fit my tongue.

XLIII.

So passed a second day; and, when the third
Was come, I tried in vain the crowd's resort.   [380]
—In deep despair, by frightful wishes stirred,
Near the sea-side I reached a ruined fort;
There, pains which nature could no more support,
With blindness linked, did on my vitals fall;
And, after many interruptions short   [385]
Of hideous sense, I sank, nor step could crawl:
Unsought for was the help that did my life recal.

XLIV.

Borne to a hospital, I lay with brain
Drowsy and weak, and shattered memory;
I heard my neighbours in their beds complain   [390]
Of many things which never troubled me—
Of feet still bustling round with busy glee,
Of looks where common kindness had no part,
Of service done with cold formality,
Fretting the fever round the languid heart,   [395]
And groans which, as they said, might make a dead man start.

---

370 sought,] sought; *1849*   adrift] adrift, *1849*

[13ʳ]

45

397   These things just served to stir the slumbering sense,
398   Nor pain nor pity in my bosom raised.
399   With strength did memory return; and, thence
400   Dismissed, again on open day I gazed,
401   At houses, men, and common light, amazed.
402   The lanes I sought, and, as the sun retired,
403   Came where beneath the trees a faggot blazed;
404   The travellers saw me weep, my fate inquired,
405   And gave me food,—} and rest, more welcome, more desired.

46

406   Rough potters seemed they, trading soberly
407   With panniered asses driven from door to door;
408   But life of happier sort set forth to me,
409   And other joys my fancy to allure;
410   The bag-pipe, dinning on the midnight moor,
411   In barn uplighted; and companions boon
412   Well met from far with revelry secure,
413   Among the forest glades, while jocund June
414   Rolled fast along the sky his warm and genial moon.

[13ᵛ]

47

415   But ill they suited me—those journeys dark
416   O'er moor and mountain, midnight theft to hatch!
417   To charm the surly house-dog's faithful bark,
418   Or hang on tiptoe at the lifted latch.
419   The gloomy lantern, and the dim blue match,
420   The black disguise, the warning whistle shrill,
421   And ear still busy on its nightly watch,
422   Were not for me, brought up in nothing ill:
423   Besides on griefs so fresh my thoughts were brooding still.

48

424   What could I do, unaided and unblest?
425   My Father! gone was every friend of thine:
426   And kindred of dead husband are at best
427   Small help; and, after marriage such as mine,
428   With little kindness would to me incline.
429   Ill was I then for toil or service fit:
430   My deep-drawn sighs no effort could confine;
431   In the open air forgetful would I sit
432   Whole hours, with idle arms in moping sorrow knit.

XLV.

These things just served to stir the slumbering sense,
Nor pain nor pity in my bosom raised.
With strength did memory return; and, thence
Dismissed, again on open day I gazed,   [400]
At houses, men, and common light, amazed.
The lanes I sought, and, as the sun retired,
Came where beneath the trees a faggot blazed;
The travellers saw me weep, my fate inquired,
And gave me food—and rest, more welcome, more desired.   [405]

XLVI.

Rough potters seemed they, trading soberly
With panniered asses driven from door to door;
But life of happier sort set forth to me,
And other joys my fancy to allure—
The bag-pipe dinning on the midnight moor   [410]
In barn uplighted; and companions boon,
Well met from far with revelry secure
Among the forest glades, while jocund June
Rolled fast along the sky his warm and genial moon.

XLVII.

But ill they suited me—those journeys dark   [415]
O'er moor and mountain, midnight theft to hatch!
To charm the surly house-dog's faithful bark,
Or hang on tip-toe at the lifted latch.
The gloomy lantern, and the dim blue match,
The black disguise, the warning whistle shrill,   [420]
And ear still busy on its nightly watch,
Were not for me, brought up in nothing ill:
Besides, on griefs so fresh my thoughts were brooding still.

XLVIII.

What could I do, unaided and unblest?
My father! gone was every friend of thine: [425]
And kindred of dead husband are at best
Small help; and, after marriage such as mine,
With little kindness would to me incline.
Nor was I then for toil or service fit;
My deep-drawn sighs no effort could confine;   [430]
In open air forgetful would I sit
Whole hours, with idle arms in moping sorrow knit.

[14ʳ]

49

433 *The roads I paced, I loitered through the fields;*
434 *Contentedly, yet sometimes self-accused,*
435 *Trusted my life to what chance-bounty yields,*
436 *Now coldly given, now utterly refused.*
437 *The ground I for my bed have often used:*
438 *But¸ what afflicts my peace with keenest ruth*
439 *Is¸ that I have my inner self abused,*
440 *Foregone the home-delight of constant truth,*

441 *And clear and open soul, so prized in fearless youth.*}

50

442 *Through tears the rising sun I oft have viewed;*
443 *Through tears have seen him towards that world descend*
444 *Where my poor heart lost all its fortitude:*
445 *Three years a w{ᵂ}anderer now my course I bend—*
446 *Oh! tell me whither—for no earthly friend*
447 *Have I—{·} She ceased, & ~~turned~~{weeping} ~~away~~{turned} away{;}—*
448 *As if because her tale was at an end*
449 *She wept—{;} because she had no more to say,*
450 *Of that perpetual weight which on her spirit lay.*

[14ᵛ]

51

451 *True sympathy the Sailor's look{s} expressed*
452 *His looks—for pondering he was mute the while.*
453 *Of Social order's care for wretchedness,*
454 *Of Times sure help—to calm & reconcile,*
455 *Joy's second spring, & Hopes long-m{tr}easured smile,*
456 *'Twas not for <u>Him</u> to speak—a man so tried.*
457 *Yet to relieve her heart in [?prince]{friend} ly style*
458 *Proverbial words of comfort he applied*
459 *And not in vain, while they went pacing side by side.*

52

460 *Ere long from heaps of turf, before their sight,*
461 *Together smoking in the sun's slant beam,*
462 *Rise various wreaths¸ that into one unite*

---

447 I.] *del to* I."— *P* (WW)
453 order's] *del to* Order's (John Carter)

---

456 *Him*] Underlined in MS.

XLIX.

The roads I paced, I loitered through the fields;
Contentedly, yet sometimes self-accused,
Trusted my life to what chance bounty yields, [435]
Now coldly given, now utterly refused.
The ground I for my bed have often used:
But what afflicts my peace with keenest ruth,
Is that I have my inner self abused,
Foregone the home delight of constant truth, [440]
And clear and open soul, so prized in fearless youth.

L.

Through tears the rising sun I oft have viewed,
Through tears have seen him towards that world descend
Where my poor heart lost all its fortitude:
Three years a wanderer now my course I bend— [445]
Oh! tell me whither—for no earthly friend
Have I."—She ceased, and weeping turned away;
As if because her tale was at an end,
She wept; because she had no more to say
Of that perpetual weight which on her spirit lay. [450]

LI.

True sympathy the Sailor's looks expressed,
His looks—for pondering he was mute the while.
Of social Order's care for wretchedness,
Of Time's sure help to calm and reconcile,
Joy's second spring and Hope's long-treasured smile, [455]
'Twas not for *him* to speak—a man so tried.
Yet, to relieve her heart, in friendly style
Proverbial words of comfort he applied,
And not in vain, while they went pacing side by side.

LII.

Ere long, from heaps of turf, before their sight, [460]
Together smoking in the sun's slant beam,
Rise various wreaths that into one unite

453–456   See Additions to MS. 1, 27ᵛ, above. In the first formulation of the lines dealing with
"social Order's care" WW suggested that such care does not exist, that it is "delusion fond"
invented by the traveler to cheer the vagrant woman. Now, in *G & S*, the suggestion is that there
is a benevolent order and that hope is possible, but that the sailor has put himself beyond them.

463   *Which high & higher mounts with silver gleam.*
464   *Fair spectacle, but instantly a scream*
465   *Thence bursting shrill did all remark prevent;*
466   *They paused, & heard a hoarser voice blaspheme*
467   *And female cries. Their course they thither bent;*
468   *And met a man who foamed with anger vehement.*

[15^r]

53

469   *A Woman stood with quivering t͡ips & pale;*
470   *And, pointing to a little Child that lay*
471   *Stretched on the ground, began a piteous tale;*
472   *How in a simple freak of thoughtless play*
473   *He had provoked his Father, who straitway,*
                        deadlier than
474   *As if each blow were ~~meant to be~~ the last,*
                        Pallid [?smitten] with dismay
475   *Struck the poor Innocent, ~~in the light of day~~*
            [?Smitten] was
                    T   heard, and
476   *~~Shuddering t~~ he Sailor's Widow stood aghast;*
477   *And stern looks on the Man her grey-haired Comrade cast.*

54

        His voice, His with   indig   rising
478   *~~And, with firm voice,~~ & ~~idignation,~~high*
479   *Such further deed in manhood's name forbade;*
            The Peasant, wild in
480   *~~He confident in~~ passion, made reply*
481   *With bitter insult & revilings sad;*
482   *Asked him in scorn what business there he had,*
483   *What kind of plunder he was hunting now;*
484   *The gallows would one day of him be glad,—*
485   *Here cold sweat started on the Sailor's brow,*
        ~~At once the griding iron~~
486   *Yet calm he seemed as thoughts so poignant would allow.*

---

476 Sailor's Widow] sailor's widow *del to* Soldier's Widow *P* (WW)
482 there] here 3a   had,] had 3a
483 now;] now 3a
484 glad,—] glad 3a
485 on] from 3a   brow,] brow 3a   Here cold sweat started on] *del to* Though inward anguish damped *P* (WW)
486 allow.] allow 3a
486/487 *No stanza number* 3a

---

478   *idignation*] MW's miswriting for "indignation." The revisions, like those to 480, are in the hand of John Carter.
486   False start to the fair copy by copying the beginning of 493.

Which high and higher mounts with silver gleam:
Fair spectacle,—but instantly a scream
Thence bursting shrill did all remark prevent;   [465]
They paused, and heard a hoarser voice blaspheme,
And female cries. Their course they thither bent,
And met a man who foamed with anger vehement.

LIII.

A woman stood with quivering lips and pale,
And, pointing to a little child that lay   [470]
Stretched on the ground, began a piteous tale;
How in a simple freak of thoughtless play
He had provoked his father, who straightway,
As if each blow were deadlier than the last,
Struck the poor innocent. Pallid with dismay   [475]
The Soldier's Widow heard and stood aghast;
And stern looks on the man her grey-haired Comrade cast.

LIV.

His voice with indignation rising high
Such further deed in manhood's name forbade;
The peasant, wild in passion, made reply   [480]
With bitter insult and revilings sad;
Asked him in scorn what business there he had;
What kind of plunder he was hunting now;
The gallows would one day of him be glad;—
Though inward anguish damped the Sailor's brow,   [485]
Yet calm he seemed as thoughts so poignant would allow.

[15ᵛ]

$$\left.\begin{array}{c}5\\56\end{array}\right\}$$

         oked ⎱
487 *Softly he str*[?]⎰ *the child who lay outstretched*
488 *With face to earth; & as the boy turned round*
489 *His battered head a groan the Sailor fetched,*

          —⎱
490 *As if he saw ,* ⎰ *then, & upon that ground—*
    Strange   *e* ⎱
491 *A̶ repetition of that*⎰ *deadly wound*
492 *He had himself inflicted. Thro' his brain*
493 *At once the griding iron passage found;*
                      en
494 *Deluge of tender thoughts that̶ rushed amain,*
                             few
               ~~some weak~~ tears refrain
495 *Nor could his sunken eyes from ~~very tears abstain~~*
                     a
              ~~some~~ few tears refrain.

          56

         —⎱
496 *Within himself he said ,* ⎰ *what hearts have we,*
497 *The blessing this a Father gives his Child!*
            B⎱
498 *Yet happy thou poor b*⎰*oy! compared with me,*
499 *Suffering not doing ill, fate far more mild.*
                 and tears
500 *The Stranger's ~~pitying~~ looks of wrath beguiled*
               l⎱
501 *The Father, & ret*⎰*enting thoughts awoke;*
         —⎱
502 *He kissed his Son ,* ⎰ *so all was reconciled;*
503 *Then with a voice which inward trouble broke*
      Ere to his lips it came
504 *I̶n̶ ̶t̶h̶e̶ ̶f̶u̶l̶l̶-̶s̶w̶e̶l̶l̶i̶n̶g̶ ̶t̶h̶r̶o̶a̶t̶ the Sailor them bespoke.*

---

487 str[?]] s[?] ed *alt* stroked 3a   child] Child 3a
488 earth;] earth 3a
489 fetched,] fetched 3a
490 saw, then,] saw—then 3a   ground—] ground 3a
491 A] *del to* Strange 3a   that] the 3a
493 found;] found 3a
494 that] then 3a   amain,] amain 3a
495 from a few tears refrain] *del to* the starting tear restrain *P* (WW)
495/496 *No stanza number* 3a
496 said, what] said What 3a   we,] we 3a
497 a] the *del to* a 3a   Child!] Child 3a
498 boy!] Boy 3a   me,] me 3a
499 mild.] mild 3a
                                        l⎱
501 awoke;] awoke 3a   ret⎰enting] relenting
502 Son,] Son 3a   reconciled;] reconciled 3a
504 them] the[?n] *overwritten* them 3a   bespoke.] bespoke 3a
504/505 *No stanza number* 3a

LV.

Softly he stroked the child, who lay outstretched
With face to earth; and, as the boy turned round
His battered head, a groan the Sailor fetched
As if he saw—there and upon that ground—   [490]
Strange repetition of the deadly wound
He had himself inflicted. Through his brain
At once the griding iron passage found;
Deluge of tender thoughts then rushed amain,
Nor could his sunken eyes the starting tear restrain.   [495]

LVI.

Within himself he said—What hearts have we!
The blessing this a father gives his child!
Yet happy thou, poor boy! compared with me,
Suffering not doing ill—fate far more mild.
The stranger's looks and tears of wrath beguiled   [500]
The father, and relenting thoughts awoke;
He kissed his son—so all was reconciled.
Then, with a voice which inward trouble broke
Ere to his lips it came, the Sailor them bespoke.

492–493   See note to ll. 645–646 of *ASP*, above.

[16ʳ]

57

505   *Bad is the world, & hard is the world's law*
506   *Even for the Man who wears the warmest fleece.*
507   *Much need have ye that time more closely draw*
508   *The bond of Nature, all unkindness cease,*
509   *And that among so few there still be peace;*
510   *Else can ye hope but with such numerous foes*
511   *Your pains shall ever with your years increase.*
                              ~~tongue~~ heart   the appropriate
512   *While from his* ~~*lips, this homely*~~ *lesson flows*
513   *A correspondent calm stole gently on his woes.*

58

              ~~The Pair then~~
514   ~~*So passing onward, down at length they look*~~
              Forthwith the Pair passed on; & down they look
515   *Where thro' a narrow valley's pleasant scene*
516   *A wreath of vapour tracked a winding brook*
517   *That babbled on thro' groves & meadows green;*
                   lowly house peeped out
518   *A* ~~*single Cottage smoked*~~ *the trees between;*
519   *The dripping groves resound with cheerful lays,*
520   *And melancholy lowings intervene*
521   *Of scattered herds that in the meadows graze,*
                   a⎫
                    ⎬mid
                   ⎭
              Some ~~in the~~ lingering shade, some touched by the sun's rays.
522   ~~*While thro the furrowed grass the lonely milk-maid strays.*~~

[16ᵛ]

59

523   *They saw & heard, & winding with the road*
524   *Down a thick wood they dropt into the vale;*
525   *Comfort by prouder mansions unbestowed*
526   *Their wearied frames she hoped would soon regale.*
              ~~Quickly~~ Soon
527   *Erelong they reached that Cottage in the dale:*

528   *It was a rustic Inn,* ⎫ *the board was spread,*

---

505 Bad] *del to* "Bad *P* (WW)   world, . . . world's] World . . . World's 3a
506 fleece.] fleece 3a
508 Nature,] Nature 3a   cease,] cease 3a
509 so] *Written over illeg word del* 3a   peace;] peace 3a
510 but] that *del to* but 3a
511 increase.] increase 3a *del to* increase?—" *P* (WW)   increase."— *del to* increase"— *P*2 (WW)
512 this homely] *del to* the appropriate 3a
513 correspondent] correspant 3a   woes.] woes 3a
515 Where thro'] Where through *del to* Into *P* (WW)
516 A wreath] *del to* Where wreath, *P* (WW) *del to* Where wreath *P*2 (WW)
523 heard, &] heard, and *del to* heard, and, *P* (?MW)

LVII.

"Bad is the world, and hard is the world's law   [505]
Even for the man who wears the warmest fleece;
Much need have ye that time more closely draw
The bond of nature, all unkindness cease,
And that among so few there still be peace:
Else can ye hope but with such numerous foes   [510]
Your pains shall ever with your years increase?"—
While from his heart the appropriate lesson flows,
A correspondent calm stole gently o'er his woes.

LVIII.

Forthwith the pair passed on; and down they look
Into a narrow valley's pleasant scene   [515]
Where wreaths of vapour tracked a winding brook,
That babbled on through groves and meadows green;
A low-roofed house peeped out the trees between;
The dripping groves resound with cheerful lays,
And melancholy lowings intervene   [520]
Of scattered herds, that in the meadow graze,
Some amid lingering shade, some touched by the sun's rays.

LIX.

They saw and heard, and, winding with the road
Down a thick wood, they dropt into the vale;
Comfort by prouder mansions unbestowed   [525]
Their wearied frames, she hoped, would soon regale.
Erelong they reached that cottage in the dale:
It was a rustic inn;—the board was spread,

529   *The milk-maid followed with her brimming pail,*
530   *And lustily the Master carved the bread;*
531   *Kindly the housewife pressed, & they in comfort fed.*

60

loth
though <s>loth</s>

532   *Their breakfast done, the <s>unhappy</s> Pair must part,*
533   *Travellers whose course no longer now agrees.*
534   *She rose & bade farewell! & while her heart*
535   *Struggled with tears nor could its sorrow ease*
536   *She left him there; for clustering round his knees*
537   *With his oak staff the cottage children played;*
538   *And soon she reached a spot oerhung with trees*
539   *And banks of ragged earth; beneath the shade*

the   road
540   *Across <s>a</s> pebbly* [—?—] *a little runner strayed.*

[17ʳ]

61

541   *A cart & horse beside the rivulet stood:*
542   *Chequering the canvass roof the sunbeams shone;*

bend
<s>bend</s>
543   *She saw the Carman* [?stop] *to scoop the flood*
544   *As the Wain fronted her,—wherein lay One*
545   *A pale-faced Woman in disease far gone:*
546   *The Carman wet her lips as well behoved;*

there was
547   *Bed under her lean Body <s>she had</s> none,*
548   *Tho' even to die near One she most had loved*
549   *She could not of herself those wasted limbs have moved.*

62

550   *The Soldier's Widow learned with honest pain*
551   *And homefelt force of sympathy sincere*

re
552   *Why thus that worn-out wretch must then sustain*

---

537 oak staff] *So P*
540 runner] runnel *del to* runner *but deletion canceled, with note* Stet *P* (WW)
540/541 61] 29 *overwritten* 28
541 stood:] stood
542 shone;] shone
543 [?stop]] bend
544 Wain] wain
545 gone:] gone
546 behoved;] behoved
547 Body she had none,] body there was none
549 moved.] moved
549/550 62] 28 *Overwritten* 29
552 then] *Overwritten* there

540/541   In MS. 3 the numbering of the stanzas has been raised by one, sometimes by erasure, sometimes by overwriting.

The milk-maid followed with her brimming pail,
And lustily the master carved the bread,   [530]
Kindly the housewife pressed, and they in comfort fed.

LX.

Their breakfast done, the pair, though loth, must part;
Wanderers whose course no longer now agrees.
She rose and bade farewell! and, while her heart
Struggled with tears nor could its sorrow ease,   [535]
She left him there; for, clustering round his knees,
With his oak-staff the cottage children played;
And soon she reached a spot o'erhung with trees
And banks of ragged earth; beneath the shade
Across the pebbly road a little runnel strayed.   [540]

LXI.

A cart and horse beside the rivulet stood;
Chequering the canvass roof the sunbeams shone.
She saw the carman bend to scoop the flood
As the wain fronted her,—wherein lay one,
A pale-faced Woman, in disease far gone.   [545]
The carman wet her lips as well behoved;
Bed under her lean body there was none,
Though even to die near one she most had loved
She could not of herself those wasted limbs have moved.

LXII.

The Soldier's Widow learned with honest pain   [550]
And homefelt force of sympathy sincere,
Why thus that worn-out wretch must there sustain

---

542 canvass] canvas *1845*–

---

540   See note to l. 693 of *ASP*, above, and the *apparatus criticus* for l. 540 of MS. 4, above. For
the proof of *G & S* the printer set up "runnel." WW deleted the "l" in favor of "r" and then
reinstated it, presumably feeling that the more commonly used term would be intelligible to a
wider readership.

553   *The jolting road, & morning air severe.*

554   *The Wain pursued its way,* *; }* *& following near*
555   *In pure compassion she her steps retraced*
556   *Far as the Cottage. "A sad sight is here"*
557   *She cried aloud—& forth ran out in haste*
558   *The friends whom she had left but a few minutes past.*

[17ᵛ]

63

                    While
559   *As to the door with eager speed they ran*
560   *From her bare straw the Woman half up-raised*
                        deadly }
561   *Her bony visage, gaunt & [?pale]} wan;*
562   *No pity asking, on the groupe she gazed*

                                — }
563   *With a dim eye, distracted & amazed, }*
564   *Then sunk upon her straw with feeble moan.*
            cried }
565   *Fervently [?]}, the Housewife "God be praised*
566   *I have a house that I can call my own;*

                                , }
567   *Nor shall she perish there,} untended & alone"!*

64

568   *So in they bear her to the chimney seat,*
569   *And busily, tho' yet with fear, untie*
570   *Her garments, &, to warm her icy feet*
571   *And chafe her temples, their careful hands apply.*
572   *Nature reviving, with a deep-drawn sigh*
573   *She strove, & not in vain, her head to rear,*

---

553 road,] road
556 Cottage.] Cottage—
558 past.] past *written over illeg word*
558/559 63] 29 *overwritten* 30
559 As] *del to* While
560 Woman] woman   up-raised] upraised
561 [?pale]] deadly   wan;] wan
562 asking,] asking   groupe] ground *overwritten* groupe
563 eye,] eye
564 amazed,—] amazed
564 moan.] moan
565 [?]] cried *written above line over caret*
566 own;] own
567 there,] there   alone"!] alone"
567/568 64] 30 *overwritten* 31
568 seat,] seat
569 fear,] fear
571 And . . . careful] With death's numb waters swoln their *del to* And chafe her temples, & their *del to* careful
572 And chafe her pulseless temples cold & dry] *del to* Nature reviving, with a deep drawn sigh,
573 She . . . her] At last she strove her languid *del to* She strove and not in vain her

---

572/573   Corrections in MS. 3 by WW.

The jolting road and morning air severe.
The wain pursued its way; and following near
In pure compassion she her steps retraced [555]
Far as the cottage. "A sad sight is here,"
She cried aloud; and forth ran out in haste
The friends whom she had left but a few minutes past.

LXIII.

While to the door with eager speed they ran,
From her bare straw the Woman half upraised [560]
Her bony visage—gaunt and deadly wan;
No pity asking, on the group she gazed
With a dim eye, distracted and amazed;
Then sank upon her straw with feeble moan.
Fervently cried the housewife—"God be praised, [565]
I have a house that I can call my own;
Nor shall she perish there, untended and alone!"

LXIV.

So in they bear her to the chimney seat,
And busily, though yet with fear, untie
Her garments, and, to warm her icy feet [570]
And chafe her temples, careful hands apply.
Nature reviving, with a deep-drawn sigh
She strove, and not in vain, her head to rear;

574   *Then said—"I thank you all, if I must die*
575   *"The God in heaven my prayers for you will hear;*
        Till now
576   ~~To day~~ *I did not think my end had been so near.*

[18ʳ]

65

577   *"Barred every comfort labour could procure,*
578   *"Suffering what no endurance could assuage,*
579   *"I was compelled to seek my Father's door*
           on
580   *"Tho' loth to be a burthen ~~to~~ his age;*
581   *"But sickness stopped me in an early stage*
          within ⎱
582   *"Of my sad journey; & [?in] ⎰ the Wain*
            life's
583   *"They placed me;—there to end ~~my~~ pilgrimage*
584   *"Unless beneath your roof I may remain;*
585   *"For I shall never see my Father's door again.*

66

         Heaven
    My life, ~~God~~ knows, hath long been burthensome
    [   ] ~~has to the full~~
586   *"~~My lot in life has long been~~ burthensome*
    But if I have not meekly
          ! ⎱
587   *"O God; ⎰ ~~if I have meekly~~ suffered, meek*
       ! ⎱ M⎱   Soon will this voice
588   *"May my end be, ⎰ m ⎰y ~~lips will soon~~ be dumb.*
589   *"Should Child of mine eer wander hither, speak*
590   *"Of me, say that the worm is on my cheek.*

---

574 Then] And *del to* Then   said—] said,   die] die,
575–612 *No opening quotation marks*
575 you] you,   hear;] hear
576 To day] *del to* Till now   near.] near
576/577 65] 31 *overwritten* 32
577 Barred] Barr'd   procure,] procure
578 assuage,] assuage
580 age;] age *and whole line inserted*
581 stopped] stopt
582 journey;] journey   [?in]] within
583 me;—] me—   my] *del to* lifes
584 remain;] remain
585 Father's] father's   again.] again *also* again. P
585/586 66] 32 *overwritten* 33
586 burthensome] burdensome
587 O God;] Oh God! *del to* But   have meekly] meekly *inserted above line then* not *written before* meekly   suffered] suffered,
588 be;] be,   dumb.] dumb
589 eer] e'er   hither,] hither
590 say] say,   cheek.] cheek

---

576   The correction here is in the hand of the revisions to 370–373, probably that of Christopher Wordsworth, Jr.

Then said—"I thank you all; if I must die,
The God in heaven my prayers for you will hear;   [575]
Till now I did not think my end had been so near.

LXV.

"Barred every comfort labour could procure,
Suffering what no endurance could assuage,
I was compelled to seek my father's door,
Though loth to be a burthen on his age.   [580]
But sickness stopped me in an early stage
Of my sad journey; and within the wain
They placed me—there to end life's pilgrimage,
Unless beneath your roof I may remain:
For I shall never see my father's door again   [585]

LXVI.

"My life, Heaven knows, hath long been burthensome;
But, if I have not meekly suffered, meek
May my end be! Soon will this voice be dumb:
Should child of mine e'er wander hither, speak
Of me, say that the worm is on my cheek.—   [590]

---

585 again] again. *1845–*

582–583 See note to ll. 735–737 of *ASP*, above. The problem of the vagrant poor was as
acute as ever in 1842, but it will be noticed that in *G & S* WW has cut out one of the bitterest
comments of *ASP* on the inhumanity of relief. This was no doubt partly because the Poor Law
Amendment Act of 1834 had seemed to offer some solution, and partly to preserve the more
generally optimistic spirit of the later poem.
590 See note to l. 743 of *ASP*, above.

591   *"In a lone hut beside the Sea we dwelt*
592   *"Near Portland light-house, in a sheltering creek,*
593   *"My Father too—the Good old Man would melt*
            were told what I have seen & felt
594   *"In tears, if he* ~~should hear of all that I have~~ *felt*
            Just God
            ~~O God~~ my life has long been burthensome
            But   meekly
            ~~But~~ if I have not suffered meek

586–594 [4a]

                        6⎫
                      67⎭

            H⎱
    "My life, h ⎰*eaven knows, hath long been burthensome;*
    "But, if I have not meekly suffered, meek
    "May my end be! Soon will this voice be dumb:
                    of mine
    "Should Child,eer wander hither, speak
    "Of me, say that the worm is on my cheek.—
            ~~Forced from our hut that stood~~
                ~~small~~   ⎱
    "~~In a~~ [—?—] ⎰ ~~hut we dwelt beside the Sea~~
            Torn from our hut that stood beside the Sea
    ~~"Near Portland Lighthouse in a lonesome creek~~
            ~~My husband served thro sad captivity~~
                        in sad
    ~~"On Ship-board toiling, bleeding as might be~~
    ~~"My husband served—fast bound till peace should set him~~ *free*
            ~~On Shipboard, served—there,~~
        "Torn from our hut that stood beside the Sea
        "Near Portland lighthouse in a lonesome creek,
        "My husband served in sad captivity
        "On Shipboard, ~~there fast~~ *bound till peace or death should*
                                set him free.

[18ᵛ]

                    67

        ~~A Soldier's wife~~
        A Sailors Wife
595   *"*~~Within that hut~~ *I knew a Widow's cares.*
        Yet two sweet Little ones partook my bed
        Yet
596   *"*~~Two little Children did partake my bed~~

---

591 In . . . hut] In a lone Hut *del to* Torn from our hut that stood   we dwelt] [?] dwelt *illeg word overwritten* We then We dwelt *del*
592 light-house,] Light-house   sheltering] *del to* lonesome   creek] *illegible word overwritten* creek *alt* creek
593 Good] good *whole line del to* My Husband served in sad captivity
594 In tears, if he should hear of all that I have felt *del to* On ship-board bound till peace or death should set him free
594/595 67] 33 *overwritten* 34
595 "Within that hut] Within that hut *del to* A Sailors wife   cares.] cares
596 "Two . . . partake] Two little Children did partake *del to* Yet two sweet Little ones partook

---

595   "A Soldier's wife" is probably in the hand of Christopher Wordsworth, Jr.

              me & to my daily prayers

        Hope cheered ~~my dreams & not unanswered prayers~~

597   "~~And strange hopes trembled thro my dreams & prayers~~

            O⎱

        ~~Asked from~~ o ⎰ur heavenly Father daily bread

598   "~~Strong was I then & labour gave us bread~~

        Till One was found by stroke of violence, [?]ad

599   "~~Until a Man was found by violence dead~~

595–599 [4ª]

    "*A Sailors wife, I knew a Widow's cares;*

             L⎱ -⎱

    "*Yet two sweet l ⎰ittle ⎰ones partook my bed;*

            y⎱ dreams

    "*Hope cheared me⎰, & to my daily prayers*

                          bread,

    "*Our heavenly Father granted each day's ~~food~~*

    "*Till One was found by stroke of violence dead*

---

                     ced⎱

600   "*Whose body near our Cottage chan*[?]⎰ *to lie.*

601   "*A dire suspicion drove us from our shed;*

602   "*In vain to find a friendly face we try,*

603   "*Nor could we live together those poor boys & I.*

                68

        For evil tongues made oath how on that day

               ~~68~~

             how⎱

       ath⎱ ~~was made that~~ ⎰ ~~on that very day.~~

604   "~~For One ⎰∧made oath how he had seen that day~~

           lurked about

605   "*My husband ~~lurking in~~ the neighbourhood,—*

606   "*Now he had fled, & whither none could say,*

607   "*And he had done the deed in the dark wood—*

                   mild

608   "*Near his own home!—but he was ~~kind~~ & good;*

---

   597 And strange hopes trembled thro my dreams & prayers *All but* prayers *del to* Hope cheered my dreams & to my daily

   598 Strong was I then, & labour gave us bread. *del to* Our heavenly Father granted each days bred

   599 Until a Man *del to* Till One

   600 chan[?]] [?chaunced] *blotted and del to* chanced   lie.] lie

   601 shed;] shed

   602 try,] try

   603 I.]   I *also* I *del to* I; *P* (?MW)

   603/604 68] 34 *overwritten* 35

   604 For one had seen he said, & swore it too *part del to* For one made oath how he had seen hat day *part del with additions to* For evil tongues made oath how on that day

   605 lurking in] *del to* lurk'd about   neighbourhood,—] neighbourhood

   606 Now he had fled, & whither no one knew *then* Now he *del to* Near his *del and* no one knew *'el to* none could say *del and entire line del*

   607 he . . . wood—] he . . . wood *and entire line del*

   608 kind] *del to* mild   good;] good

   607   *he*] Underlined in MS.

Torn from our hut, that stood beside the sea
Near Portland lighthouse in a lonesome creek,
My husband served in sad captivity
On shipboard, bound till peace or death should set him free.

LXVII.

"A sailor's wife I knew a widow's cares,
Yet two sweet little ones partook my bed;

Hope cheered my dreams, and to my daily prayers
Our heavenly Father granted each day's bread;
Till one was found by stroke of violence dead,
Whose body near our cottage chanced to lie;   [600]
A dire suspicion drove us from our shed;
In vain to find a friendly face we try,
Nor could we live together those poor boys and I;

LXVIII.

"For evil tongues made oath how on that day
My husband lurked about the neighbourhood;   [605]
Now he had fled, and whither none could say,
And *he* had done the deed in the dark wood—
Near his own home!—but he was mild and good;

                                    gentler
609   "*Never on earth was ~~milder~~ Creature seen;*
610   "*He'd not have robbed the raven of its food*
              O   dear   ~~lived he would have been~~
611   "*Oh had my husband ~~'mong the living been~~*
                 ~~My true & sure defence~~ For me my tender husband stood between
612   "*~~My days had passed secure from misery so keen~~*"
                 ~~My tender husband stood [?by] me, between~~

                 ~~Among the living had my husband been~~
                 [   ] The ~~The world & all its wrongs & pains~~ however
                         passed   ⎫
                 ~~My days had~~ [?   ] ⎬ *from misery*
                            [?] ⎭
                 The world & all its wrongs ⎰ *& pains* [*?however*] *keen*

610-612 [4a]

                 "*He'd not have robbed the Raven of its food.*
                   My Husbands loving kindness
                 "*~~For me my tender Husband~~* stood between
                   ~~All hardships of this~~   rongs ⎱
                   ~~The wrongs of this bad world,~~ & w[?] ⎰ *however keen.*
                   Me and all worldly harms

[19ʳ]

                         69
613   *Alas, the thing she told with labouring breath*
                              ⎱ T⎱
614   *The Sailor knew too well;* ⎰ t ⎰*hat wickedness*
                                 the
615   *His hand had wrought; & when in ~~her~~ hour of death*
616   *He saw his Wife's lips move his name to bless*
                 ~~With~~ her last words unable to suppress
617   *~~At such a sight he could no more suppress~~*
                 ~~His agony; with tears he ceased to~~
618   *~~Feelings that did within his bosom strive~~*
             Such⎱   is⎱   he⎱
          His ~~His~~ ⎰ anguish; with her⎰ heart ~~she~~ ⎰ ceased to strive
                                 his
                            ' "T⎱   "⎱
619   *And weeping loud* i ⎰n *this extreme distress* ⎰

---

609 milder] *del to* gentler   Creature seen;] creature seen
611 Oh had my husband mong the living been *part del to* My husbands loving kindness stood
between
612 "My . . . so] My days had passed secure from misery so *del to* Me & all worldly pains &
wrongs however   keen] keen"
612/613 69] 35 *overwritten* 36
613 Alas,] Alas! *First five words written over erasure*
614 *First five words written over erasure*
615 wrought; & when] wrought, when *then* & *inserted in line before* when *and semicolon written
over comma*
617 At . . . more] At such a sight he could no more *del to* With her last words unable to
618 Feelings that did within his bosom strive] *del to* His anguish with his heart he ceased to
strive
619 And . . . loud] And, . . . loud,

Never on earth was gentler creature seen;
He'd not have robbed the raven of its food.   [610]
My husband's loving kindness stood between
Me and all wordly harms and wrongs however keen."

LXIX.

Alas! the thing she told with labouring breath
The Sailor knew too well. That wickedness
His hand had wrought; and when, in the hour of death,   [615]
He saw his Wife's lips move his name to bless
With her last words, unable to suppress
His anguish, with his heart he ceased to strive;
And, weeping loud in this extreme distress,

---

611 loving kindness] loving-kindness *1846*

<pre>
                           do
620   He cried—"Oḥ pity me! that thou shouldst live
         neither   n⎫
621   I do not ask, ⎬ or wish—forgive me, but forgive!"
                        ⎭
</pre>

617–621 [4a]

> With her last words, unable to suppress
> His anguish, with his heart he ceased to strive;
>   I⎫ t
> And weeping loud, "i⎬n his extreme distress
> He cried—"Do pity me! That thou should live
>   ;⎫
> I neither ask nor wish—⎬forgive me, me, but forgive!"
>   ⎭

<pre>
                       70
        tell   V⎫
622   To speak the change that v ⎬oice within her wrought
623   Nature by sign or sound made no essay;
624   A sudden joy surprized expiring thought
625   And every mortal pang dissolved away.
626   Borne gently to a bed, there in death she lay;
627   Yet still, while over her the husband bent,
628   A look was in her face which seemed to say,
629   "Be blest;"—by sight of thee from heaven was sent
                               ;⎫
630   Peace to my parting Soul—⎬ the fullness of content."
                               ⎭
</pre>

[19ᵛ]

<pre>
                    ı⎫
                   72⎭
631   She slept in peace,—his pulses throbbed & stopped;
</pre>

---

620 Oh] *Oh (underlined) overwritten* do   pity me] *written over erasure*
  621 do not] *del to* neither   or] *made into* nor   but] *written over illeg word*   forgive!"]
forgive"
  621/622 70] 36 *overwritten* 37
  622 speak] *alt* tell
  623 or] *written* nor *then* n *erased*   essay;] essay
  626 bed,] bed   there in death] there dead *del to* in death   lay;] lay—
  627 Yet . . . her] Silently oer her face *del to* Yet still while over her   bent,] bent
  628 in her face] on her lips *del to* in her face   say,] say
  629 Comfort to thee my parting Soul hath sent *del to* Be blest!, by sight of thee from heaven is
sent *then* is *del to* was
  630 But not to him it seemed on other thoughts intent. *del to* Peace to my parting Soul—the
fullness of content.
  630/631 72] 37 *overwritten* 38
  631 peace,—] peace—   stopped;] stopped

  630/631   In the fair copy, MS. 4, stanzas 71–74 were misnumbered and have been corrected
by overwriting. In MS. 3 the fair copy jumped from 630 to 649 (the two stanzas 631–648 were
written at the end); at 630–631 the copyist is directed to insert the stanzas in the final order by
the note "She slept in peace (see for / Stanza [miswritten "Statza"] at the end)" and by the
insertion of the stanza number "38." At the foot of the additional stanzas at the end MW has
written "Confirmed of purpose (turn back)."
  631   *She*] underlined in MS.

He cried—"Do pity me! That thou shouldst live [620]
I neither ask nor wish—forgive me, but forgive!"

LXX.

To tell the change that Voice within her wrought
Nature by sign or sound made no essay;
A sudden joy surprised expiring thought,
And every mortal pang dissolved away. [625]
Borne gently to a bed, in death she lay;
Yet still while over her the husband bent,
A look was in her face which seemed to say,
"Be blest; by sight of thee from heaven was sent
Peace to my parting soul, the fulness of content." [630]

LXXI.

She slept in peace,—his pulses throbbed and stopped,

632 *Breathless he gazed upon her face* ⌉ *then took*
633 *Her hand in his, & raised it, but both dropped*
634 *When on his own he cast a rueful look.*
635 *His ears were never silent; sleep forsook*
636 *His burning eyelids, stretched & stiff as lead;*
                         under
637 *All night from time to time* ~~beneath~~ *him shook*
638 *The floor as he lay shuddering on his bed;*
639 *And oft he groaned aloud, "O God that I were dead!"*

               2 ⌉
             73 ⌠

640 *The Soldier's Widow lingered in the Cot;*
641 *And, when he rose, he thanked her pious care*

642 *Thro' which his Wife, to that kind shelter brought,* ⌉
           ; ⌉
643 *Died in his arms——* ⌠ *and with those thanks a prayer*
644 *He breathed for her, & for that merciful Pair.——*
645 *The Corse interred, not one hour he remained*
         Beneath
646 ~~*Under*~~ *their roof; but to the open air*

647 *A burthen* ⌉ *now, with fortitude sustained* ⌉
648 *He bore, within a breast where dreadful quiet reigned.*

[20ʳ]

             3 ⌉
            74 ⌠

649 *Confirmed of purpose, fearlessly prepared*

---

632 face—] face,
634 on] in *overwritten on*   look.] look
635 silent;] silent
636 eyelids,] eyelids   lead;] lead
637 beneath] *del to* under
638 bed;] bed
639/640 73] 38
640 Soldier's Widow] *Written over erasure*   Cot;] Cot
641 And,] And   rose,] rose
642 Wife,] Wife   brought,] brought
643 and] *inserted above line*
644 breathed] Breathed *then* He *inserted above line*   Pair.—] Pair.
645 interred,] interred   hour] *written over illeg word*   remained] remain'd
646 Under] *del to* Beneath   roof;] roof
647 burthen,] burthen   now,] now   sustained,] sustained
648 bore, within] carried [?in] *del to* bore within
648/649 74] 38 *overwritten* 39
649–651 *The following full transcription will make the complicated readings of MS. 3 clearer:*
                                         ly ⌉
   Confirmed of purpose   fearless & ⌠ prepared

640–651 See additions to MS. 2, 79ᵛ, above, for MW's copy of these lines at the back of that notebook. The stanza 640–648 is also one of the additional stanzas written after the end of the fair copy in MS. 3.
    649–651 In the addition to MS. 3, "For act & suffering" is in WW's hand.

Breathless he gazed upon her face,—then took
Her hand in his, and raised it, but both dropped,
When on his own he cast a rueful look.
His ears were never silent; sleep forsook   [635]
His burning eyelids stretched and stiff as lead;
All night from time to time under him shook
The floor as he lay shuddering on his bed;
And oft he groaned aloud, "O God, that I were dead!"

LXXII.

The Soldier's Widow lingered in the cot;   [640]
And, when he rose, he thanked her pious care
Through which his Wife, to that kind shelter brought,
Died in his arms; and with those thanks a prayer
He breathed for her, and for that merciful pair.
The corse interred, not one hour he remained   [645]
Beneath their roof, but to the open air
A burthen, now with fortitude sustained,
He bore within a breast where dreadful quiet reigned.

LXXIII.

Confirmed of purpose, fearlessly prepared

646 their] her *1846*

650   *For act & suffering, to the City strait*
651   *He journeyed, & forthwith his crime declared:*
652   *"And from your doom" he added "now I wait,*
653   *"Nor let it linger long, the Murderer's fate."*
654   *Not ineffectual was that piteous claim.*

              _{w⎱}
      A O W⎰elcome ~~the~~   which
655   *"O ~~welcome sentence that~~ will end tho' late,"*
656   *He said, "the pangs that to my conscience came*

657   *Out of that deed⫽⎱ My trust Saviour, is in thy Name!"*

            4⎱
           75⎰

           H⎱
658   *His fate was pitied. h⎰im in iron case,*

659   *(Reader forgive the intolerable thoughts⎰⫽)*

    For act & suffering
  ~~The corse was buried, to the City strait~~
    ~~From that last office,~~ to the City strait
    ⎰journeyed
  He ⎱went   ~~& all which he had done declared~~
         & forthwith his crime declared
652 doom] hands *overwritten* doom
653 "Nor] Nor   it] them *del to* it
654 Not] Nor *overwritten* Not
655 "O welcome] "Blest be the *del to* O welcome   end] end,   late,"] late"
657 trust] trust,   Saviour,] Saviour!   Name] name
657/658 75] 40
658–666 *Full transcription of MS. 3 is again helpful:*
  His fate was pitied—him in iron case
  ~~They left him hung on high in iron case~~
  (Reader forgive the intolerable thought)
  ~~Warning for Men unthinking & untaught~~
  They hung not—no one on his form or face
  ~~And such would come to gaze upon his face~~
  Would gaze as on ~~which~~ a show by idlers sought,
  ~~And to that spot in idle numbers sought~~
  No kindred Sufferer to his death-place brought
  ~~Women & children were by Fathers brought~~
  By lawless curiosity or chance
  ~~And now some kindred sufferer⎰ driven perchance~~
       W⎱   evening
  ~~That way,~~ w⎰hen into storm the sky is wrought
    his   an   could
  Upon ~~the~~ swinging corpse ~~his~~ eye ~~may~~ glance
  And drop as ~~he~~ once dropped in miserable trance
On the opposite verso WW has penciled:
  His fate was pitied—him in iron case
  (Reader forgive the intolerable thought
                on his form or
  They hung not—~~so that~~ no one ~~on his~~ face c
  Could gaze as on a show by idlers sought
  Nor could a kindred Sufferer thither brought
  By urgent curiosity or ch

658–663   On MS. 3, 48ʳ, with the notebook inverted, WW has penciled the greatly revised version of these lines of the last stanza. His version, in a slightly corrected state, was then interlined in ink on the fair copy. In MS. 4, of course, the new version has become the base text.

For act and suffering, to the city straight   [650]
He journeyed, and forthwith his crime declared:
"And from your doom," he added, "now I wait,
Nor let it linger long, the murderer's fate."
Not ineffectual was that piteous claim:
"O welcome sentence which will end though late,"   [655]
He said, "the pangs that to my conscience came
"Out of that deed. My trust, Saviour! is in thy name!"

LXXIV.

His fate was pitied. Him in iron case
(Reader, forgive the intolerable thought)

---

657 "Out] Out *1845–*

660   *They hung not;—no one on <u>his</u> form or face*

661   *Could gaze as on a she}w, by idlers sought;*

662   *No kindred sufferer to his death-place brought*

663   *By lawless curiosity, or chance,*

664   *When into storm the evening sky is wrought[—?—]}*

665   *Upon his swinging corpse an eye can } glance,*

666   *And drop, as he once dropped, in miserable trance.*

---

665 corpse] *del to* corse *P* (John Carter)   could] *del to* can *P* (WW)
666 *After line 666 in* P2 *WW has added* 1793−4

---

660   *his*] underlined in MS.

They hung not:—no one on *his* form or face [660]
Could gaze, as on a show by idlers sought;
No kindred sufferer, to his death-place brought
By lawless curiosity or chance,
When into storm the evening sky is wrought,
Upon his swinging corse an eye can glance, [665]
And drop, as he once dropped, in miserable trance.

1793–4.

Appendixes

Appendix I

Fragments Related to the Salisbury Plain Poems in DC MS. 2

Dove Cottage MS. 2 contains two fragmentary pieces, edited by de Selin-court as Juvenilia, numbers XVI (a) and (b), *PW*, I, 292–295, with notes on 371. His text necessarily left out all the draft material toward the more finished versions of each fragment. As these are of considerable interest, they are presented below, following edited reading texts.

Juvenilia No. XV, in debased Spenserians, which de Selincourt also presents in a reading text, is most closely related to *The Borderers*, especially to Act II, scene ii, but some of its lines are repeated at the opening of the second part of *ASP* in MS. 2; see XV, 200–202 (*PW*, I, 292), and *ASP*, 412–414. Fragments XVI (a) and (b), cited hereafter as (a) and (b), in blank verse and debased Spenserian stanzas respectively, are also connected with *The Borderers* in that lines 28–32 of (a) show a few verbal parallels with the beggar's speech in *The Borderers*, MS. B, Act I, scene iii, 420–428 (*PW*, I, 144). The fragments are most obviously connected, however, with the Salisbury Plain poems. Lines 88–90 of (b) appear also in MS. 2, where WW attempted a fresh opening for the woman's story; see above, *ASP* transcription, 40^r. Odd details suggest also that the fragments are closely linked in WW's mind with the Salisbury Plain poems. In one version of (b), lines 25–26, the traveler hears the clock toll out "from the Minster tower," the minster tower the sailor looks for in vain as he toils up onto the Plain. Lines 76–79 of (b) compress into finer poetry *SP*, 204–205 and 218:

> Her cheek, the beauty of whose doubtful hues
> Showed like a rose, its time of blowing past,
> Wet with the morning's ineffectual dews.[1]

Lines 24–26 of (b) recall *SP*, 115 and 118–119.

There are parallels, too, of situation. The incident in which the woman offers hospitality to the vagrant, for example, is a fusion of the details in *ASP* from the episodes where the Female Vagrant tells her story to the sailor and

---

[1] Carol Landon, "Wordsworth's Racedown Period: Some Uncertainties Resolved," *BNYPL*, LXVIII (1964), 100–109. See especially 103.

where they meet the poor woman whose husband maltreats their child. The narrative strategy is repeated where the traveler's sympathy draws the mother on to tell her story, just as in *ASP* the sailor's sympathy encourages the Female Vagrant to continue. The difference is that the bond of sympathy is now felt between two women and not between the woman and the sailor.

It is difficult, however, to understand the relationship of (a) and (b) to the Salisbury Plain poems and to WW's development. De Selincourt dated the passages 1791 and thus saw them as early work on themes for *The Borderers* and *SP*. This dating is convincingly challenged in the article by Carol Landon cited above, which places them between late 1795 and late 1796—that is, when the two early versions of the Salisbury Plain poems were substantially complete. It thus seems likely that the fragments belong, not to work toward *SP* or *ASP*, but to a development of certain aspects of these poems. They would seem to belong to that period between the completion of *ASP* and the beginning of *The Borderers* in which WW was working toward the more ambitious themes and form of the tragedy. In XV some details of the psychology of the sailor in *ASP* are developed. The motives of the murderer and the feelings of guilt and doubt that possess him, future focuses of interest in *The Borderers*, are high-lighted. In (a) and (b) a new emphasis is placed on the sympathy between the two women, which develops the earlier idea of the emotional bond between the sailor and his chance companion, the woman. Most important of all, in (a) WW makes his first significant use of blank verse, which was to become his medium for sustained poetry. Emerging from this work, *The Borderers* brought to a focus WW's development as a philosophical poet.

The Text

In presenting the materials in DC MS. 2 which are related to the Salisbury Plain poems, I follow the conventions adopted for presentation of the poems themselves. Transcriptions of the fragments are preceded by edited reading texts, which represent the fragments in their most advanced state.

Texts

(a)

The road extended o'er a heath
Weary and bleak: no cottager had there
Won from the waste a rood of ground, no hearth
Of Traveller's half-way house with its turf smoke
Scented the air through which the plover wings   5
His solitary flight. The sun was sunk
And, fresh-indented, the white road proclaimed
The self-provided waggoner gone by.
Me from the public way the [common] hope
Of shorter path seduced, and led me on   10
Where smooth-green sheep-tracks thridded the sharp furze
And kept the choice suspended, having chosen.
The time exacted haste and steps secure
From such perplexity, so to regain
The road now more than a long mile remote   15
My course I slanted, when at once winds rose
And from the rainy east a bellying cloud
Met the first star and hurried on the night.
Now fast against my cheek and whistling ears
My loose wet hair and tattered bonnet flapped   20
With thought-perplexing noise, that seemed to make
The universal darkness that ensued
More dark and desolate. Though I had seen
Worse storm, no stranger to such nights as these
Yet had I fears from which a life like mine   25
Might long have rested, and remember well
That as I floundered on, disheartened sore
With the rough element and pelting shower,
I saw safe sheltered by the viewless furze   30
The tiny glowworm, lowliest child of earth,
From his green lodge with undiminished light
Shine through the rain, and strange comparison
Of Envy linked with pity touched my heart
And such reproach of heavenly ordonnance
As shall not need forgiveness.   35

(b)

1

No spade for leagues had won a rood of earth
From that bleak common, of all covert bare;
From traveller's half-way house no genial hearth
Scented with its turf smoke the desart air,
Through which the plover wings his lonely course,   5
Nor aught that might detain the sight was there,
Only a blossomed slope of dazzling gorse
Gave back the deep light of the setting sun;
All else was dreary dark—sad course her feet must run.

2

The road's white surface fresh indented showed   10
The self-provided waggoner gone by,
Yet oft her eye retraced the backward road
Some coal-team or night-going wain to spy;
At last for nearer path she turned aside
And strayed where numerous sheep-tracks green and dry   15
The sharp furze thridding did all choice divide.
And now with slanted course again she sought
The road whose winding reach was now a mile remote.

3

Her heart recovered but the time allowed
No further stay and less her late affright,   20
And from the rainy east a bellying cloud
Met the first star and hurried on the night;
The shower o'erblown the air was cold and clear,
The desart opening in the moon's pale light,
Nor sound save her own steps she seemed to hear   25
For ten long miles: from the Minster tower,
The distant clock tolled out the morning's second hour.

4

And from the facing of a hill she viewed
A taper twinkling through a wicker hole,
Whence through the still depth of the air subdued   30
Forthwith a sound of singing upward stole,
So plaintive sad the cadence might agree
With one who sang from very grief of soul,

More likely at such hour the lullaby
Of some poor mother o'er a sleepless child: 35
The house was soon attained—it was a dwelling wild.

5

Gently she knocked and prayed they would not blame
A Traveller weary-worn and needing rest;
Strait to the door a ragged woman came
Who with arms linked and huddling elbows press'd   40
By either hand, a tattered jacket drew
With modest care across her hollow breast,
That showed a skin of sickly yellow hue.
"With travel spent," she cried, "you needs must be
If from the heath arrived; come in and rest with me.   45

6

How could I fear that I, whose winter nights
Once stole such merry festivals from sleep,
Should pine, in youth outliving youth's delights,
Here in the eye of hunger doomed to weep?
Here of my better days no trace is seen,   50
Yet in my breast the shadow still I keep
Of Happiness gone by, with years between,
And but that Nature feels these corporal aches
My life might seem a dream, the thing a vision makes."

7

So praying her to come more near she threw   55
A knot of heath upon the embers cold,
Which with her breath [   ] anon she blew
And talked between of that unfriendly wold;
Then from a mat of straw a boy she raised
Who seemed though weak in growth three winters old,   60
And with a fruitless look of fondness gazed
On his pale face; she held him at her breast
If nourishment thence drawn might lead at length to rest.

8

The stranger, whom such sight not failed to touch,
Tenderly said, "In truth you are to blame,   65
For you are feeble and 'twill waste you much,
That office asks indeed a stronger frame."

At this [?meek] proof of sympathy so given
In to the mother's eye a big tear came.
"To wean the boy," she said, "I oft have striven,   70
But we are poor and when no bread is nigh
It is a piteous thing to hear an infant cry."

9

At once a thousand Dreams through memory rushed
And from the heart its present sorrow chased;
While down her cheek by feverish watching flushed   75
Th' o'erflow of inmost weakness trickled fast,
Her cheek, the beauty of whose doubtful hues
Showed like a rose, its time of blowing past,
Wet with the morning's ineffectual dews.
Then while the stranger warmed her torpid feet,   80
So willing seemed her ear, she gan her tale repeat.

10

"A little farm, my husband's own domain,
Beheld the promise of my bridal day,
And when the dancing eddy of the brain
Was past, through many months that rolled away   85
Their calmer progress, sober reason blest
Each hope that Youth can feed or years betray.
Our farm was sheltered like a little nest,
No greener fields than ours could eye survey,
Pleasant the fields without, and all within as gay.   90

11

From homely labour and appearance plain
Round the light heart such steady pleasure shone,
Thankful I lived, nor tongue pronounced me vain.
I bore my fortunes meekly and was one
Whom softened envy might have learned to bless;   95
Nor needed that my summer should be flown
To teach my heart the claims of wretchedness.
But [   ]
Nor may it well be said by one so fallen as I.

Transcriptions

[Inside front cover]

     her hair upon her shoulders spread
Not ~~she~~ lovelier shows the oak through sunny showers
The first light yellow of his budding head

[52^v]

Her heart recovered but the time allowed
No further search and less her late affright
[?Now]⎱
 And ⎰from the rainy east a bellying cloud
Met the first star and hurried on the night

No cottager had won a rood of earth
               [?cutting]
From that dark common of all ~~verdure~~ bare
From travellers half way house no genial hear
      ed
~~Did~~ scent   with its turf smoke the vacant air
~~The~~ [?plovers] [?range] the [?sunk] had left the sky,
And fresh indented did the road declare
The self provided waggoner gone by

[53^r]

              ~~And I can well conceive~~
~~That wandring after sunset oer some heath~~
~~The self-provided Waggoner gone by~~
The public way extended   It was a heath
Weary and bleak no cottager had there
                  no hearth
Won from the waste a rood of earth, ~~or fixed no smoke~~
    [−?−] ⎱   T⎱
Hi[?s] Hearth⎰ [−?−] of t ⎰ravellers half way house with
~~From hearth of any dwelling with turf~~ smoke
Scented the air throug which the plover wings
His lonely flight. The sun was setting

[53^v]

The public way extended oer a heath
Weary and bleak no cottager had there
Won from the waste a rood of earth no hearth
Of Travellers half way house with its turf smoke
Scented the air through which the plover wings
            [?sinking]
His lonely flight. The [?sunk] was ~~setting~~ [?down] sinking low
   in   fresh   the white
And ~~on the~~ indented road ~~the recent track~~ proclaimed
The self-provided waggoner gone by.
  Me ⎱
[?]⎰ from the publick way the the common hope

                       shorter
Of ~~nearer~~ path seduced and led me on

                                t ⎫
                 m ⎫   [?]⎰racks   furze
Where ~~numerous~~ s[h]⎰ooth green sheep ~~walks~~ thridded the sharp ~~gorse~~
And kept the choice suspended having chosen.
             ~~Now And yet not long for from the rainy east~~
When⎫
[?]⎰ from the rainy east a bellying cloud
             Yet long it was not so for from the [?east]
Met the first star and hurried on the night.
     [?Roaring] and [?dreary] and wild
                    [?then]
~~Lost~~ In the total darkness ~~that~~ ensued winds rose a
And whistled round my ears and my loose hair
And tattered bonnet flapped with deafening sound
                  wind blast a load
And my legs struggled with the ~~wind storm~~ [?and] weight
Of garments heavy with the ~~battering~~ soaking shower
              against
                   ~~And with~~ the blast my legs
Struggled and with a weight of garments soak[?s]
~~With~~ ⎫ [?] In the
~~by~~ ⎰ hard shower. Though I had seen
                such night as
Worse storm no stranger to a night like this
              from which
Yet I had fears ~~about me such as~~ a life like mine
              well   And remember   [?]
Might [——?——?——] be spared   Nor ~~had I strength to view~~

[54ʳ]

~~At~~⎫
[?]⎰ ~~such a time~~
Flou[?n]edring ~~through that~~ oer that dark heath nor house
~~In~~ [?view] ~~nor hous~~ The glowworm sheltered by the unseen furze
Shine through the rain [?thro][?] the rain with undiminishe light
        strong
And ~~such~~ comparison rose in my heart
        lit by   [?patient]
~~Of envy~~ [?mixed] ~~with~~ pity and such reproach of
As will not need forgiveness

          I cannot

Winds sounds against my face and whistling ears
My loose [?] wet hair and tattered bonnet flapped
     thought-perplexing   deaf and thought-perp
With ~~deafening~~ noise ~~against the blast my legs~~
~~Again struggled~~

53ᵛ   The hanging "a" at the end of the line ending "winds rose" is perhaps the result of WW's
writing in the flow of composition the first letter of the next line.

      make
To ~~give~~ the [?motal] Darkness that [?ens]
   [?~~blu~~]
Mor ~~wild~~ and

[54ᵛ]

               Though I had seen
Worse storm, no stranger to such nights as these
Yet I had fears from which a life like mine
Might long have rested   and ~~I~~ remember well
   As on   [?daught] as I was
~~That as I~~ floundered ~~oer that~~   ~~heath~~
   Of man
       bed   that night   such
~~No house in~~ view ~~that~~ strange comparison
Of ~~Pity~~ Envy linked with pity wracked my heart
And such reproach of heavenly ordonnance
                   I marked⎫
As shall not need forgiveness when [?]⎰
The glowworm sheltered by the viewless furze
Shine through the shower with undiminished light
        rueful
When [?stat] ~~a~~ sound that seemed the ~~rueful~~ [?voice]
Of [?heart] in sorrow pining smote her ear
~~Follow~~ [————?————] [?this]
Erelong succeeded by a groan

           the cotters ponies pastured near
Mute as the ground nor other living thing
Appeared through all the waste; only the geese
          om⎫
Were heard to send fr[?]⎰ far a dreary cry
   a [?]   succeed
And ~~some~~thing   a [?given]

And, fresh-indented the white road declared
The self-provided waggoner gone by

[55ʳ]

           —the road extended oer a heath
Weary and bleak: no cottager had there
          ground
Won from the waste a rood of ~~earth~~ no hearth
Of Traveller's half-way house with its turf smoke
Scented the air through which the plover wings
His solitary flight. The sun was sunk
And, fresh-indented, the white road proclaimed
The self-provided waggoner gone by
Me from the public way   the   hope
Of shorter path seduced, and led me on
Where smooth-green sheep-tracks thridded the sharp furze
And kept the choice suspended having chosen.
~~But such perplexity endured not long~~

                          h ⎫
The time exacted [?]⎫ aste and steps secure
From such perplexity, so to regain
The road now more than a long mile remote
  change'd my course I slanted
I turned when all at once winds rose
And from the rainy east a bellying cloud
Met the first star & hurried on the night.
      fast   cheek
And now‸against my face and whistling ears
My loose wet hair and tattered bonnet flapped
                        that seemed to make
With thought-perplexing noise. Though I had seen
    The universal darkness that ensued

[55ᵛ]

    More dark and desolate   though I had seen
Worse storm, no stranger to such nights as these
Yet had I fears from which a life like mine
Might long have rested, and remember well
That as I floundered on dishearted sore
With⎫
 By ⎭ the rough element and pelting shower
   I   safe sheltered by the viewless furze
And saw‸   the lowliest child of earth
    The tiny glow-worm lowliest child of earth
The gloworm sheltered by the viewless furze
              dge⎫
    From his green lo[?]⎭
Shine through the rain with undiminished light
                        and
Shine through the rain, such strange comparison
Of Envy linked with pity touched my heart
And such reproach of heavenly ordonnance
As shall not need forgiveness

[58ʳ]

No spade for leagues had won a rood of earth
From that bleak common of all covert bare
From travellers half-way house no genial hearth
Scented with its turf smoke the desart air
                wheels   screaming
Through which the plover wings his lonely course
Nor aught that might detain the sight was there
Only a blossomed slope of dazzling gorse
Gave back the deep light of the setting sun
                              [?race]
All else was dreary-dark—sad course her feet must run.

    58ʳ   Just preceding this page is a stub with the following visible: A/ of/ Wa/ So/ Lik/ Clap/
                                                          Or
Fro/ Mea. Then in different ink appears: And/ Of/ Ere/ As a/ Tha/ She/ [?]/ Whe/ An.

did her eye retrace the backward road
Oft look~~ed she back~~ward for night-going wain
    Some   to
~~Nor~~ coal-team or night-going wain ~~could~~ spy
    The roads white surface, fresh indented showed
And the white road declared indented plain
The self-provided waggoner gone by
    She
Then turned aside for nearer path and strayed
            where ⎫ ~~but~~
Onward, [?when] ⎭ numerous sheep-tracks green and dry
Thrid the sharp furze and after choice is made
Keep choice suspended—so, again she sought
With slanted course the road a long mile now remote

The road's white surface fresh indented showed
The self provided waggoner gone by
Yet oft her eye retraced the backward road
Some coal team or night going wain to spy

[58ᵛ]

Her heart recovered but the time allowed
            stay
No further ~~search~~ and less her late affright
And from the rainy east a bellying cloud
Met the first star & hurried on the night
                the air was cold & clear
The shower o'erblown ~~she urged her lonely way~~
The desart opening in the moon's pale light
    ~~Long was her course~~
~~And marked at last a taper's twinkling ray~~
    ~~Nor sound~~   from the Minster
~~Then little hoped for in the moon's pale light~~
                from the Minster tower
The distant clock tolled out the morning's second hour

            save
Nor sound ~~but~~ her own steps she seemed to hear
For ten long miles.

The roads white surface fresh indented showed
The self-provided waggoner gone by
Yet oft here eye retraced the backward road
Some coal-team or night-going wain to spy
    At last for
In hope of nearer path she turned aside
And strayed where numerous sheep track's green and dry
The sharp furze thridding did all choice divide
    And now
At last with slanted course again she sought

W
~~The~~   stretching road a ~~a~~ long mile now remote
The road whose winding reach was now a mile remote

[59ʳ]

It was a lofty hill that to the ear
Gave large command and now from wicker hole
below
Of ~~hut~~ beneath that taper twinkled clear
And thence a sound of singing upward stole
cadence
So plaintive-sad the ~~tones~~ might ~~well~~ agree
With one who sang from very grief of soul
More likely at such hour the lullaby
Of some poor mother oer a sleepless child
Sad

And thence along the night air clear and still

at   a hills inpending brow
And from the facing of a hill she viewd
A taper twinkling through a wicker hole
Whence through the still depth of the air subdued
Forthwith a sound of singing upward stole
So plaintive sad the cadence might agree

Who with arms linkt and huddeling elbows drew
A [?packing] round her body ~~stiff~~ and bent

[59ᵛ]

~~And~~ [?an] woman met her view
And strait a ragged woman met her
Cla~~d in a jacket half sleeve~~less
Whose [?frail] [?half] jacket
That showed an arm of sickly yellow hue
[?from]
All [?] the Shoulder to the elbow bare
In
The jacket ~~clad~~ [?] which had mock'd repair
Half-sleeveless shewed an arm of yellow hue
All fro

[62ᵛ]

Backward she often looked and might have spared
Those backward loo   for nothing met her eye
And fresh indented the white road declared
The self-provided ~~gone b~~ waggoner gone by
turned and
So from the public way ~~she~~ strayed
for nearer path [?wer] sheep track smooth and try
Thrid the sharp furze and after choice was made
Still kept the choice suspended; ~~turning~~ back she sought
~~With~~ slanted [?course] the road now more [?]

　　　　　　　[?in]　　　　　　　out the road
For nearer path from ~~public that public way~~ she strayed
Led on where numerous sheep tracks green and dry
Thrid
Then from the road for nearer   so she turned and sought
With slanted course the road a[?lo]

[65ʳ]

　　[?she]　　r ⎫　　declared
The ~~white~~ [?]⎰oad ~~told~~ ~~indented fresh~~ and plain
The self provided waggoner gone by
For coal team or night-going limeston wain
　　　　　she often
Backward ~~she~~ cast in [?vain] [?] a [?]
　　　　she looked
~~And fresh-indented the white road declared~~
The self-provided waggoner gone by
Then from the road for nearer path she strayed
　　Onward
Led on   where numerous sheep-tracks ~~smoo~~   green and dry
Thrid the sharp furze and after choice is made
[—]⎫
The⎰ Keep choice suspended   so she turned—and sought
With slanted course, the road a long mile now remote
For coal-team or night-going limestone wain
Backward she looked nor man or team could spy
And the white road declared indented plain
The self-provided waggoner gone by
[?Then] ~~for a   In hope of nearer path~~
　　　　　　　　　She turned aside for nearer path
　　　　　　　　　　　　　and stray

[65ᵛ]

W⎫　　　So that ~~the~~ she soon should
T⎰hen And soon could she regain the public way
For now all colour was extinguished quite

When long she travelled on exhausted quite
　　　saw at last
And ~~lost she saw~~ a taper's twinkling ray
　　[—?—] Thither [?gained]
And ~~gained~~ the spot   when from the minster tow
　　　　　　　　twice
The distant clock tolled ~~out the~~ mornings second hour

[71ʳ]

　　　　　　　　　　　crazy hut
The house was soon attained—it was a dwelling wild
Gently she knock'd and prayed they would not blame

71ʳ Just preceding this page is a stub with the following visible: A/ W/ W/ An/ [?]est/ ~~So the~~/
[?]
As/ And/ When/ He[?]/ And/ Then/ Of.

A Traveller weary-worn and needing rest
Strait to the door a ragged woman came
Who with arms linked and huddling elbows press'd
By either hand a tattered jacket drew
With modest care across her hollow brest
That showed a skin of sickly yellow hue
With travel spent" she cried "you needs must be
If from the heath arrived come in and rest with me

How could I fear that I whose winter nights
    Once stole such   s
Won many a̱merry festival from sleep
    Should
~~Must~~ pine, in youth outliving youth's delights,
Here in the eye of hunger doomed to weep:
Here of my better days no trace is seen
Yet in my breast the shadow still I keep
Of Happiness gone by, with years between,
And but that Nature feels these corpo'ral aches
My life might seem a dream the thing a vision makes

[71ᵛ]
       So praying her to come more near
~~Praying~~ the stranger to approach she threw
      heath⎱
A knot of turf⎰ upon the embers cold
Which with her breath   anon she blew
And talked between, of that unfriendly wold
   Then   from a mat of straw ~~a child~~ a boy she
~~And shortly~~ from a bed adjoined she took
~~A That seemed but little less than three years old~~
         at to   [?tender]
~~And placed him on her breast; with piteous look~~
Then from a mat of straw a boy she raised
Who seemed though weak in growth three winters old
~~Then~~ And with a fruitless look of ~~love~~ fondness gazed
         she held
On his pale face and ~~placed~~ him at her breast
       kindred thought
~~Sight which with [——?——] grief the strangers heart oppres~~
If nourishment thence drawn might lead at length to rest
Th⎱
Su⎰
    The stranger whom such sight not failed to touch
         you⎱
Tenderly said in truth ye⎰ are to blame
For you are feeble and twill wast you much
    That office
  ~~Such~~ ⎱ service⎱
~~As service~~⎰ [?]⎰ asks indeed a stronger frame.
At this [?meek] proof of sympathy so given
I⎱
T⎰n to the mothers eye a big tear came

                       oft
~~She said~~ To wean the boy she said I long have striven
But [?have] we are poor and when no bread is nigh
It is a piteous thing to hear an infants cry
In this [?peat] hut a pipe for every blast
To blow wild music in the ear of cold

[72ᵛ]

    & this in memory,   sorrow
And from her heart the present chased
    The tears of
~~And tears~~ from ~~weakness inmost~~ inmost weakness trickled fast
   And   [?in]
Down her ~~worn~~ cheek by feverish watching flushed
Her cheek the beauty of whose doubtful hues
Showed like a rose, its time of blowing past,
Wet with the mornings ineffectual dews
And while the stranger sat to warm her feet
She gan ~~as grief is wont~~ her sorrow to repeat

[73ᵛ]

                 with sudden apparition melts its way
A little farm my husbands own domain
Beheld the promise of my bridal day.
   W ⎱ ~~While~~
And ⎰ ᴧhomely labour and appearance plain
    For months made all within
Preserved the conscious heart serene and gay,
For many a month, while sober reason blest
  E ⎱
  S ⎰ ach hope that Youth can feed or years betray

             sober reason blest
Each hope that youth can feed or years betray
Our farm was sheltered like a little nest
No greener fields than ours could eye survey
Pleasant the field without and all within as gay

From homely labour and appearance plain
     certain   on
Such ~~such our~~ pleasure ~~on the~~ [?] shone
Yet none   pronounced me vain
     fortune
I bore my meekly and I was one
One whom softened envy might have learned to bless

[74ʳ]

A little farm [–?–] my husband's own ~~domain~~ demesne
Beheld the promise of my bridal day
And when the dancing eddy of the brain
Was past, through many months that rolled away
Their calmer progress, sober reason blest

Each hope that Youth can feed or years betray.
Our farm was sheltered like a little nest
No greener fields than ours could eye survey,
Pleasant the fields without, and all within as gay.

From homely labour and appearance plain
                     pleasure
Round the ~~bright~~ light heart such steady   shone
     Yet never tongue
~~Thankful I lived nor,~~tongue pronounced me vain
I bore my fortunes meekly and was one
Whom softened envy might have learned to bless
     ~~did I need my~~ my store summer should be flown
Nor needed that ~~these joys should all be gone~~
To teach my heart the claims of wretchedness
But
Nor may it well be said by one so fallen as I

                      wish
              wish and brooding wish
        oh I could ~~brood on~~ [?these] [?things]
      Till Memory owned the [?courage] of Desire

[75^r]
    once
At ~~this~~ a thousand Dreams through memory rushed,
        the   its
And from her heart the present sorrow chased;
While⎱
And⎰ Down her cheek by feverish watching flushed
Th'oerflow of inmost weakness trickled fast,
—Her cheek, the beauty of whose doubtful hues
Showed like a rose, its time of blowing past,
Wet with the mornings inefectual dews.
                      torpid feet
Then while ~~the stranger sat to~~ warmd her ~~feet~~
                  [?gand]   grief
~~Her~~ so willing seemed seemed ~~her~~ she [?did] ~~her tale~~ repeat
                    [?be]
So willing seemed her ear, she gan her tale repeat

[76^v]

A little farm my husbands own domain
~~With feast~~
~~With feast received me on my wedding~~
                   bridal
Beheld the   of my ~~wedding~~ day
There ~~sober~~ steady labour and appearance plain
Preserved the conscious serene and gay

   74^r The word "pleasure" in the line beginning "Round" is in pencil; in the following line "Yet never tongue" is in pencil, as are the deletion line and caret. Three lines below, "did I need my" is deleted in pencil; "these" through "gone" is deleted in pencil as well as ink.

~~Through~~
~~An~~

Or stole from househould prudence one [?resolve]

[77^r]

A little farm my husbands own domain
With feast received me on my bridal day,
And homely labour and "appearance plain"
Preserved the conscious heart serene and gay;
Through

Can [?Hope]{ ^{Youth} } can measure out or years betray

[101^v]

My happiness gone by with years between

[Rear end paper]

Where a full-blossomed slope of dazzling furze
Gave back the ~~rich~~ ^{deep} light of the setting sun
But now from human voice no [?Peace] [?]

Like the clear brilliance of the evening star
Mid the dull red of heavens inferior fires

Appendix II

The Prose Note for the Sailor's Story

Evidence of the early development of Wordsworth's conception of the sailor's role is recorded in DC MS. 11, usually called the Racedown Notebook. The manuscript has 32 leaves intact: 9, 14–24, 27–38, and 43–50. Leaves 4–5 and 8 are only partially intact (about a third of each leaf has been lost). Stubs only remain at 1–3, 6–7, 10–13, 25–26, and 39–42. The white laid paper, with chain lines at intervals of 2.6 centimeters, is watermarked with a fleur-de-lys within a highly ornamented frame surmounted by a trefoil device, and is countermarked TP.

The prose note that follows is on stubs 3^v–4^r in Wordsworth's hand. So little is left of 3^v that it is by no means certain that the words do in fact belong to the *SP* drafting. The narrow page 4^r is progressively torn away, so that toward its foot it is possible to see only parts of single words. The notebook was in use, as its name suggests, largely during the period of the Wordsworths' stay at Racedown. The draft is followed by the poems *In vain have Time & Nature toiled to throw*, *How sweet the walk along the woody steep*, and *Imitation of Juvenal*. In view of Wordsworth's letter to Wrangham of 20 November 1795, in which the revision of *Salisbury Plain* is dated "since I came to Racedown," it is reasonable to see the prose note as part of this work and to date it accordingly soon after 26 September 1795.

Text

[3ᵛ]
[?Never] [?] [?in] [?]
[?recommended.] Praise of the
[?individuals] [?conclusion]

[4ʳ]
The Woman continues her story
Her feelings and forlorn situation.
                          sailor
Sympathy of the ~~traveller~~
and his benevolent exertions
to console her [?distress] [?]
still further exhibiting
the sad choice to which the
       he
~~sailor~~ is exposed and his humanity
          They arrived at Cottage—
Where the woman ~~for~~ leaves him—
          Ere she is gone far
~~and She soon~~ meets ~~an object~~
with an occurrence which
                        ~~to him~~
induces her to ~~return~~ [—?—]
       seek him again
~~hope of finding her friend~~ [?this]
[?] ~~to seek her friend~~
[?] of cottgers wife
of parish officers
which afflicts the
remorse
[?] [?~~noble~~] resolve
Salisbury
       over ages
[—?—] of
[?] [?many]
[?p]rogress
[?]inance
[?]ciety
[—?—]
[?]

Appendix III

A Possible Source for the Sailor's Story

In a note on *Guilt and Sorrow* in his edition *Wordsworth: Representative Poems* (New York, 1937), Arthur Beatty records the opinion which was repeated by Ernest de Selincourt (*PW*, I, 334) that the story of one Jarvis Matchem, reported in the *New Annual Register* for 1786, was the source for the story of Wordsworth's sailor.

I present below a composite account of what could be the inspiration for Wordsworth's plot.

Sources

New Annual Register . . . For the Year 1786 [Part II], 27–28, 37.

Gentleman's Magazine, LVI (June 1786), 521.

R. H. Dalton Barham, *The Life and Letters of the Rev. Richard Harris Barham* (2 vols.; London, 1870), II, 3–4; and Barham, ed., *The Ingoldsby Legends: or, Mirth and Marvels* (2 vols.; London, 1870), II, 237–255.

Charles G. Harper, *The Ingoldsby Country* (London, 1904), 264–269.

Philip G. M. Dickinson, "Drummerboy Murdered at Alconbury . . .," *Hunts County Magazine*, I, No. 2 (1946), 65–66.

A basic source for all acounts must be the pamphlet *A Narrative of the Life, Confession, and Dying Speech of Jarvis Matchan*, signed by the Reverend J. Nicholson who attended him as minister. This is mentioned by R. H. Dalton Barham in his discussion of his father's version of the story in "The Dead Drummer," *The Ingoldsby Legends* (1840–1847), and quoted in his edition (II, 253–255). I have been unable to trace the pamphlet. The versions in the *New Annual Register* and the *Gentleman's Magazine* differ much in detail, but remarkable similarities in phrasing in their accounts of the sailor's tortured state of mind point to a common source. The sailor's name is spelled variously as Jarvis and Gervase, Matcham, Matchan, and Matchem. I shall refer to him as Gervas Matchan, following the first record of his name in the register of the church where he was baptized.

The Story

Gervas, son of David Matchan of Frodingham, was baptized and entered in the register of Owthorne Parish Church, East Riding, on 29 September 1756.[1] At the age of twelve he ran away from home and became a stable boy with a family named Bethell at Rise, also in the East Riding. At seventeen he was sent in charge of horses presented by the Duke of Northumberland to the Empress of Russia (to the Emperor, Dickinson says). On his return he enlisted on the man-of-war *Medway* but he deserted. He was then pressed into the crew of the *Ariadne*. While the ship was anchored off Yarmouth, Matchan escaped and enlisted in the 13th Regiment of Foot. Near Chatham he deserted and spent some time as a vagrant before being arrested at Huntingdon races. He talked his way out of detention and (perhaps as a condition of his release) enlisted in the 49th Regiment of Foot, then recruiting in the county town.

On 18 August 1780 (the nineteenth in all accounts save Dickinson's) Matchan went with Benjamin Jones, the drummer-boy son of a quartermaster (recruiting sergeant), to fetch subsistence money from a Major Reynolds at Diddington Hall, about five miles from Huntingdon. On the return journey, carrying £6 7s. in gold, they lost their way at the junction of the Huntingdon road with the Great North Road, half a mile north of Buckden, and arrived eventually at Alconbury, where they stayed the night (reported by Dickinson only). As they set off next morning Matchan cut Jones's throat and made his way to Stamford, where he picked up the north-bound coach. Having visited his mother (Harper says he went to London only), Matchan enlisted again in the navy, and was paid off finally at Plymouth from H.M.S. *Sampson* on 15 June 1786.

Together with a friend named John Shepherd (Sheppard, Shepperd) Matchan set off to tramp along the old coach road from Plymouth to London. They had only reached the stretch between Blandford and Salisbury, however, passing Woodyates Inn, when they were overtaken by a fierce storm.[2] Accounts of what actually happened now differ, but as this is the only section of the narrative quoted by R. H. Dalton Barham, and since all other versions are diluted, I cite it in full:

> Matchan being a little way apart from Shepherd,
> the latter called to the former, and said, "Jarvis,

---

[1] I am most grateful to Mr. N. Higson, county archivist for the East Riding of Yorkshire, and to the Reverend Harry Eastwood, vicar of Withernsea with Owthorne, for their help in tracing this record. Dickinson says (65) that Huntingdon tradition has it that Matchan was born at a village called Fradlingham, rightly identified as Frodingham by Harper, who does not, however, distinguish between North and South Frodingham.

[2] William Stukeley, *Stonehenge: A Temple Restor'd to the British Druids* (1740), has an illustration (opposite p. 6) of a section of Salisbury Plain "a little beyond Woodyates."